INDUSTRY OF DEVOTION

Industry of Devotion

THE TRANSFORMATION OF WOMEN'S WORK IN ENGLAND, 1500–1660

Susan Cahn

1987

COLUMBIA UNIVERSITY PRESS

New York

The Andrew W. Mellon Foundation, through a special grant,
has assisted the Press in publishing this volume.

Columbia University Press
New York   Guildford, Surrey
Copyright © 1987 Columbia University Press

Library of Congress Cataloging-in-Publication Data

Cahn, Susan.
    Industry of devotion.

    Bibliography: p.
    Includes index.
    1. Women—England—Social conditions.   2. Women—
England—Economic conditions.   3. Housewives—
England—History—16th century.   4. Housewives—
England History—17th century.   I. Title.
HQ1599.E5C34   1987   305.4'2'0942   87-5832
ISBN 0-231-06500-0

Clothbound editions of Columbia University Press are
Smyth-sewn and printed on permanent and durable
acid-free paper.

Book design by J. S. Roberts

To Judah with Love

CONTENTS

ACKNOWLEDGMENTS

I thank the staff at the J. P. Morgan Library for their assistance. I also thank the staff of the Union Theological Seminary, especially Mr. Seth Kasten, for their help. They made the splendid UTS collection of sermons available to me in most comfortable circumstances.

Thomas N. Tentler read an earlier draft of this manuscript and made many useful suggestions, some of which I have implemented. I thank him.

I am grateful for the suggestions and encouragement provided me by William Hunt, Victoria List, and Penelope Butler. A work like mine which takes decided positions in particular political and historiographical debates encounters sometimes unexpected obstacles on the road to publication. Their questions helped me to refine, clarify, and even modify some of those positions. Their support helped me surmount the obstacles. The almost off-hand confidence of Kathleen Shanley and Ellen Houlihan that my work should be published means a great deal to me.

I give special thanks to Manuel Sclar and Gale Swann. Early drafts owe much to the work and counsel of Dr. Sclar, and the decision to do something further is one that could not have been implemented without both Drs. Sclar and Swann.

I also thank Kathy Hollen who coped with sloppy corrections, untidy additions, and the sometimes dilatory U.S. Postal Service and turned out a beautiful manuscript for me.

Finally, I thank Steve Downs, without whom anything I accomplish would be as ashes in my mouth.

England is the paradise of women, the purgatory of men, and the hell of horses.

John Florio (1553?–1625)
Second Frutes

INTRODUCTION

Pieces of a Puzzle: Putting Women in Their Place

The two hundred years from 1500 to 1700 were a period of tremendous upheaval and change in England, and the changes that occurred then shaped the course of English—and world—history thereafter.[1] Traditional historiography has concentrated on three areas of change—political, economic, and religious. This book does not dispute the importance of these changes but, instead, adds a fourth area of major change, that of relations between men and women. It proposes that the changes in politics, in economics, and in religion are the context in which the changes in women's lives must be understood, and equally that to understand the political, economic, and religious changes traditionally deemed significant, it is necessary to examine the changes in the sex-gender system. The brief discussion which follows of the fundamental changes traditionally considered crucial here sets the stage for an extended look at fundamental changes in women's lives.

Politically, England was transformed from a weakly and loosely governed land into a modern nation-state. In the sixteenth century, England was only beginning to recover from the Wars of the Roses, during which two factions of the Plantagenet royal family periodically engaged in battles over which was to possess the crown. During this time, legitimacy had to be established—and reestablished—on the battlefield, and the reigning monarch had to rely on the great feudal lords, with their armies of retainers, servants, and tenants, for maintenance. The next two hundred years saw the monarchy so firmly establish its own power that it tamed the great feudal lords. The Tudors created and consolidated a state governmental machinery, whose control became itself the object of war between the crown and the Parliament by the mid-seventeenth century. The monarchy was then tamed in its turn by the national Parliament of propertied men. In 1688, Parliament's consent to a monarch's accession was taken to be a more reliable sign of "divine right" than legitimate dynastic rights of succession.[2]

The social and economic changes England underwent are less easily characterized. Today's dominant view of the sixteenth and seventeenth centuries is that they were transitional years during which the conditions necessary for the success of capitalism were established in England. The country was transformed from a precapitalist and, in many ways, even premarket economy to a modern capitalist state, on the brink of an industrial revolution.[3]

During these two hundred years, England also took part in the religious reformation of Europe, and, again, this book shares the traditional views of this process. Despite Henry VIII's initial defense of the Roman Catholic faith in reply to Luther's challenges, Henry himself broke with Rome and set England surely on a path to Protestantism from which it scarcely strayed, although the degree of its Protestantism varied. To a large extent, England did succeed in finding a "middle way" of reform.[4]

Historians have usually described these centuries as generally liberating for the English people. This viewpoint reflects a failure, only now being remedied, to analyze the situation of women: while men may have been liberated, women faced new constraints. Those historians who have examined the changing nature of the family have largely argued that the net changes in women's roles and in ideas about women were positive and that women enjoyed increased status within the family.[5] Attention to the particular case of women reveals that, on the contrary, the role of the housewife was diminished and that patriarchy became so firmly enshrined within the family that it remains today a basic feature of the modern family.

All these epochal changes were processes which were worked out through decades and even centuries, with few moments of cataclysmic break. There was no moment, for instance, when England became capitalist or when Elizabeth knew her crown rested secure from the dangers of "overmighty subjects."[6] Yet, contemporaries were well aware that their world was changing. At the turn of the seventeenth century, John Donne lamented,

> Tis all in pieces, all coherence gone,
> All just supply, and all relation:
> Prince, Subject, Father, Son, are things forgot,
> For every man alone thinks he hath got
> To be a Phoenix, and that there can be
> None of that kind which he is, but he.
> This is the world's condition now.[7]

Throughout the two hundred years from 1500 to 1700, English men and women of various strata and occupations mourned the passing of the old world and welcomed the opportunities of the new. They bemoaned change and celebrated the improvements in living standards fostered by change. Some individuals consistently rejected the new social and political mores; others accepted and rejected with discrimination.

But the changes affected everyone. The literate aristocracy and the growing middle classes had the greatest opportunity to express their views of the upheaval around them in ways we can easily understand and interpret,[8] but even the poorest peasant families in the most isolated rural areas of England experienced some adjustments in their daily lives. All English men and women, for example, were legally obligated to attend church services, where there was a new emphasis on the sermon or homily, in contrast to the traditional (Roman Catholic) mass, with its emphasis on ritual and the miracle of consecration. However minute such an adjustment might appear to later, more secular generations, it required some rethinking on the part of individuals and families in the sixteenth century.

The Missing Pieces

Once looked for, the changes in women's lives are as visible as the changes in politics, economics, and religion, and their effects in society may be seen to be as pervasive. Women lost certain roles in economic production; they took on new and subordinated roles in economic consumption. They lost their place in public society and found themselves newly enclosed in the private society of their families. Like changes in politics, economics, and religion, these changes required rethinking: in this case, rethinking of ideas about women. This book examines an aspect of the complex relationship between ideological and material change in England, of how the ideas through which the English people understood their lives interacted with the physical circumstances in which they lived. The interaction occurred in all areas of change: here, the focus is the way in which it changed women's lives. The basic argument is that women's position in society, measured by status and opportunities, declined both absolutely and relative to that of men during the sixteenth and seventeenth centuries in England and that the decline, far from being either natural or inevitable, was the result of a complex interaction of social, political, and economic forces.

Two fundamental propositions underlie this argument. First, it is assumed that the changes in ideas about women and in women's social roles were part of the other changes outlined above. What was happening to women, that is, cannot be divorced from what was happening in the rest of society—where, historians agree, tradition was being turned on its head. As one example, new attitudes toward the market were taking root throughout this period. These attitudes, in combination with both the steady growth of market production and the accessibility of markets, affected women directly insofar as they undermined the traditional household division of labor. The result was, as will be discussed in chapters 3 and 5, that wives became increasingly dependent upon their husbands' income to meet the needs of their families. But the significance of this new dependence is inextricably bound up with other changes, and it becomes clear only in their context.

The housewife's newly increased dependence on her husband, that is, was not, in itself, necessarily debilitating to women. It became so, however, in conjunction with two other changes. First, the traditional idea that property and wages were gifts from God, intended for family and community needs, was gradually superseded by the idea that property was private and free from any family or social obligations. Second, the ability to provide one's own living without dependence on another became a criterion for participation in political society.[9]

Thus, the proposition that changes in ideas about women and their social roles were part of broad social changes has itself two aspects. One, that the reconsideration of women and their place was part of a broad ideological transformation. People were rethinking everything—from the name given to church services to the "just price" to the relationship between king and parliament. And two, that the significance of the specific changes affecting women can be understood only in the context of the English society these changes helped to create.

The second proposition underlying this study is that the causes of the changes in ideas about women were diverse and that the effects of them were varied and unevenly felt. Historians have shown that changes in ideas about property and political allegiance stemmed from disparate sources and that the effects of these changes varied among social strata. So, too, changes in ideas about women and their place were sparked by several causes and were experienced differently by women in different places in society. In some cases, traditional formulations about women were visibly out of touch with current practices. In other cases, the traditional ideas and practices achieved ends which some individuals no longer considered desirable. Ideas about what women could and should do changed as what women did changed. But once formulated, the ideas began to shape and limit what women did.

In all cases, the new ideas were part of a gradual and diffuse process. The new ideas about the market price did not spring forth full-blown from some nascent bourgeois's head and immediately dominate society. Neither did the new ideas restricting women spring forth full-blown from some patriarch's head and immediately succeed in confining women to their homes. As this book will show, many of the ideas about women which served to restrict them in seventeeth-century England were already present, without such restrictive effect, in fifteenth-century England and were repeated with only rephrasings or new emphasis. To attain their restrictive effects, these ideas were reworked by new phrasing, new contexts, or some other shift, either in material conditions or in ideas. As with the more radical reworking of political and economic ideas, the changes in ideas about women occurred slowly. The ideas were thought out gradually and developed and tested against reality and reworked again. Their ultimate success depended upon their ability to explain and justify social reality as well as to evoke what was considered a desirable social reality. As a result, it often happened that an idea might be unattainable for most people yet still succeed as a model of social reality. As with changes in material conditions, changes in ideas could affect different social classes at varying speeds and in various ways.

Ideology and real life act together dialectically, each constantly limiting, shaping, and legitimizing the other. For the most part, this book examines the ideas articulated by the middle and upper strata of English society. It argues that the ideas became elements in the hegemonic ideology of England, and their validity gradually extended down the social scale. Although the ideas discussed here were first given voice by wealthy and socially prominent English men and women, they were accepted and internalized by many who were neither wealthy nor socially prominent. Acceptance of these ideas became, in fact, for a time, the price of upward social mobility, the ticket to a place among the "substantial sort" or the "better inhabitants" of a community. Eventually, of course, these ideas were accepted and internalized even by the poor and laboring men and women of England and, indeed, of western capitalist society.

The success of these ideas stemmed from their ability to explain and, importantly, to justify social or economic or political facts. Although many of the ideas discussed here were not immediately applicable to all social strata or geographic regions, their espousal by men and women of high social and moral prestige lent these ideas an initial legitimacy. Their legitimacy was reinforced by the spread of changes in material conditions which slowly allowed broader elements of society actually to implement in their own lives the ideas and practices their ministers and political and social superiors had been inculcating.[10]

Returning to the example of the household division of labor will illustrate the way that material and ideological changes developed in uneven and dialectical relationships. In early modern England, the growing market orientation undermined the ability of all housewives to meet the needs of their families without resorting to markets, but the injury was not felt by all women at the same time or in the same ways. In many rural areas, women continued to provide for the needs of their families directly through their own labor. In manufacturing or market centers, other women used the wages from their labor to provide for their families. Some wealthy women entered the market economy solely as consumers because, while they had no need to earn money, their social status and wealth required them to display products outside the purview of the traditional housewife. Others participated as consumers because they no longer had the means to perform traditional housewifely labor.

The actual overturning of the household division of labor was a lengthy process which, for many families, was incomplete in 1700. But the ideas by which the overturning was explained, such as that the responsibility to provide for the family, and the honor for doing so, belonged solely to the husband, had been articulated and were accepted even by many of the families in which the wife remained a co-equal or the primary provider, as well as by those families in which the wife lived idly and luxuriously off the fruits of her husband's labor.[11]

Moreover, the successful spread of ideas which made natural or even holy those practices which were at odds with tradition and with the immediate needs and interests of many families helped to spread the practices themselves. That it was constantly taught that women were unable to earn their own living, for example, is one reason why English people of the sixteenth and seventeenth centuries did not demand that the wages for the work that women did should be raised or that women should learn new, profitable trades but, instead, advised families not to waste their resources in training daughters, since those daughters would not be able to support themselves without husbands, much less to repay the family's investment. The fewer women trained in skills that could earn livings, the fewer women who did earn livings and the more women accounted for by the new truism that women were dependent on their husbands.

These changes were part of the general overturning of values—the reassessment of the roles of mothers, fathers, employers, clergy, even kings—necessitated by changing material conditions and studied at length by other historians. But they are aspects of change which historians have overlooked and left unsatisfactorily explained, if explained at all. In 1500, England was described by a European visitor as a hell for horses but paradise for women. By 1700, partially through women's own labor, their industry of devotion, paradise had been transformed.[12] Women's industry created havens for men; it left women unprepared to meet the challenges of an industrial age. The constriction of the work women did is the subject of this book.

The Plan of the Book

In examining women's descent from paradise, the book is concerned with the growing differentiation between the public and the private and between the productive and the nonproductive which is a central feature of capitalism. It examines the expansion of the public economy and constriction of the private or domestic economy from the perspective of women's place in them, looking for the connections between women's shrinking and debased role outside the family economy and their changed role within their families. It also examines the ways in which these changes were both a consequence and a cause of ideological change, suggesting that the specific changes affecting women in sixteenth- and seventeenth-century England were the product of the dialectical interaction of ideology and material conditions and that they could have occurred only within the context of this interaction.

The term "ideology" as used in the text refers to a world view that orders and organizes thought, defining what is "natural," "possible," and "appropriate," and explaining social reality in such a way as to make it appear legitimate and worthy of reproduction. It is conceived of as a cause and, at the same time, a reflection of material change.

The appendix describes the major sources used to reveal this ideology. These sources include popular literature, both lay and religious, and the biographies, autobiographies, memoirs, and correspondence of men and women of sixteenth- and seventeenth-century England. Although chapter 1 turns to secondary sources to present an overview of the basic material changes England experienced during these years, and chapter 2 pinpoints their material effects on women, the rest of the book relies heavily on these literary sources. Using them, chapter 3 examines general changes in the English social structure and social values, looking at how general changes in ideas about society affected particular ideas about women's place in society. Chapters 4 and 5 use the literary sources to explore the role of women within the home, with chapter 4 focusing on the role of the housewife and chapter 5 on the woman's new family roles. Chapter 6 looks in greater detail at particular aspects of the more general changes described in chapters 4 and 5, illuminating the interaction between objective material conditions and the perceptions of these conditions.

CHAPTER ONE

The Beginning
of a New Age:
Social Stratification
and Order

The increasing differentiation among what the English called "degrees of men" was one of the major social changes of sixteenth- and seventeenth-century England. The very structure of English society was changing. Some powerful new social groups were emerging while other, traditional social groups were declining. At the same time, traditional methods of preserving social order and stability were being transformed. Briefly examining these fundamental social and economic changes helps to provide the context necessary to understand women's changing place in English society.

The Ruling Class

The changes were obvious to contemporaries. In 1500, English society was divided into two main groups: the gentry and the nongentry—or, as contemporaries saw it, those who could afford to live without manual labor and those who labored for their subsistence.[1] Conventionally, the gentry were characterized by "gentle" birth, their possession of landed wealth, their mode of living—what we today call "lifestyle"—and their political power.[2] Although there were differences within the gentry, separating, for example, the aristocracy from "those that be no lords," the mere knights and gentlemen, English people had no doubt that the gentry occupied a special place in the social order and could readily be distinguished from their inferior countrymen.[3]

But this simple two-part system was already breaking down. In the mid-sixteenth century, William Harrison, a London cleric, described England as composed of people of four different degrees:[4] the gentry, the citizens and burgesses, the yeomanry, and the rest—those with "neither voice nor authority in the commonwealth, but [who] are to be ruled and not to rule others." Although Harrison still believed that the gentry could readily be distinguished from everyone else—by their ability to "live without manual labor" and yet sustain "the port, charge and countenance" of gentlemen—he no longer attributed political power to the gentry alone, and he recognized that men could move from one degree to another. In addition to the gentry, Harrison regarded citizens and burgesses, a category defined by occupation and legal privileges, and the yeomanry, a category rather vaguely defined by "a certain pre-eminence and . . . estimation," and, implicitly by wealth, as bearers of rule within the nation and their local communities. He also noted that the sons of these men were very often gentlemen. Moreover, Harrison accorded a kind of honorary gentry status to members of certain professions and to university graduates who, although overwhelmingly the sons of gentry, were not entirely so descended and who labored in some trades or professions in order both to maintain and to upgrade their social and economic status. For Harrison and many of his contemporaries, education apparently so raised its recipient from the mass of his fellows that alone it could confer gentry status.

Harrison's analysis reveals that, by the mid-sixteenth

century, the criteria by which social status was accorded were somewhat fluid and that the traditional social division was no longer sufficient to account for the complex structure of society. Birth and landed wealth still counted for much, but new roads to power and to wealth were opening up and contemporaries were struggling with how to rank them. In the final analysis, contemporaries continued to rate landed wealth as *the* essential characteristic of gentility, but they placed increasing weight on elements of lifestyle, such as clothing, leisure activities, diet, house, the number and kinds of servants employed, on education and occupation and on the exercise of authority as indices of status.[5] As is discussed below, labor, too, was gaining in importance as a criterion. Because it was increasingly possible to meet some but not all of the various criteria for gentry status, many individuals felt what modern researchers call "status anxiety" as they sought to maintain or improve their social ranking in the face of the new criteria.[6] Thus, in 1616, William Whately, the minister of Banbury, observed that "Many a yeoman is far wealthier than some Justices of the Peace that dwell near him," and admonished the yeomen to live in accord with their place rather than their wealth.[7] The yeomanry, that is, were to continue to defer to their social superiors (including the clergy) and to maintain a level of consumption and display below that of the gentry, despite their greater share of landed wealth.

In mid-sixteenth-century descriptions of English society, commentators had distinguished the yeomanry from the gentry as much by their manner of living and their use of wealth as by the amount of wealth they possessed. Sir Thomas Smith, for example, had provided this definition:

This sort of people confess themselves to be no gentlemen. . . . Yet they have a certain pre-eminence and more estimation than labourers and artificers, and commonly live wealthily, keep good houses, and do their business and travail to acquire riches: these be (for the most part) farmers unto gentlemen, which, with grazing, frequenting of markets, and keeping of servants not idle as the gentlemen doth, but *such as get both their own living and parts of their masters* [emphasis added].[8]

By the turn of the seventeenth century, however, none of these criteria could be applied consistently to differentiate yeoman from gentleman. As a rule, gentry were no longer keeping idle servants—even the aristocracy had reduced their numbers of retainers; the gentry had begun to take active interest in their own farming operations and those of their tenants; and successful yeomen had displaced "unthrifty gentlemen" in wealth and, sometimes, in community power.

Just as confusing, to contemporaries and to twentieth-century historians, were the places of the urban elite—the professional lawyer or cleric and the merchant and trader—whom Harrison had tentatively assigned gentry status. These men clearly lived by their labor, spent much of their time attending to business (and little of their time in the traditional leisure pursuits of the country gentleman), and, at least initially, possessed no landed wealth. But they were related to the gentry—they were its sons, sons-in-law, brothers—they wielded considerable power within the cities in which they lived and at law and royal courts; they often also acquired land, which may then have been used to maintain themselves and their families in Harrison's "port, charge and countenance" of the gentry. These men did not fit the traditional definition of gentry but they mingled with and married the gentry, and their ungenteel labor might well have been rewarded with a title, an office, or land.

Throughout the time period under study, the numbers of these anomalous urban men were increasing, as were the numbers of their rural counterparts, the yeomanry, and both groups prospered in wealth as well as in numbers.[9] The rich, in other words, were getting richer and more numerous, and they were jostling among themselves for pride of place. Because, as will be discussed in more detail in later chapters, social status was conventionally taken to be a reflection of moral worth, the jockeying for position among the gentry and near-gentry, those whom the historian Lawrence Stone calls the "squirearchy," often took on moral overtones. Those who were challenging the exclusive right of the traditional gentry to rule also challenged the monopoly of the traditional gentry to high moral worth. As they based their claim to political or social power on their achievements rather than their birth, so, too, the challengers based their claim to moral worth on their achievement rather than on their bloodlines. They deserved power in the commonwealth because they had demonstrated success in providing for and governing others; they demonstrated their moral worth—or nobility—by turning their success to the benefit of the commonwealth.

Thus, the merchant who had been excoriated in fifteenth-century England as a bloodsucker preened himself in seventeenth-century England for the multiplicity of benefits he had brought the kingdom. Over the course of the sixteenth and seventeenth centuries, more and more of England's elite came to esteem the merchant at his own evaluation.[10] Such a reevaluation of the role of the merchant obviously involved the reexamination of the most basic social values and relationships.

A significant feature of this reexamination, and one with marked implications for England's future, was that it did not repudiate traditional notions: it expanded them. Rather than deny the traditional elements of nobility, for example, Sir Thomas Smith in 1560 showed how they had operated: "the example of progenitors . . . encourages [virtue] . . . the education . . . enables [a knowledge of virtue] . . . the love of tenants . . . pricks forward [to virtue]."[11] These advantages, he suggested, made virtue—true gentility—more easily accessible to the nobleman nobly and wealthily born, but, he added, they did not give the aristocracy a monopoly on virtue. The citizen born without these advantages might have a harder time achieving gentility but his success might, therefore, be the more savored. In actually contesting the traditional holders of political power for rule, again, the challengers or "new men" did not violently overthrow the aristocracy; on the contrary, they assisted them in the difficult task of maintaining order, diluting the power of the aristocracy through sharing and expanding their political and social rule.

In the sixteenth and seventeenth centuries, then, the new men sought to adapt and incorporate the traditional values rather than to negate them. The old gentry, for their part, aided this process by the actions they took to maintain their supremacy. They continued to laud landed wealth and birth as the primary sources of power and prestige, but they began to use their land in new and "ungenteel" ways. The yeomanry were rising—ofttimes right into the gentry—through their rational and capitalistic exploitation of land; those gentry who retained or improved their place did so by a similar adaptation to agrarian capitalism.[12] As the yeoman prospered through attention to markets, convertible husbandry, and rational deployment of labor, so the gentleman, and even the peer, was forced—if he desired to maintain his superiority to the yeoman—to do the same. Fortunes were made or increased through private enterprise on land, and the gentry found themselves compelled to be as enterprising as the yeomanry or to fall outside the gentry.[13]

The Lower "Orders"

The obverse side of the rich getting richer, however, and of the prosperity enjoyed by the yeomanry and the other middle and upper elements of society, was that the poor were getting poorer. Historians are now generally agreed that the sixteenth and seventeenth centuries witnessed the crucial period "in the demise of the peasantry in England," or in R. H. Tawney's words, "the decline of the subsistent husbandman."[14]

In the traditional view of English society, those who constituted the overwhelming majority of the population (by some estimates, as much as 98 percent), the nongentry, were seen as subsistence farmers, husbandmen who farmed a plot of land and survived on its fruits. Some of these husbandmen, admittedly, plied other trades, such as small handicrafts, textile work, smithing, carpentry, in addition to maintaining their small farms. Others regularly took on wage work, having so small a plot of land that their families could not be maintained by its fruits alone. Nonetheless, the traditional, rather idealized view held that England was a nation of self-sufficient farmers and, through the fifteenth century, this view was, largely, an accurate view of society. In the sixteenth and seventeenth centuries, this view became increasingly untenable. By the second half of the sixteenth century, only small pockets of subsistence farming remained, and even the farmers of these pockets were finding themselves hard pressed and, sometimes, forced off their lands, by rising rents.[15] Throughout England in the sixteenth and seventeenth centuries, the trend was away from subsistence farming and toward "commercial cropping," or market agriculture. This trend was stimulated by and, in turn, reinforced the process of the enclosure of common fields. In combination, these forces devastated the traditional rural economy and the social relations which had supported and expressed it.

Although contemporaries laid the blame for enclosure on the gentry and accused them of heartlessly depopulating their lands in order to feed sheep (and sell the wool), in fact, the yeomanry initiated enclosures at least as often as the gentry. Furthermore, only a minority of enclosures were done to convert arable land into pasture. Most enclosures took the form of "engrossment" of land for the purpose of rationalizing agricultural production and allowing individual farmers to make their own, individual decisions about what and how to grow, thus enabling them to run their farms as private businesses. The gentry and yeomanry alike, on the whole, benefited from these processes—the yeomanry succeeding so well that contemporaries began to regard them as an estimable "degree," raised above their rural fellows.

Those social strata below the yeomanry in the country and the merchant-traders in the city did not fare so well. Harrison offered no analysis of this social grouping—by far the majority of his countrymen—implying that there was no noticeable difference in prestige or access to social resources among day laborers, skilled journeymen, and husbandmen. In fact, there were differences—and men of Harrison's rank came to acknowledge them—but the people of these strata shared a characteristic which bound them more closely together than their differences could distinguish them: they were poor, and over the course of the sixteenth and seventeenth centuries, they were getting poorer. Inflation played a big part in this. Foods led the price rise—multiplying sixfold while the price of manufactured goods "only" doubled—and the price of the cheaper foodstuffs, the basic necessities, rose more quickly and sharply than luxury food items. Rents skyrocketed and real wages *fell* by one-half.[16]

But inflation alone did not pauperize the husbandmen. Inflation together with the consolidation and improvement of farmland and the population increase led to more and more husbandmen—the subsistence farmers par excellence—living at, and falling off, the edge into landlessness. The husbandman was, by definition, a small farmer, and he rarely had resources comparable to those of the gentry to improve his land. As rents increased and larger shares of his produce went toward paying his "rack-rent"—the highest rent the market would bear—many families of husbandmen found themselves unable to survive on the land. Husbandmen grew more and more dependent on wages and whatever nonagricultural work they could get. The husbandman was the first to suffer in times of dearth since he, almost by definition, had little reserve, and even in times of good harvest, his inability to withhold his produce from the market meant he was unable to obtain the highest price for it. In order to buy at the market, then, husbandmen increasingly sold their labor.

The landless or near landless were, over the course of these centuries, sinking deeper into poverty. That they had much company probably was not very comforting to the laborers whose loss of traditional rights to commons land might mean the inability to keep *any* livestock or grow any food, and thus the loss of any possibility of supporting their families without some form of assistance, or in times of real dearth might mean starvation. The rural landless who were employed in such rural industries as textiles or nail-making as well as in seasonal agricultural work were at the mercy not only of harvests, as in the past, but now also of trade cycles. The urban poor, whose numbers were also rapidly growing, were, like the rural poor, dependent on wages; and, like the rural poor, they suffered from the same economic changes which were such a boon to the middle and upper layers of society. Indeed, the disparities between the rich and poor became so great during this time period that some historians point to the seventeenth century as that which gave rise to a "culture of poverty."[17]

In sum, the sixteenth and seventeenth centuries saw the collapse of the social structure composed of gentry and everyone else. By the late seventeenth century, it was the poor who occupied a special place in the social order and could most readily be distinguished from their superior countryfolk—who devoted much of their labor and material wealth toward demonstrating that they were not of the poor and toward making plain exactly how high was their own place in the social order. Because the criteria by which these higher places were assigned were so fluid, these efforts, as will be discussed in the next two chapters, took many forms.

Capitalism and Its Implications

The shifts in the social structure of England reflected and reinforced the development of capitalism. It was, historians today recognize as contemporaries could not, the increasing dominance of capital and of capitalist relations which was changing the face of both English society and the English countryside.[18] The numbers of landless laborers dependent on wages for subsistence grew both absolutely and relatively during these two centuries,[19] because landlords and tenants were using their landholdings as commodities and sources of profit, rather than for patronage or subsistence. The sophisticated market system being born in sixteenth-century England was predicated on free and mobile wage labor and on economic, not personal, relationships between worker and employer.[20]

Contemporaries did have some inklings of the nature of the changes. Sir Thomas Smith, for example, had noted that the yeomanry amassed wealth through the labor of their servants, labor so productive that it paid their wage and added to the wealth of the yeomen masters. By the turn of the century, the gentry had recognized that, if they were to retain their superior wealth, then they would have to employ servants who could, as Smith had put it, "get" some of that wealth. Although they rarely articulated this change of attitude toward property and servants, they began to act as if land and the labor to work it were the objects of economic calculation rather than, as in the past, the expression of relationships between persons.

Increasingly, landlords and tenants both were seeking to realize profit from their landholdings, and increasingly, this involved raising marketable crops at the lowest possible cost. The enclosure of farmland allowed individual farmers to make decisions and investments which could raise the productivity and profitability of the land. Those who invested in drainage systems, took advantage of new, more productive agricultural techniques, and reduced their labor costs could—and did—realize ever greater profits.

Those landlords and farmers who clung to the old ways of farming and deploying labor found themselves falling behind in the new competition for land and profit as, for example, farmers not bound by the aristocratic ethos hired only those laborers they needed and only for so long as the labor was needed, saving themselves the costs of feeding and/or lodging "idle" servants and thus adding to their profits. The landlord who did not "rack-rent" found his own real income falling in the face of inflation, while the tenant farmer who had to pay the racked rent found he could not afford labor which did not pay for itself and "somewhat" more. The enclosed agricultural units were private *competitive* enterprises: those who won, won new prestige and wealth; those who lost, lost everything but their labor power. They joined the growing army of landless, whose members were "free" and had no option other than to sell that labor power to an employer who would use it, as Smith said, to pay the servant's wage and the master's profit.

Trade and manufacturing, too, were being reshaped by developing capitalism. Although the great merchants of the London elite often enjoyed extraordinary prosperity as a result of risky but enormously profitable long-distance trade, some merchants, traders, and even master craftsmen were beginning to recognize the possibilities of increasing their profits from the sale of manufactured goods by exercising tighter control of production costs. Thus they, like their agricultural counterparts, sought to reduce the cost of the labor they employed, by hiring it, for example, only for specific tasks and only as necessary, or by encouraging a greater specialization of labor among their workers. Some sought to evade onerous or costly city regulations by employing labor outside cities, where also the rents and/or wages were lower.

In manufacturing, as in agriculture, individuals and enterprises were competing for markets and for raw materials. The smaller producers—the master arisans and small traders—found life more precarious than did the great merchants and financiers of the urban elites. The smaller men, without the resources to risk in cornering a market or investing in long-distance trade, often tried to save their position by using more traditional and conservative methods, by restricting competition, for example, rather than trying to undersell it.

Some master craftsmen, affected by rising rents and costs, found the prices of their wares rising more slowly than the price of food and other necessities. While this meant that the market for these goods could—and did—expand, because it became relatively cheaper to buy than to make some basic household items (including even bread and cloth) as well as some more luxurious goods, some of the craftsmen feared that the "cheapness" of their products would ruin them. Accordingly, they sought to limit their competition—the supply of their products—and thereby raise prices, by making it more difficult and expensive to set up shop as masters. Their guilds—those organizations which conferred status and benefits among artisans—increased the fees for attaining a master's status and lengthened the terms of apprenticeships.

Measures like these did not reduce output. Ironically, the way in which these measures benefited the master craftsmen who imposed them was by lowering the cost of the labor they used, and thus the cost of output. By imposing restrictions which froze apprentices and journeypeople into their places at low "trainee" wages, master craftsmen acquired workers ever more skilled and productive at what they did, but who did not receive increased payment. They remained instead wholly dependent on their employers for wages which, so far from enabling journeypeople to save up their masters' initiation fee or the money to buy for themselves the tools of their trades, barely provided them with subsistence. The low value of their labor meant that they could not afford to withdraw it from paid employment long enough to create their "masterpiece," another prerequisite for attaining full membership or "freedom" of the guild whose attainment was made stiffer over the course of the sixteenth and seventeenth centuries. It also meant that their employers could hire more journeypeople, expanding output and achieving economies both of scale and of a more complex division of labor.[21]

Urban workers, thus, like the agricultural workers from whose ranks they often came and to whose ranks they often returned, were at the mercy of their employers, of harvests, of trade cycles. Workers of both kinds were also at the mercy of each other. Their numbers increasing as a consequence of both population pressure and the spread of market relations, they competed with each other for what work was available. Many of them traveled the length and breadth of England to do so.

Over the course of the sixteenth and seventeenth centuries, these travelers or, as their contemporaries called them, "vagabonds," crossed a nation which was becoming rapidly, if unevenly, dominated by capitalism.[22] Its influence was everywhere evident: in the new and better-maintained roads by which foodstuffs and manufactured items were more rapidly transported from region to region; in the market towns and urban areas where populations were growing at an astounding rate, fed by the landless who came seeking work (England's population as a whole doubled from 1500 to 1700, but London's expanded sixfold, and other cities also grew faster than the nation); in the more specialized production and division of labor developed to feed these population centers and utilize their primary asset, human labor; in the proliferation of "professional" and other services available in these centers—doctors, lawyers, booksellers, starchers, launderers, makers of gloves, hats, and farthingales; and, finally, in the rootlessness and mobility of the people themselves. Free from ties to land or landlord, these people struggled to find their place in society.

Responses to Change

Some of the changes which are evident to the historian were not quite so evident to the men and women of sixteenth- and seventeenth-century England. Contemporaries saw the traditional order of society breaking down; they only dimly glimpsed how it might be reconstituted on new terms. Their attitudes toward the changes in their world were shaped by their (traditional) conception of how society should function—in an orderly and hierarchical way—and their response to the changes was, therefore, to try to reinforce the toppling order and hierarchy. Within the new elite strata, individuals and groups strove to reestablish credentials of status. Thus, for example, lawyers sought to lay down more rigorous criteria for inclusion in the profession, asserting more vociferously their specialized knowledge. In the Royal College of Physicians the same struggle occurred. Founded in the early sixteenth century, the college devoted itself to convincing laypeople of the superiority of physicians, that is, university-trained experts in scientific knowledge and natural philosophy, over traditional healers, whether barber-surgeons, herbalists, or midwives. Guilds, as noted above, tightened their own requirements of admission, insisting that the "mysteries" of their crafts demanded long years of training. The gentry and the near-gentry provided the college of heralds with booming business as families sought to display coats-of-arms in order to demonstrate their genealogical superiority.

Among this new elite, then, there was differentiation and dissension. Did the lawyer rank above the physician? Must the Mayor of London yield precedence to the country knight? Uncertain of their standing in relation to each other, the upper and middle strata of society were wholly convinced of how to address the poor: the lower orders were to be repressed, restrained, "mastered."

What concerned the upper and middle strata most was the threat to order and property posed by the vagabonds, whom they characterized, tellingly, as "masterless men." England had no police force, no standing army: the traditional means of enforcing order had been personal. Personal relationships between landlords and tenants, servants and masters, parents and children had provided some guarantees of appropriate behavior. The servants of the gentry may have been idle, but they were under the eye of their lord (employer) and would be punished for disruptive behavior displeasing to the employer. The very fact of employment reduced the opportunities of servants to wreak havoc as their activities and physical space were circumscribed.

Eviction for enclosure, economic rents, and the more rational deployment of labor undermined this system of social control and loosed what those who owned property saw as hordes of masterless men upon the land. Those who evicted these men or turned away their servants feared the consequences of their actions, believing the poor to be, as Sir John Oglander put it, "always apt to rebel and mutiny."[23] Sir Richard Morison wrote in 1537 that the "worser sort" were jealous of their betters and would take up arms against them at any opportunity. Morison warned his peers that they must take care to prevent opportunities for rebellion and to instill in all "sorts" proper regard for proper place.[24]

The fears of the wealthy increased as the numbers of poor grew. In 1589, Sir John Smith wrote to Elizabeth's chief adviser that the growth of poverty and vagabondism "may turn this realm to great danger" and cited the slave rebellions of ancient Rome as instances of what he expected. In 1605, the Earl of Dorset claimed that "the poor people are ready to mutiny" over the high cost of corn.[25] Although the earl managed to suppress the mutiny, in fact, the fears of the property owners were not groundless. In 1536 and again in 1549, the poor staged massive uprisings involving thousands of people and terrorizing the rich through whose property they "passed." In 1549, they succeeded in taking over the city of Norwich: they threw down enclosures and burned 20,000 sheep before they were subdued.[26]

Until the civil war, no other social disturbance achieved the scale of the Norfolk rebellion in 1549. Yet, property owners were confronted with periodic food riots and attacks on enclosures throughout the sixteenth and seventeenth centuries, and they lived in dread that one of these would gain the widespread support that had conquered Norwich. The food riots were particularly associated with years of harvest failure, but enclosure riots showed no such pattern, leaving the government and local property owners and enclosers with unspecific, vague worries about what would set off the "many-headed monster," the poor. A weaver in Ardleigh in 1596, for example, proposed himself as a captain of an army which would "cut the throats of the rich churls and cornmongers" because, he said, things would never improve for the poor "until men did rise." A laborer in Hatfield in 1594 threatened to gather a band of men to go take the food they could not afford to buy, asking, "What can rich men do against poor men, if poor men rise and hold together?"[27]

Furthermore, the middle and upper classes feared not only collective action by the poor but also individual "criminal" acts. According to the rich, the poor easily fell into theft or pilferage, if only to feed their hungry stomachs, and their hatred and jealousy of their superiors inclined them to assault. These fears of the rich, too, found bases in fact. Court records indicate increasing prosecutions for theft, particularly during years of harvest failure or seasons of trade depression. They also reveal that many of the poor "pilfered" as a matter of course.[28] Many peasants, for instance, failed to yield their traditional commons rights when the commons were enclosed. In the late sixteenth and early seventeenth centuries, property owners were redefining time-honored customs such as gleaning or gathering of kindling as crimes against the newly sacrosanct private property, and they were persecuting the poor as criminals for adherence to the old ways.

The efforts of the "better sort" to defuse what they saw as threats to their property and security took many forms. As will be discussed in chapters 5 and 6, they mounted a vigorous ideological campaign to reassert ever more strongly their version of order and hierarchy. They also, however, took direct steps to control the unruly multitudes.

They continued, for example, efforts to restrict the mobility of the poor. Various localities imposed settlement restrictions, banning the entry and residence of those who might require financial assistance. Justices of the Peace—gentry all (and all male)—enforced regulations requiring poor travelers to carry certificates attesting to their masters' knowledge and approval of their travels. Immigrants without employment or even, sometimes, without guaranteed or "covenanted" long-term employment were denied housing—and those who gave them lodging were prosecuted. In 1589 Parliament passed the Statute of Cottagers which forbade the erection of housing on lots of less than four acres. The rationale behind the statute was the belief that no family could subsist with lesser acreage. In fact, Parliament's assessment was low: most families with only four acres of land needed to supplement their husbandry with wage work so that they could buy at the market necessary items that those four acres could not produce; the number of acres necessary for self-sufficiency varied considerably by region.

All these measures addressed the issue of masterless men, and all these measures failed to solve it. In part, the failure stemmed from the unwillingness of local authorities to enforce the legislation. The men charged with doing so, after all, were the employers, the very men who benefited from the low cost of labor. Thus, enforcement was always selective. Men, for example, were permitted to settle where women were not, because men, since they received higher wages than women, even for the same work,[29] and were unlikely to become unable to work or add to the parish population through pregnancy, were seen as less liable to become "chargeable" to the parish and more able either to subsist alone or to move along if subsistence was impossible. The Cottagers Act might be ignored during times of prosperity, when laborers were welcome; in times of bad harvests or commercial down cycles, families would find themselves evicted from their homes and turned into criminals instead of legitimate residents entitled to community aid.[30]

The failure also, however, stemmed from the very nature of the measures. They were attempts to evade the problems of the landless poor and of masterless men, not to solve them. Ultimately, the men without employment and the families without housing had to live somewhere; these measures offered local authorities lawful ways to try to force these people to go to some other community, but finally, some community was going to have to deal with them.

Towns faced this sooner than did rural areas and made serious and innovative efforts to deal with the influx of vagabonds by the mid-sixteenth century.[31] At that time, several towns instituted various programs designed to deal with what is now recognized to have been structural unemployment—more laborers than could be absorbed into the existing economic structure. It is important to recall the way in which the sixteenth-century English posed the problem. What the town sought to provide was not only employment but also, through employment, control. The most pressing need they sought to fulfill was that for disciplining or regulating the lower orders.[32] Certainly, the poor must be fed—but they must be fed in such a way as to repress their wicked jealousy of their betters and to subdue their rebellious impulses. The goal of making work for the unemployed was subsumed in that of giving masters to the masterless.

Workhouses were established in mid-sixteenth-century London that the poor might be "set at work." London city officials began to distinguish among the poor, separating those who would not work, who were punished, from those who could not find work, who were "set to work," at subsistence (or below subsistence) wages, either in the specially created and endowed workhouses or for some private employer who had contracted with the city. In 1597 and 1601, Parliament codified and extended London's system of poor relief throughout the nation. The Poor Law legislated punishment for the lazy, work for those who could do it, and relief for the young, infirm, and workers whose wages did not meet their needs. The legislation, understandably, left much discretion to the local authorities who would have to implement its basic principles. It is worth noting that many local authorities attempted to force fathers to bear responsibility for their young and infirm. Apparently, by the turn of the century, the authorities had little hope that unmarried mothers or abandoned wives could maintain their children without assistance. Accordingly, they sought to identify fathers and hold them liable for their wives and children; and they also sought, with increasing severity throughout this time period, to punish unwed mothers.[33]

State and local authorities tried to set the poor to work because they believed this would reduce the poor's opportunities to sin, inculcate in them "saving" (both financially and morally) habits, and place them in a proper relation of subordination to their superiors. The authorities appear, as well, to have hoped to foster among masters and those they set to work the personal relations which, traditionally, had been such important and successful elements of social control. Several local authorities, for instance, turned to employers to discipline those of their servants who committed civil offenses, and at both national and local levels, regulations were passed forbidding employers to turn out workers during slack times.[34]

These attempts at workfare foundered on some of the same shoals which shipwrecked the legislation restricting mobility. Again, the men charged with implementing these measures were the employers, who benefited from the low cost of labor, who suffered by being forced to keep on idle servants, and whose products competed on the marketplace with those of the workhouses. These men were rarely eager to endow their competition, and their reluctance was only increased by the possibility that workhouses might attract to the neighborhood enough poor people to fill or overflow the workhouses.

More fundamentally, all these measures proposed by the propertied classes to deal with the growing numbers of mobile, landless poor suffered from the contradictions of the emerging capitalist society. Property owners feared the anger of evicted tenants, but few of them were ready to forego the economic rents they could achieve by evicting "unproductive" tenants and turning lands to new uses. The wealthy feared the "idle loitering people who break hedges and steal wood,"[35] but few of them were ready to hire workers who could not be continuously employed in profit-making tasks. Few employers were willing, even, to pay their workers subsistence wages, if that could be avoided. The example of wages, in fact, clearly illuminates the contradictions of these policies and shows how these contradictions could be resolved only by going outside the realm of economics, by appealing, that is, to a vision of society and social order.

Justices of the Peace were empowered, throughout this time period, to set wage rates. At the beginning of the sixteenth century, before the "labor glut," employers were fined by the justices for offering excessive wages in order to attract workers. By the late sixteenth century, as the population increased and so did the consolidation of farmland, the bidding for wages by employers had entered a downward spiral; wages, whose maximum was set by the justices of each county, rose far more slowly than prices.[36]

County wage commissions took few steps to bring the value of wages into line with the rising cost of living. Indeed,

many commissions set wage rates so low that even fully employed laboring families could not survive without public assistance.[37] With some rare exceptions, this aid was forthcoming.
By the early seventeenth century, the assistance was institutionalized through the poor rate, imposed, in accordance with the
Poor Law, on all parish residents (except those being aided).
The poor rate spread the cost of maintaining labor over the entire community. This system allowed employers to reap more
profit from their workers. Large employers of labor, frequently
the very men setting the wage rate, got off relatively cheaply,
while those who employed few or no servants subsidized the
profits of the wealthy.[38]

Moreover, the smaller employers of labor, compelled
to pay poor rates, were increasingly motivated to insist that the
poor be disciplined and carefully supervised in order to ensure
that the "largesse" of the parish was not squandered in, say, taverns. Since it was these smaller employers, the "less substantial" men of the parish who actually performed the day-to-day
work of "overseeing" the poor, their cooperation in the large
task of repressing "the people of mean condition [who] are apt
to turn every pretence and colour of grievance into uproar and
seditious mutiny" was valuable, indeed, to those with much to
lose in an uproar.[39]

The setting of wages "according to the scarcity or
plenty of the time" thus was one more instrument of the
wealthy in defending the order they considered at once precarious and vital. Low wages not only contributed to the employers' share of the value of his servants' labor but also helped to
differentiate, mark as outcast, and repress the poor, distinguishing them from the "better part of the inhabitants," i.e., those
who were paying, not receiving, the poor rate. Additionally,
they compelled laboring families—dependent on their em-
ployer/masters and on the local overseers—to adhere to the domestic order deemed proper by those in authority over them.

This last effect of the wage rates may be seen most
clearly in the differentials provided by the justices. County
wage assessments, for example, as mentioned, continued to

mandate higher wages for men than for women. They also differentiated the labor of married men from that of unmarried and began to direct that married men, despite their higher wages, be hired in preference to the unmarried. The reason for this, said the commissioners, was that married men bore responsibility for entire families while the unmarried supported only themselves.[40] Providing married men with work and wages could, therefore, *reduce* although rarely eliminating the burden of the man's family on the parish. But, the commissioners also argued, it would allow the man to assume his proper role as master within his family. That the family would require some additional assistance only permitted a closer oversight of the family's life; it did not detract from the benefits of imposing dependency on wives. The inability of married women to earn subsistence wages helped to impress upon the poor what the commissioners and their peers believed to be the correct ordering of relations between husbands and wives.

The preferential hiring of men over women which, during this time period, became notable even in fields previously monopolized by women (as will be discussed later) may be explained partially by material facts: in this age of increasing specialization, men were more likely than women to have received specialized training; men were more able to migrate into areas of high employment and to be permitted to settle there than women; men were perceived to be more productive in certain tasks (usually requiring strength) than women. Yet the material facts do not explain it all: men were hired over women for unskilled labor; men faced fewer settlement restrictions than women precisely because they were perceived as more likely to gain employment; and finally, women's lower productivity in heavy labor was always offset, at least to some degree, by their lower wages. An additional explanation is that the preferential hiring of men over women did increase the numbers of men provided with masters, men who might otherwise be masterless and dangerous.

To those who might have proposed increasing female wages or female employment, the newly obvious answer was that the wages of women served merely as what was coming to be called "pin money," while the wages of men fed families. As married men should be hired in preference to bachelors, therefore, all men should be hired in preference to women. This rationalization was self-fulfilling. If women's wages were set at pin-money rates, then they could not support families—although many women without husbands strove to do so.[41] The rationalization was new in the sixteenth century; earlier organized discrimination against women in employment opportunities had been based on male contributions to the state.[42] By the late seventeenth century, however, this new justification for hiring men over women had become a commonplace, and it was a commonplace which buttressed the new social order. It imposed a rigid gender division of labor and allowed employers to segment the glutted labor market in a way which rid them of their most overriding fear—the sturdy vagabonds who stole and the evicted husbandmen who tore down enclosures. These men were the omnipresent and most alarming specter of those poor who, as Thomas Delony explained at the turn of the century, "hate the rich because they will not set them on work."[43]

Unable or unwilling to set all the able-bodied poor on work, the rich concentrated on finding work for the able-bodied men. Men employed through this novel policy were doubly mastered: subject to the discipline of the master at work and the discipline of maintaining a family at home. They did, of course, receive in return the mastery of their families and a near monopoly over the best paying and most prestigious jobs in the restructured labor market.

In sixteenth-century England, the abject poverty of the laboring classes may have blinded them to the value of these trade-offs. Not so the upper classes and those industrious middle strata who labored industriously that they might not be taken for laborers. These classes found in the new gender division of labor and the internal family relations which expressed and sustained them the ultimate guarantors of vital hierarchy and, as chapters 5 and 6 will show, turned to them as bulwarks of social order and havens in a tempestuous world.

CHAPTER TWO

Women and the New Economic Order

Historians have only rarely asked what the social and economic changes just described meant to women.[1] Yet the effects on women can scarcely be overstated: if the prevailing ideology saw England in 1500 as a nation of self-sufficient husbandmen, divided only between those who worked and those who ruled the workers, it saw no division at all among its women. Women were housewives, first and foremost, and housewives were the ultimate guarantors of all this self-sufficiency. From the wife of the shepherd right up the social and economic ladders to the Countess of Shrewsbury, housewives ensured the provision of the basic needs—food, drink, clothing, furnishings, medicine—of their households. The way in which women did this varied: the Countess of Shrewsbury, for example, would direct her servants to brew the household's ale while the wife of the shepherd would brew her own or would sell some other product she had produced, such as wool, in order to buy the necessary ale.[2] But all wives had as their province the maintenance of the household; the decline of the subsistence household, which inevitably meant the decline of the self-sufficient housewife, thus struck at all women.

The social and economic changes which were part of England's transition to capitalism initiated the erosion of the housewife's traditional role by altering the ways in which housewives performed their traditional roles and contributing to a new assessment of women's rightful place in society. The changes earlier described affected women both as housewives and as potential entrants in the glutted labor market. In the changing society characterized by the growth of markets, cities, and the class of landless laborers, and by the increasing complexity of social stratification and of the division of labor, women found tradition an uncertain and often inadequate guide to survival, much less success.

HER PRICE ABOVE RUBIES

The Traditional Housewife
and Woman's Place in Society

In 1500, England was an overwhelmingly rural society. It was not as self-sufficient as contemporaries imagined: markets were proliferating, and housewives increasingly used them to exchange their surplus produce—cheese, butter, yarn, ale—for necessities they did not produce. But the English self-image still had strong roots in reality: most households were still substantially self-sufficient. Many housewives met almost all the basic needs of the household "of their own," as the English called it. They grew their own grains and other foodstuffs; they preserved their own meats; they brewed their own beverages; they spun the yarn with which they made their own clothes and linens; they concocted their own elixirs and medicines from the herbs and flowers they grew in their own gardens. Written laws, the statutes of Parliaments, guilds, and municipalities, and customs show that the English recognized that women were important contributors to the English economy, both as housewives and as individuals with economic functions outside the home, partly because the housewife's role in guaranteeing her family's subsistence could take her outside the realm of subsistence production and into the world of markets and skilled labor.

In addition to being the supplier and overseer of family needs, the housewife was generally understood to be her husband's helper in the family enterprise. Widows' rights clearly demonstrate this: widows of husbandmen and yeomen customarily inherited the right to all or a portion of their husbands' lands, while guilds generally granted "freedom" or full memberships to the widows of members. These customs imply that the division of labor was not rigid, and that women were perceived as having become skilled workers through the joint practice of a craft or a farm with their husbands.

Women had traditionally received little recognition in statutes. As one early sixteenth-century European visitor put it, English wives had so few legal rights that they were "entirely in the power of their husbands, their lives only excepted."[3]

The prominent English jurist Sir Thomas Smith in the mid-sixteenth century confirmed this view of women's legal rights, noting,

> The wife is so much in the power of her husband, not only her goods by marriage are straight made her husband's, and she loses administration which she had of them but also where all English men have names and surnames . . . our daughters as soon as they are married lose the surname of their family, and of the family and stock whereof they come, and take the surname of their husbands.[4]

Smith added that, in the eyes of the law, "Whatsoever [wives] get after marriage, they get to their husbands. They neither can give nor sell either of their husbands or their own" without the permission of their husbands.[5] This comment suggests that women in mid-sixteenth-century England were participating in the market economy, selling either their labor or products of their labor for money. It also suggests that married women who did so without benefit of a special legal status were denied control over their wages or their profits and, thus, effectively denied the opportunity to treat their labor or their businesses as the objects of their own economic calculations. Married women were legally denied the opportunities—which, as has been stated, were opening up for men—to invest and reinvest profits in such a way as to increase them. What Smith's addition means, plainly put, is that in this age of nascent capitalism, written law was denying women the role of capitalist.

But there were exceptions to the traditional law which bound a married woman's property and labor to her husband, and the exceptions attest to women's traditional participation in skilled work. There was, in fact, a special legal status which granted women's control of their wages or profits. This status was called "femme sole" and it granted married women the rights and status of single women before the law. As it did on many areas of the continent, this special status enabled married women to operate businesses independently of their husbands and to control the assets of their businesses. It also freed husbands from liability for the debts their wives might incur in the course of business. Although the numbers of women who claimed this status were never great, its existence testifies that married women took part in economic production, both skilled and unskilled, as independent workers, not solely as housewives. Moreover, the evident care with which various city regulations specified that "femmes soles" might practice any craft reinforces the claim that the division of labor by gender was not rigidly enforced in precapitalist England.[6]

Written law also made special provisions ensuring women's rights to own and administer land, traditionally, one recalls, the primary source of status and power in English society. Statutes guaranteed the rights of women to inherit lands and titles and the political rights associated with them. The law even offered protection against husbands who might squander the landed property. While married or "under couverture" of their husbands, women lost their rights to administer their inherited property, but they retained control over its sale and at widowhood regained full control.[7]

The women thus protected by statute law, most notably landed heiresses and "femmes soles," were, almost by definition, exceptional. They were the women whom social custom and what is called "common law" did not protect. Early modern statutes took up where custom and the common law inferred from it left off; they show us the unusual, the novel approaches to old dilemmas which custom no longer satisfactorily resolved. That laws were enacted to provide for them indicates that these women were not an insignificant minority and that they had achieved recognition at the highest level of society, among those who made law, but it also underlines their relative rarity.

But there were also more common exceptions to the laws which bound married women's property and labor to their husbands. Custom decreed that those women who "got" as part of their housewifery controlled their proceeds.[8] Traditional social customs, in other words, recognized and protected women's widespread economic activities. Thus, widows whose husbands left no wills received, by custom, the third part (or more, depending on the locality) of their husbands' lands to do with as they would or could. More to the point, housewives customarily controlled whatever surplus they accrued from the production they undertook in their role as housewives. Dairying is an obvious case. In 1500, dairying was already a stereotypically feminine activity and was viewed as an essential element in the housewife's maintenance of her household. Most rural families kept one cow (or more), and urban families could even rent a cow to supply their household needs. Any surplus that women achieved in their dairying, any extra cheese or butter, for example, they sold at the market—and custom gave them control over their proceeds.[9] Because women mainly engaged in dairying as part of their efforts to feed their families, the profits were rarely large, and they were likely to be thrown back into the household pool— to be spent on feeding the family.

Yet the custom which held that her proceeds from these activities belonged to the housewife was significant. It shows that women did engage in market activity as part of the housewife's role, underlining that what was exceptional about the "femme sole" was not her market activity. What made the "femme sole" special was that she engaged in market activity for profit *outside* her role as housewife or as helper to her husband. Women who participated in the market as part of the role of housewife had no need for the special protections available to the femme sole: custom guaranteed them their profit, and their housewifely duties prevented them from using that profit as a stepping stone to risky business ventures—for whose failures the husband and family would be held liable—which might yield high profits.

The custom is also significant because, with the aid of hindsight, it shows how the rights and roles of women of all strata were threatened by the economic changes occurring in sixteenth- and seventeenth-century England. As the husbandman lost his land, his wife often no longer could keep a cow or use dairying as a means of feeding the family "of her own." Dairying, once one of the housewife's basic means of providing for her family's needs—and for herself—grew beyond the means of many rural families. The women of these lower strata may have been forced to sell their labor for wages, over which, as Smith pointed out, they did not have the same control custom had given them over the activities traditionally associated with housewifery.

Richer women, too, found their control of dairying and its profits threatened as the profits to be made in dairying began to justify its erection into a full-fledged and full-time business. No longer the "extra" means by which, as an instance, the mid-sixteenth-century cleric Hugh Latimer's mother had provided dowries for her daughters,[10] dairying grew into a strictly commercial activity as more and more families relied exclusively on markets instead of themselves or their neighborhood to provide them with what the English had once called "poor men's meats." The women of these families lost not only a traditional task and the opportunity to "get" an income, they lost also the rights and prestige which had derived from their successful efforts to fulfill these tasks.

Other customs which had similarly recognized and reinforced the importance of the housewife's skilled contribution to her family, and her national economy, were similarly eroding, and the erosion threatened what might be called the "traditional rights of the Englishwoman." The freedom of movement, for example, which visitors from the continent considered so noteworthy and about which the Englishmen preened themselves was intimately connected to the housewife's customary role of provider of family subsistence. Traditionally, English women had gone everywhere. Rural women attended markets, buying and selling according to the needs and abilities of their families. Urban women, especially poor urban women, obtained the money necessary for their own and their families' subsistence by purchasing goods at central markets and then "hawking" them at points throughout the city or door-to-door. Wealthy women and even, one shocked visitor noted, "ladies of distinction," dined and drank in taverns, often owned and staffed by women.[11] Traditionally, in other words, women moved about in public. But they did so in order to fulfill their housewifely responsibility to provide for their families.

All this movement gave women collectively a powerful role in economic affairs, which again was part of their housewifery. Housewives, as the primary purchasers of household goods, set "market values" on these goods. The housewives arrived at their appraisal of market value through barter and information exchanged at taverns, markets, and childbed. Historians today are rediscovering that it was women, not men, who precipitated food riots when prices rose in what the women believed to be unconscionable ways or when they suspected merchants of hoarding.[12] Women's "gossip," that is, customarily served as an important source of political, economic, and social intelligence and contributed to the formulation of what is now called public opinion. It enabled women to be more efficient housewives while at the same time it granted them importance beyond their households. The varied social strata of the women participating in the creation of gossip, moreover, may well have promoted among some women an awareness that their status and occupation were determined by gender as much as by the birth and wealth so important for men.

The information gained by women as they "gadded about" did not always lead to the immediate pecuniary advantage of the family. The social contacts they made and maintained did not always provide immediate benefits. Their contribution to public opinion could be small. Yet, men recognized that freedom of movement and association allowed women to hone their trading skills and provided them with the experience necessary for intelligent discrimination, that their immersion in the social economy enabled women to help their husbands prosper in business, and that families could rise socially through the connections made by women, connections whose continuance demanded the continued mobility of women. The customary rights and liberties of Englishwomen allowed women to be successful housewives and husbanders of their goods through allowing families to use the skills of women to the best advantage of the family, without regard to rigid gender conventions. These customs had grown up and thrived in the traditional English society peopled by subsistence farmers, a society whose primary social division was between the gentry and the nongentry, who were everyone else. As has been seen, however, by the mid-sixteenth century, this society no longer existed.

Status Differentiation, Markets, and Housewives

In the years between 1500 and 1660, English society could still be seen as composed of two classes if those two classes were defined the ruling class and those who were ruled. The ruling class included, in significant numbers, merchants, traders, and yeomen—men who worked—and self-sufficient husbandmen were disappearing. A large and growing segment of the population had lost any claims on the land, and many who continued to farm were growing crops for the market as often as for their own use. Indeed, the profit orientation was proving so strong that rural areas began to suffer from shortages of dairy products—as Harrison noted, they were "wont to be accounted as one of the chief stays throughout the island"—because dairy farmers were sending their products to urban markets where prices and profits were higher.[13] The changes in the structure of English society affected all housewives, but, as the instance of dairying has already suggested, they affected housewives differently. All housewives faced new dependence on the market, and the nature of the dependence varied according to the social and economic status of the housewife's family.

It is worth noting that the English were unprepared for any variation among housewives, for this partly explains how slow they were to acknowledge it. For generations, all housewives had performed the same tasks in essentially the same ways. Although wealthy wives delegated more tasks than they performed themselves, rich and poor housewives alike had focused their attention and energies on providing "of their own" what their households needed to survive. In 1500, the wife of the London merchant had occupations very similar to those of a wife of a Lancaster farmer. In 1650, the two had little in common except for the distance each had traveled, separately, from self-sufficiency. Class, education, area of residence—these traits were coming to play an increasingly significant role in differentiating the lives of women. The examination of how women were affected by the increasing accessibility, regularity, and broadening of markets, themselves a primary cause of the erosion of the housewife's traditional role, illustrates both the general erosion and the particular variations.

For housewives of the landless strata, the growing market network was both a blessing and a curse. At the market, they could buy the basic necessities of life—but only if they or their husbands managed to sell enough labor power to cover the price. The markets provided the means of subsistence, but they did so at wrenching cost to those who had no choice but the market. Housewives of the lower strata, in other words, looked to the market to fulfill their new needs for subsistence goods, and the housewives hoped to sell their labor in order to buy what they could not produce. For housewives of the landed and professional strata, on the contrary, the growth of the market economy was, at least in the short-term, more unequivocally a boon. These housewives found more manufactured goods available than ever before, and these goods were relatively cheaper than they had been. The price of luxury items rose far more slowly than the price of basic foodstuffs. Housewives of the upper and middling strata thus also looked to the market to fulfill new needs, but these "needs" were for white bread, wax candles, and imported wines to replace mixed-grain bread, homemade candles, and home-brewed ale, and the housewives hoped to reduce their own labor burden. In all classes, the traditional role of the housewife was eroding because women were fulfilling their role of providing household needs through purchase rather than production, but the erosion was felt differently by women of different strata.

The increasing emphasis on lifestyle as a criterion of status added to the general erosion of the housewife's role as well as to the differential between housewives of different strata. Food provides perhaps the premier example of how the struggle for status interacted with the expansion of markets, each stimulating the other. As the identification of dairy products as "poor men's meats" suggests, food was a traditional symbol of status.

William Harrison observed in the mid-sixteenth century that

> The bread throughout the land is made of such grain as the soil yields; nevertheless, the gentility commonly provide themselves sufficiently of wheat for their own tables, while their household servants and poor neighbors in some shires are forced to content themselves with rye, or barley, yea, and in time of dearth, many with bread made either of beans, peas or oats.[14]

Families with pretensions to gentility obviously ate wheat bread. Ironically, however, poor families with no pretensions to gentility were coming to eat wheat bread too, because bakers, having found they could make a higher profit from wheat than from mixed-grain bread, manufactured more wheat bread, and poor women were dependent on what the baker manufactured. In both kinds of family, what had been a traditional task of the housewife—the production of bread—shifted to the market. The wealthier families went in search of status or because they did not have the milling equipment and ovens necessary to produce high-status wheat bread at home; the poorer families went because they had no choice: without their own grains and ovens, they could produce no bread at all.[15] In both instances, the role of the housewife changed but it changed for different reasons, and the housewives themselves reacted to the changes differently.

As the case of bread shows, wives in the middle and upper strata had continually to seek out new items, not yet accessible to the poor, which could proclaim the family's high status. Moreover, although dramatists frequently targeted women as the source of a family's pretensions in diet,[16] the concern with status was common to both genders, and conspicuous consumption was a popular means for social climbing by both genders.[17] William Harrison acknowledged, without making distinctions of gender, that "the kind of meat which is obtained with most difficulty and cost is commonly taken for most delicate and thereupon will each guest soonest feed."[18] The housewife whose family would climb into the upper ranks of society was well advised to forget her basic cookery and cultivate a new refinement of taste.

Gervase Markham, for example, in his early seventeenth-century housewifery manual, appropriately entitled *The English Housewife*, praised the housewife who produced her own food but warned that the failure to develop skills in wine selection and preservation "could turn the husband much loss."[19] Markham's message was plain: the social prestige of the family was at stake with each morsel guests lifted to their delicate mouths. Both "sparing tables" and tables laden down with such coarse "country" fare as housewives were wont to prepare were social liabilities. The wife who supervised a chef (preferably, of the most prestigious kind, male) capable of rising to heights of culinary skill helped her husband more than the wife who insisted on performing the old tasks in the old ways.

Indeed, the wife's very effort to share in the preparation of the banquet could mark her as ungenteel, for as the gentleman was traditionally identified by his lack of labor, so, too, as many women were learning, there was much work the lady did not do. Families unsure of their place—but hoping for high rankings—often deemed it better to be safe than *déclassé*, and many wives of the middle but aspiring strata found themselves delegating many tasks it did not "do" for them to perform on their own.[20]

In England's new market society, then, housewives of all strata lost—or failed to perform—traditional tasks, but women of the various strata lost them for different reasons and with some different consequences. Where, in 1500, many housewives did meet almost all the basic needs of their households for food, clothing, medicine, and so on of their own, in 1650, many housewives filled these basic needs at the market.

Landless women obviously did so because of their landlessness; they had nothing "of their own" with which to meet family needs. Housewives did not receive the rights to lands from which their husbands were evicted. Without land, they could neither grow their own foods nor raise their own cattle. Landless, they failed to fulfill their traditional responsibilities, and if they tried to compensate by earning money through wage labor, they found themselves disadvantaged by both their traditionally low wage rates and employers' strong concern with "placing" men. Increasingly, these wives depended on the money wages brought in by their husbands and developed skills in consuming and "making do" rather than producing.

Although contemporaries made no distinctions between them, the failure of the middle- and upper-class women to continue production and the increasing dependence of these women, too, on the money provided by husbands are rather more complicated than they were for poor women. Many of the rich and middling women did not lose their traditional means of production, but they did find the value of their production diminished, both relatively and absolutely. Because, traditionally, the purpose of the housewife's production was not simply to keep her busy but to meet her family's needs most effectively—in terms both of economic cost and social status—these housewives, too, found themselves drawn into the market to buy their necessities and increasingly dependent on money income, for which, as is discussed below, they, too, depended on their husbands.

The reasons for the diminishing value of the housewife's production were multiple. Some, as already mentioned, were directly related to the new complexity of social stratification: if a housewife's labor degraded her husband and the family's status, then, whatever its use in feeding or clothing the family, its value was low. Others were related more directly to the process of urbanization England experienced in these centuries or to the mobility engendered in landless and landed families alike as the search for economic opportunities and profit became more widespread. All these forces could—and did—help to erode the traditional role of the housewife.

Brewing provides a classic example of how urbanization and mobility could affect the housewife's traditional role. In 1500, most households produced their own beer and ale. By 1650, so much beer and ale were sold that taxation on their sale netted the king a substantial revenue. Throughout the sixteenth and seventeenth centuries, the cost of "stillery" equipment remained relatively high, while the price of purchased beverages, thanks to volume production and sale, remained low and supplies were easily accessible. Distilling equipment was huge, costly, and difficult to transport—clearly a worthwhile investment for the commercial producer but not so clearly worthwhile to the small family. Mobile families might find the expense of transportation not justified by the savings of home brew; urban families had to consider not only the cost of the equipment itself but also the cost of the space to house it—and urban space was at a premium. Lady Margaret Hoby, a wealthy gentlewoman of the late sixteenth century, divided her time between residence at her country property and visits to London and other cities. While in the country, she drank the ale she brewed herself. While living in cities, even when she stayed for lengthy periods of time, she purchased her beverages on the market, evidently concluding it did not pay to transport her equipment.

Families more permanently resident in the city—and by 1660, 7 percent of English people lived in London alone—had to consider whether the capital invested in distilling equipment and its housing might not be put to more efficient use—assuming, of course, they had the capital in the first place, for cities were populated by the poor in even greater numbers than the rich. For all these poor people and for those wealthier families who prudently questioned the outlay of capital, the ready availability and low price of beer at the market eased the transition from producing-consumers to consumers.[21] The transition was made even less painful by the more tasty beer which was often available in commercial outlets, which often could afford to allow a longer period of aging than could housewives. The conviviality and gossip available in pubs and taverns made the transition close to a pleasure for many poor families—so close, in fact, that local and national authorities sought to suppress the taverns as hotbeds of the vice so endemic to the poor.[22]

Between Husbands and Wives

The social and economic processes which were part of England's transition to capitalism, besides eroding the housewife's role in providing her family's subsistence, also eroded her role in providing her husband with help in his own trade or craft. The increasing availability and relative cheapness of wage labor allowed even small masters to afford to employ journeymen laborers rather than to rely on their wives as their primary helpers. The masters, moreover, were encouraged to do so by guild regulations and status prescribing the hiring of skilled labor to assist in some production processes. The purpose of these regulations was to provide employment for masterless men, but there were benefits to masters. The hired laborer could focus his attention on the task at hand in a way that housewives, who had to attend to child care, housekeeping, spinning, and the multifarious other tasks of housewifery, could not. The hired laborers could thus repay the cost of their wage through their higher productivity, and the family need for the wife to second her husband—which, again, distracted her from her own tasks—was diminished among both rural and urban small property owners. The need disappeared entirely among the wealthy where, in fact, the wife's participation in the family enterprise was coming to be seen as a blot on the husband's reputation rather than the natural consequence of marital union.[23] Housewives who did not help their husbands did not learn their husbands' skills and did not earn, as once they had done, a place in skilled market production through their role as housewives.

The decreasing likelihood of a wife's active participation in what was, increasingly, the husband's business was reflected in both urban guild regulations and yeomen wills. In the early seventeenth century, guilds began to distinguish between the freedom of the full member of the company, achieved through apprenticeship, purchase, or patrimony, and the freedom of the widow of a member. The freedom of the widow began to be treated as a capital good, which would be sold, leased, or passed on through remarriage rather than used to continue in the business oneself. Wills of both urban and rural property owners less frequently in the seventeenth century than before appointed widows as executors of estates and guardians of children.[24] These two phenomena suggest that husbands were losing confidence in the abilities or desires of their wives simply to take over the husband's place in the "family" enterprise.

At the same time, of course, the husband was encroaching on the housewife's place and denying her the traditional access to markets available to the housewife engaged in subsistence production, closing the gap through which the housewife might have legitimately entered into profit-oriented market activity. The case of dairying is once again a good example. When, as suggested above, it grew apparent that well-managed dairying could become a regular source of great profit rather than simply an irregular means by which housewives earned some "extra" money, many wives lost control of dairying. Where dairying was still part of the housewife's subsistence production, it remained under the wife's control. But where dairying had become primarily a market activity, husbands took over.

Thomas Tusser's mid-sixteenth-century manual on farming demonstrates the shift. Tusser told husbands to learn from their wives how to set up a dairy, but he clearly assumed that the husband would make and implement marketing decisions for the dairy business he established with the help of his wife.[25] The housewife on whose skill the sixteenth-century husband relied was an "expert" consultant; she was not a partner. Still occupied with meeting the wide range of daily needs of the family, this housewife, like the wife of the craftsman, could not devote the constant attention, travail, and travel necessary for the best advantage of the business. Hence, as dairying—and poultrying, market gardening, and other activities once part of the housewife's effort to provide her family's basic needs— shifted to profit-making capitalist enterprises, housewives lost their traditional place in them.

The cumulative effect of these changes in traditional social relations and household patterns of production and consumption was to deprive the housewife of many of her traditional tasks as well as of the prestige within her family and society which she had once won by her success in meeting household needs through her accomplishment of them. The social perceptions of what was occurring increased the devaluation of women caused by the actual erosion of their housewifely role, since, while the failure of many wives to perform their traditional tasks and achieve their traditional results was obvious to contemporary eyes, the reasons for the failures were not obvious. Women had not, after all, won prestige because their labor was so prestigious—the prestige of labor, as will be seen, was only beginning to be recognized—but rather because the fruits of their labor resulted in the family's well-being. And it was the lack of these fruits, not women's failure to perform any specific tasks, for which contemporaries condemned women. The individual husband and wife may have recognized the need for the wife to change the way she provided for the family's needs, but collectively men saw only that women were not doing what they had done: indeed, they were *failing* to do it.

Contemporaries did not blame the "failure" on changing economic conditions; they failed to see that women without land cannot grow the food with which to feed their families and women without brewing equipment cannot brew. Contemporaries also did not see the housewife's "failure" as a temporary phenomenon: something to be endured while women "retooled" their skills and figured out how best to meet old—and new—needs in the new ways demanded by the new social and economic conditions. On the contrary, contemporaries saw in the wife's "failure" proof of deep-rooted female inferiority and, as is discussed below, reason to shift the entire financial responsibility for the family onto the husband, obviating, in the process, any economic retooling by the wife.

Consequently, the sixteenth and seventeenth centuries in England marked a crucial turning point in the lives of English women: these years witnessed the beginning of the decline of the role of housewife as, in these transitional centuries, what housewives could fulfill of their traditional roles very untraditionally depended largely on their money income and what they could do with it. This placed them at an untraditional day-to-day dependence on their husbands, historically the better provider of cash income, and often the sole provider. As is discussed in considerably more detail below (chapters 4–6), this economic dependence contributed to the subordination of women within their families and within society.

WOMEN IN AND OUT
OF THE LABOR MARKET

As the status "femme sole" and the stereotypical female trades of dairymaid, fishwife, and tavern hostess make clear, however, women in the sixteenth century were not only housewives. Housewifery was their most important social role, but women also performed other roles in the social economy, sometimes as a means of fulfilling their housewifely duty of provisioning, sometimes as a means of providing for themselves outside marriage. In the investigation of the effects of the social and economic changes of sixteenth- and seventeenth-century England on women, therefore, women's opportunities as wage laborers or capitalists must be considered. They were, it is obvious, quite restricted.

In some ways, the restrictions of women's opportunities outside the home corresponded to their constriction within the home. Women lost skills and opportunities to learn them within the home for the same reasons that they lost opportunities to obtain and exercise skills outside the home. There is, however, a significance difference. The devaluation of women as economic producers in the public sphere was both more clear-cut and more final than their devaluation within the family. Within their households, women remained, depending on social status and individual arrangements, to a greater or lesser extent, the partners and helpers of their husbands, and what they lost in productive functions, they could replace, to a greater or lesser extent, by reproductive functions. In other words, despite the general erosion of the housewife's role, some wives continued to play important roles in their family economies, and other women began to perform different roles within the families, most notably that of nurturing mother. As is shown in chapter 4, the role of mother could be a source of both power and prestige.

Outside the family, there was less room for the negotiation about roles and responsibilities within the working unit formed by husbands and wives. Individual deviations from the more rigid gender division of labor characteristic of capitalist society could still occur within the family but were rarer outside the home. Women did perform new tasks outside the home, as the changing economy opened up new occupations, but the occupations which opened up for women were uniformly at the bottom of the social and economic ladders. Outside the family, the gender segregation of labor was becoming more firmly fixed and more hierarchical. Moreover, the exclusion of women from crafts and trades and the debasement of "woman's work" took on great significance as the crafts and trades rose in prestige and men interpreted women's absence from them as proof of women's natural inability to attain skills, and women's heavy presence in low-skilled arenas of work as proof that these tasks were all women were fit to do.[26]

To understand why this had so severe and permanent an effect on women workers, one must reconsider some of the basic socioeconomic changes in sixteenth- and seventeenth-century England. The increasing numbers of landless changed the English employment structure. Historians have commonly singled out two important elements of this change. There were relatively more persons available for wage labor than ever before, and there was developing a more complex and stratified division of labor.[27] As was discussed in chapter 1, the increase in the size of the labor pool and its new division were factors dialectically contributing to the relative cheapness of manufactured goods, the spread of markets, and the changing social structure. And the number of wage laborers increased as it became increasingly difficult to move out of that status. For the agricultural worker, the obstacle was land. For the artisan or craftsperson, the obstacle was, more often than not, the accumulation of capital—capital to pay the master's entry fee at the guild or trade association or to buy or rent a shop and to stock raw materials and labor, the costs of which were rising as both inflation and the efforts of masters to safeguard their superior position took their toll. One seventeenth-century minister warned his congregants that, unless parents provided their children with some initial capital, the children would be unable to achieve real economic independence: "in regard whereof the times we live, it is . . . needful for setting up in a good calling and for obtaining a good match that children have some stock or portion."[28]

The more specialized division of labor widened the gap between the master artisan and his journeypeople. The masters (most of them men) controlled the guilds, and in their effort to maintain and increase their own income and prestige in the swiftly changing society, they used this control to limit their own numbers and to control competition. To ply any skilled trade in urban areas, one needed the "freedom" of a guild, yet guilds were making this more and more difficult to obtain. They raised fees, lengthened terms, and increased costs of apprenticeships. These measures directly affected opportunities for women to participate as skilled laborers and as capitalists. Some crafts explicitly excluded women; others simply raised the apprenticeship fees so high that it was unlikely any father would pay such a sum for the training of a daughter, whose earnings would go to the man whose name she took, her husband.[29] Most guilds worked hard at convincing society that their particular craft was highly skilled, a "mystery" whose penetration deserved monetary and prestige rewards. The "prospering middle strata" were found in large numbers in those guilds which succeeded in creating "professions" out of what had once been work. In so doing they almost always created male monopolies.

The following pages examine in more detail exactly what the effects of these trends toward a more complex and stratified division of labor had on women. By looking at what women did and ceased to do in the textile crafts, in brewing, and in medicine, one may gain an understanding of what the changing structure of the labor market meant to women. It is not simply the case that women were excluded: women were pushed out of some crafts, but they never dropped out of the labor market entirely.

Textiles

Before the sixteenth century, women had been prominently and prestigiously employed in various textile crafts, as both part-time and full-time workers. But by 1650, those textile crafts in which women predominated were not prestigious. As a general rule, in fact, the more predominantly female the trade, the lower its social prestige and remuneration. Even silk-weaving, which in the fifteenth and sixteenth centuries had included aristocratic women among its practitioners, had sunk to the level of a poorly paid and poorly esteemed occupation.[30]

Modern accounts of the textile industry note that, already by 1500, weaving had been transferred from the housewife to the "professional" male weaver.[31] The transfer elevated weaving from an easily acquired skill, practiced by most women as a basic aspect of housewifery, to a special craft which only men could practice and for which special equipment (requiring a capital investment) was necessary. This was a typical process in the sixteenth and seventeenth centuries, but the instance of weaving is especially revealing because some of the mechanics of the transference are visible.

Existing records show that in the late fifteenth century male weavers and would-be weavers, unable to find work, consciously took steps to prevent women from competing with them for work. Groups of male weavers petitioned the king to bar women from the trade of weaving. They gave two reasons for the proposed ban. First, they claimed, women were not strong enough to operate looms without help. Until the development of the power loom, it is true that women needed help to operate looms most efficiently. But so did men. Statutes and by-laws of weaving companies throughout England testify to the dependence of male weavers on additional sets of arms and hands. They also testify that the gender of the helping hands had no necessary or, even, conventional connection with the quality of the help. While excluding women from entering the trade on their own, the regulations expressly allow the weaver to accept help from his wife and daughters, equating the wife's aid with that of a competent journeyman. The woman's strength was clearly not the real issue.

The second claim the weavers made to justify women's debarment from the trade does bring the real issue into clear focus. They complained that there was not enough work available to employ all the male and female weavers seeking it. Like most of their contemporaries, they did not envisage an expanding market (demand) providing employment for all suppliers, and they proposed to reduce artificially the number of suppliers to meet the naturally limited demand. They chose to do this by eliminating the competition of women because, they asserted, men were more deserving of employment than women. King and nation owed male weavers surety of employment because male weavers could serve as soldiers and defend king and country against attack. For this reason, men were more valuable to the state than women (who, however, did bear these potential soldiers). The weavers claimed that, in exchange for the protection they would provide the state in wartime, the state owed them protection of their livelihoods in peacetime.[32] There was, incidentally, no claim that men were more valuable to their families and needed to bring in a "family wage."

Spinning, another of the textile crafts, remained the province of women. But, while weaving was upgraded to professional status—albeit low professional status—spinning remained the stereotypical by-industry. As Anthony FitzHerbert, an early sixteenth-century writer on husbandry, noted, "A woman cannot get her living honestly on the distaff [yet] it stoppeth a gap and must needs be had."[33] Spinning was an activity women could pick up and discard at will; it was a skill shared by almost every woman and most female children. No "mystery" into whose secrets one had to be initiated, its remuneration was low and fell even lower in the course of the sixteenth and seventeenth centuries just as the "gap" needing to be filled by cash widened. Yet women span in ever greater numbers, both for their families and for what was virtually an inexhaustible market. It took eight spinners to provide enough yarn for one weaver, an index of the low productivity of spinning but also assurance of a market.[34]

Other crafts, in and out of the textile industry, followed this same pattern. The crafts in which women predominated were characterized by low initiation investments (in either equipment or training), low skills, low pay, and low prestige. Never having had access to specialized training in equal numbers with men, now that training was the surest means for economic success, they were even less likely to receive it. There are two basic reasons for this. First, families were notoriously unwilling to make such long-term investments in daughters whose husbands reaped the rewards. Second, their lack of power or organized presence within the crafts rendered them unable to influence guild regulations aimed at restricting competition and easy targets for the regulations.

There were, however, certain advantages to women's failure to specialize, especially if the woman's income did serve as only a nonessential supplement to the husband's. What women lacked in sophisticated skills, they made up for in versatility. Particularly in the textile trade, this could assure them steady access to an income. General sewing was less prestigious and profitable than haberdashery, for example, but more families could afford the irregular services of a cheap seamstress. The ability of women, moreover, to perform general tasks on the periphery of the textile trade such as sewing, laundering, and starching reinforced the trend toward the "socialization" of such tasks, the removal of them from the private household to the market. Because women performed these tasks for low wages, it began to make economic sense for more families to hire such tasks out to women who specialized in them than for the housewife, for whom sewing was but one task of many, to do her own.[35] The implications of this shift to the market for the housewife/consumer have been discussed.

Brewing

Brewing, already mentioned as a central task of the housewife, illustrates how women were affected by apparently impersonal, not gender-related, forces. As brewing became more large-scale and regular a trade, supposedly involving skills so great as to constitute a "mystery," men, more likely than women to gain parental backing in the form of training or capital, outnumbered women and used their dominance to prevent the small-scale competition women might have offered. The way in which this occurred demonstrates that there need have been no conscious conspiracy to exclude women or to degrade their skills for women to be pushed out of a trade or their skills devalued: the new market forces could simply interact with the old social practices and women would lose ground.

The first brewers guild in London had been founded in the late fourteenth century with female as well as male members. Outside the limits of London, it was the custom that anyone could sell ale as long as he or she announced the sale and permitted local authorities to inspect the ale for contamination. The most common sellers were women who had made too much ale for household consumption. Because so many housewives sold ale in these circumstances, brewing carried no special esteem as a craft.

In the sixteenth century, the London guild began to insist that the brewing of acceptable ales to beers was a special skill, a "mystery" into which apprentices must be initiated rather than something girls imbibed at mother's knee. Members put through by-laws requiring training of prospective brewers, thereby limiting entry to the field, giving themselves control over that entry, and suggesting that brewing for sale was qualitatively different from brewing for household use. There was, in fact, a qualitative difference between home brew and "store-bought." The early sixteenth-century introduction of hops enabled brewers to store and age their product. Hops, not any arcane mystery, accounted for the frequent superiority of purchased ale. The royal determination to increase revenues from the sale of ale coupled with the efforts of national and local authorities to reduce opportunities for the poor to congregate, to wallow in the vice of drunkenness, or to engage in the "lewd" behavior stimulated by drink, aided the company in its efforts to separate brewing for use, an easy, nonmysterious process, from brewing for sale, a mystery. In 1552, the king forbade household sale of ale. Ale could be sold only from alehouses which were licensed—for a fee—by (male) Justices of the Peace. In the early seventeenth century, royal edicts prevented women from selling their surplus to these alehouses by requiring alehouses to purchase their own stocks only from licensed wholesalers, i.e., wholesalers who paid a fee to the crown.[36]

It does not seem that the king or the brewers guild or even the local justices were consciously attempting to prevent women from brewing. The brewers simply wanted to ensure themselves an income and saw limiting the number of brewers as their best chance. The king wanted to ensure the most successful collection of taxes and saw limiting the numbers of persons from whom he collected them as his best hope. The local authorities wanted to keep a strict eye on the poor. The steps taken to limit the numbers of brewers—requiring licenses and apprenticeships, with apprenticeship fees—however, affected men and women differently. The unwillingness of fathers to invest in their daughters made their establishment as professional brewers less likely and, over time, contributed to the belief that the manufacture of home brew, a process requiring less skill than producing for sale, was all women could do. The local authorities, moreover, were probably more likely to license male tavern keepers than female ones in the belief that men could better control unruly customers.

Medicine

Medicine, the last example studied here of the more complex and stratified division of labor, shows how women's traditional exclusion from higher education affected their position in the labor market both relatively—as with brewing, women possessed the basic skills but the basic skills became notedly "inferior" to those of professionals—and absolutely—women were expressly forbidden to attend institutions of higher learning, thus expressly forbidden from becoming physicians or lawyers. The major vehicle for this exclusion and devaluation in the field of medicine was, as already mentioned, the male Royal College of Physicians, founded early in the sixteenth century. Its greatest achievement over the next one hundred and fifty years was convincing the general populace that, despite its poor success rate, the medicine practiced by male physicians was based on expert, scientific knowledge and therefore far superior to the physic of women without university educations. In the words of Gervase Markham, the popular early seventeenth-century writer of how-to manuals for women, "The depth and secrets of the most excellent art of physic is beyond the capacity of the most skillful woman . . . lodging in the breast of learned professors."[37] Women, whose abilities as healers had been based on knowledge passed down from mother to daughter or on instruction from learned men,[38] could not counteract this pretension to scientific knowledge and suffered a marked decline in prestige relative to physicians as a consequence.

The vocation of midwifery, which did not succeed in establishing itself as a "profession," epitomizes the trend. Until the early sixteenth century women enjoyed a monopoly over the practice, mainly because of the social conventions deploring the presence of men at childbed. By the mid-sixteenth century, the monopoly had been breached, and by mid-seventeenth century, male midwives (especially those with access to forceps) were in demand. Significantly, although some urban midwives had offered apprenticeships, the midwives had not banded together and/or set up any form of regular training for their numbers. Women acted as midwives not because they had received training but because they were in the neighborhood, might have experience at childbed, might be close friends of the family, and, without doubt, were willing to earn money.

The first efforts to regulate midwifery occurred in the early sixteenth century and had little to do with medical skill. They aimed at guaranteeing the moral acceptability of the midwife who, in clerical acknowledgment of the dangers of childbed, had been granted the authority to baptize infants. Thus, in 1512, the church was given the power to license midwives. Church rules made the licenses dependent on the midwives taking courses in religious and medical instruction and passing examinations given by clergy and by physicians and other midwives. These regulations were rarely enforced, usually only in towns. In 1557, the English Church denied women the authority to baptize even in emergency. In itself, this is a sign of the declining esteem in which women were held. More than this, it ended all official attempts to regulate and train midwives.

The midwives themselves did not step into the breach until the early seventeenth century. They made no efforts to form guilds or to impose standards of training or practice. Then, in 1616, distressed by the low esteem in which midwifery had fallen and the inroads male midwives had made into the female practice and fearful of being subjected to male control, London midwives sought to incorporate. They asked King James for permission to form a guild in order to provide professional training and raise standards of practice among midwives. James, well known for his low opinion of women, asked the Royal College of Physicians for advice. The physicians readily agreed with the midwives that standards were low but disagreed with their schemes to raise them. The physicians condemned the midwives' attempts to be self-governing. The doctors proposed, and James agreed, that the midwives be made subject to the Royal College of Physicians, who could provide training for them. As James noted in his response to the midwives' request, midwifery was still a predominantly female occupation and thus incapable of self-government.[39]

Not surprisingly, given their newly obvious lack of training, the status of midwives in general and relative to physicians declined. The physicians who competed with midwives for clients, and thus had something of a vested interest in downgrading midwife skills, shared Markham's belief that women could not understand the "deep mysteries" of medical science and made no effort to explain these mysteries to them.

THE OVERVIEW

What happened to women working in the textile crafts and as brewers and midwives was part of the general trend in the sixteenth through the nineteenth centuries to a more specialized division of labor throughout society and to an economy characterized by commodity production. Women, starting without "special skills," were unable to turn what skills they did have into special, professional skills. Some specific failures were because of the conscious and organized opposition of men as men, some because of the conscious and organized opposition of men as practitioners of a trade, opposing competition from anyone, woman or man. Others involved less conscious human agency. The results, however, were that, by about 1650, the trades in which women predominated were characterized by low pay and low prestige. The trades did require skills, but the skills involved were disparaged by society: after all, if any woman could spin, then spinning could not be special. Much of "woman's work" did involve low levels of productivity and required many hours of work to realize a profit or product. The work was, generally, of a kind which could easily be interrupted and started again, giving women who worked for wages the opportunity to do so in moments free from housewifery.[40]

There were some women, throughout the seventeenth century, who were active in highly skilled crafts and trades, members of guilds which fought hard to upgrade the craft in the eyes of society. But, increasingly, women were members of guilds by right of their husbands and were unable to ply the trade themselves: they had neither the skills nor the rights to conduct business or direct production on their own. The widow's freedom of her husband's company no longer involved her own participation in his craft. As mentioned, guild regulations began to distinguish between the freedom of those who earned it by apprenticeship and widows who gained it by marriage. The freedom of the widow was comparable to a marriage settlement, a means of income which she realized by leasing it out rather than working it herself. The widow's freedom could also serve as a dowry, luring a second husband who could use the freedom, not merely lease it or sell its products. The widow was a *rentier*, but it was the capitalist who was remaking the world in his own image.

Furthermore, there is some evidence that, even where women continued to participate in the family enterprise, the nature of their participation changed from the sixteenth to the seventeenth centuries. Rather than help to make the product or supervise the labor, wives directed their efforts simply to selling the product. One historian has commented that "the wit and beauty" of the seventeenth-century wives of London Cheapside merchants was a legend. The wit and beauty were bait luring customers into shops but were totally unconnected with the merchandise for sale.[41] Women sat outside their husbands' shops and bantered with prospective buyers; they no longer participated in the inside, productive work.

For women of the growing landless strata, who were "free" to work and forced by economics to take any work they could get, the most favorable position was that of domestic servant in a prospering family. The servant had a good chance of obtaining enough to eat and an opportunity to learn domestic skills which could be of use, either in her own family or in another wage position.[42] As these positions became increasingly valuable, however, they became harder to get. More women desired them; fewer women left them for marriage and their own families, and finally, employers were more careful of the costs of servants.[43]

Some families paid employers to hire their daughters, terming the household service "apprenticeship." Indeed, the only occupation to which girls were apprenticed in sizable numbers in the seventeenth century was that of "housewife."[44] Married women found it almost impossible to obtain secure service positions like this, regardless of apprenticeship, both because employers preferred unmarried women with no conflicting loyalties or family responsibilities and because their family responsibilities required their presence at home. Married women usually engaged in wage-producing tasks which permitted them to live at home, providing what family care and what wage they could.[45] Few succeeded in achieving "middling" status for themselves or their families by their own unaided efforts. More succeeded, despite the new assumption that widows could not take over their husbands' responsibilities, in maintaining the status and wealth he had achieved. But, of course, no seventeenth-century housewives succeeded in running their households as truly self-sufficient units. For this, all women suffered.

The market economy was clearly taking over England by 1600. Social expectations of what housewives should and could do did not keep pace with the fast-changing economy; and seventeenth-century housewives, judged by the standard of their grandmothers, were failures. They depended on money brought in by their husbands to buy even essential foodstuffs; products they could and did make at home suffered in the comparison to more prestigious store-bought products—white bread replacing brown and wine or purchased ale replacing home brew—and they no longer participated regularly in the information network which had kept them in touch with the world outside their doors. The women of sixteenth- and seventeenth-century England did much of the work necessary to keep their families and, thus, society going. But, where six-teenth-century women had made necessary objects, seven-teenth-century women were more likely to purchase them. In the labor market, seventeenth-century women formed the low-skilled cellar, and in their homes, they acted the drudge.

CHAPTER THREE

Women and Place

It did not escape the notice of sharp-eyed Englishfolk in the late sixteenth and seventeenth centuries either that women's housewifery was not what once it had been or that women were finding gainful employment increasingly difficult to come by. But the way in which the English interpreted these facts contributed to a devaluation of women. For the English interpreted women's obvious material difficulties as proof of women's inferiority and turned the economic problems women faced in the transitional society of the sixteenth and seventeenth centuries into permanent liabilities in the newly emergent capitalist society.

Take But Degree Away: Order and Hierarchy

As discussed earlier, English society in 1500 was hierarchical and the English intended that it remain so. At no time during the sixteenth or seventeenth centuries does anyone in England seem seriously to have espoused the creation of an egalitarian society, although many offered various suggestions about how society might be differently ordered.[1] People conceived of society as ordered or graded as all of creation was ordered, by God. The dominant view, actively promoted by both state and church, was, as mentioned in chapter 2, that the social hierarchy was a reflection of the moral hierarchy. In other words, the aristocracy—the nobility—were noble in mind as well as birth. Those lower down the social scale were lower or coarser in spirit and build as well as social place; they were "the inferior sort . . . the meaner sort" and naturally subject to their "betters." As Henry Smith, a popular clergyman of the late sixteenth century, put it, "It is not right that the worse should rule the better, but that the better should rule the worse."[2] That the English conflated social status, moral worth, and political power helps to explain their preoccupation with status. For the sixteenth- and seventeenth-century English, the question was, in the face of evident social disarray, how to know who was better because, unquestionably, someone had to rule.

The power to rule, after all, came from God, according to scripture, and God meant it as a gift both to those who wielded it and to those under it, according to the English. John Aylmer, propagandist for Elizabeth, explained in the mid-sixteenth century that God had ordained

that some ruling and some obeying, concord and tranquillity might continue. For if all should rule, there should be none to obey. Or, if all should obey, there should be none to rule. Wherefore, God has so disposed his creatures in the world that such as He will deck and beautify with His singular gifts should by ruling others that lack them be means to aid and help them.[3]

Thomas Gataker, a prominent seventeenth-century clergyman, observed that the need of people for some sort of hierarchy was so urgent that

there can be no ordinary intercourse and commerce or conversing between person and person, but there must be precedency on the one part and a yielding of it on the other. Now where they be equals, there may be some question, some difficulty.[4]

God himself did not, of course, esteem the prince more highly than the peasant. But men were less acute than God in discerning inner thoughts and souls, in appreciating inner worth, and the English believed that God gave them the outward signs of the social hierarchy to help them avoid the questions and difficulties mentioned by Gataker. That the best should rule, they were born into the best rank of society. That the worst should be the most hard-pressed, with the least opportunity for vice to crop up, they were born into the worst, or lowest, rank of society. For ordinary conversing, God permitted little signposts to indicate status. Apparel was one of these: while "extravagance" in apparel was condemned on the whole, persons of high social status were allowed and, sometimes, encouraged to wear sumptuous apparel, "for the distinction of them from the inferior sort."[5]

Women's place in the hierarchy was at the bottom. Again, God did not automatically rate men higher than women. The influential preacher Thomas Becon reminded his mid-sixteenth-century congregation that "Before God, there is no respect of persons. Neither is man better than woman."[6] In the mid-seventeenth century, ministers were still repeating this: salvation came, they said, "not by sex, but by mind and constant purpose."[7] Salvation, however, came in the next world, and in this world, it was clear there was respect of genders.

Moreover, it was clear to many Englishmen that sexual inequality was the result of God's providence. The judicious Richard Hooker explained women's inferiority as part of God's plan to help society function smoothly: gender hierarchy was a necessary part of an orderly society. If men and women were— or could be—equal, there might be some question or difficulty in resolving family disputes. In Hooker's words,

It was not possible [husband and wife] could concur unless there were subalternation between them, which subalternation is naturally grounded upon inequality because things equal in every respect are never willingly directed one by another: woman *therefore* was even in her first estate framed by nature not only after in time but inferior in excellency also to man. [Emphasis added.][8]

God might make no distinction between persons but the family and the society based on the family would grind to a halt unless these distinctions were made and observed.

Calling

Yet, and this was the problem for the sixteenth- and seventeenth-century English, traditional distinctions and signs no longer sufficed. The rising middle layers of society were contesting the aristocracy's exclusive claim to high moral worth and arguing for new ways of assessing social and thus moral worth. Although the traditional division of society into gentry and nongentry or "better" and "inferior" turned on labor—the gentry were those who did no manual labor—wealth and the power which derived from it were increasingly accruing to those who visibly labored. Those "laborers" were recasting social divisions and emphasizing the noble qualities of work.

The Puritans were extreme in the extent to which they exalted labor, but they were clearly part of a general European trend toward defining social ranks in terms of what one did rather than what one's parents and grandparents had done.[9] The rising classes argued that not birth but what one did with one's birthright was the determining element of social status and worth. Where Phillip Stubbes, the sixteenth-century social critic, saw apparel as a means of differentiating between nobility and the inferior sort, the seventeenth-century minister William Whately told his congregants that "attire is to represent the differences of men's *calling*" [emphasis added].[10]

The Puritan doctrine of calling held that each individual, in addition to one's general calling of Christian, had a particular calling, a vocation, and through its practice a person added to God's glory, to the commonwealth, and to one's own certainty of salvation. Diligent labor in one's calling did not win heaven but could serve as a sign that heaven was won. Understandably enough, the less-educated laity tended to equate material success—acceptable evidence of diligent labor in one's calling—with "election," or God's grace. The equation was the more easily made because material success was so often rewarded with power, which, traditionally, the English held to be a visible symbol of moral worth and of God's blessing. The clergy aided in the collapse of material into social into moral worth. Although they continually pointed out that "saving" labor was for the general social benefit, not simply to increase one's own wealth, they also attributed social benefit to a wide range of activities whose most tangible results were the increase of individual wealth. Thus, one famous clergyman insisted that it was only by doing good to others that men were "most properly" counted members of the commonwealth but held up as models of "doing good" marriage and trading. As Christopher Hill has shown, ministers claimed that those who were properly fulfilling their duty to labor would be able "not only to sustain themselves competently, but also to relieve and supply the necessity and want of others."[11] What was good for East Anglia textiles was good for society. And it was good for the East Anglian merchant's social status. And it was, it seemed, a good omen for the East Anglian merchant's salvation.

The already-mentioned struggle to "professionalize" crafts was part of the recasting of the social hierarchy and exalting of labor. The practitioners of the new professions and those newly prestigious crafts argued that their labor provided multitudinous benefits to the commonwealth and also that it required a special knowledge whose possession lifted its holders above the common rank. Thus, the university-trained physicians based their claim of superiority to the barber-surgeons and midwives they supplanted on their scientific knowledge, which gave them special insight into God's works, as much as their record of cures, which, after all, was not so much better than that of their competitors. Lawyers preened themselves on their university and professional training, which gave them, too, a more expert knowledge than was available to the average man, as well as on their service to society.

The emphasis on skill and knowledge helped to raise

the status of a craft or profession in two primary ways. First, of course, in practical terms, it made the craft more exclusive, differentiating practitioners from everyone else. But, second, in a more abstract sense, the claim of a greater knowledge of a particular skill or of science or of law was also a claim of a greater knowledge of God and His providence and, often, of a greater ability to contribute not only to the commonwealth but also to God's glory. The lawyer had a greater understanding of law (still seen in sixteenth- and seventeenth-century England to be derived from God's law) and of justice than the average person, and his calling could be seen as daily to do God's work—ensure justice on earth. The goldsmith had a more intimate acquaintance than the average person with the nature and properties of some of the most precious gems of God's creation, and his calling was daily to make the wonders of God's creation more apparent to the less expert eye.

The doctrine of calling, then, while in theory glorifying all labor, in English practice glorified some labor more than others. Some callings, because they contributed more to God's glory and to the commonwealth, were more exalted than other callings. Which callings were most exalted was the subject of intense debate throughout this time period, a debate made even hotter because also at issue was precisely how to define social benefits. Who, for example, added more to the commonwealth—and God's glory: the merchant who brought in spices—thereby permitting food supplies to be stretched and adding to the English people's knowledge of the infinite variety of God's creation; or the clothier who organized the production of cloth—thereby providing work, wages, and some "mastery" to many of the poor and relieving communities of heavy burdens of poor relief (while trade was good, of course); or the gentleman who managed his estate—thereby improving agricultural productivity and ensuring the presence of the country's "natural rulers" in the countryside?[12]

The new emphasis on labor had different consequences for men than for women. For some men, the doctrine of calling increased opportunities for upward social mobility, because it allowed men not born to wealth and power to achieve them by dint of their own diligent study and actions. It never, however, allowed women to do so. Indeed, the way in which the doctrine actually operated in late sixteenth- and seventeenth-century England served to degrade women and exclude them from public esteem and power, rather than to offer them new opportunities. The use of "callings" as understood by the English to determine status closed women out of the competition for status.

There were two main reasons for this effect. The first is obviously exactly the English emphasis on skill and knowledge just discussed. English women never had access to formal higher education in the universities and law courts; they never had the same access as men to training in productive skills, and, by the seventeenth century, they were losing much of their traditional access as guilds closed their doors to women or raised fees so high that few parents were willing to enroll daughters, whose labor and wages, one recalls, belonged to their husbands. As chapter 2 has shown, women were slow to grasp the importance of professionalization and did not succeed in holding their own on the labor market.

This failure to hold their own in the public labor market contributed to the second reason why the doctrine of calling worked to women's disadvantage: women were perceived as practicing callings different from and inferior to men's. Women were increasingly excluded from the callings which were rising in social esteem, and the callings they did follow were seen as very different from those men pursued. And, finally, what women contributed through their callings was newly defined to be of little social benefit. Women, in other words, were not lawyers or clerics and were increasingly rarely merchants, and they were denied credit for other kinds of contributions to the commonwealth. Men received such credit, even, sometimes, credit for contributions women made. Marriage is a case in point. As mentioned earlier, ministers claimed that men performed a "public good" by marrying. In words representative of many other seventeenth-century clerical treaties on marriage, Matthew Griffith in 1632 explained how men did "good" by marriage. The man, he said, "doth good to others, as good 1) to her whom he (under God) takes into his protection 2) to the church in begetting an holy seed 3) to the world in replenishing it with people."[13]

Now, women *could* have been considered as contributing equally with men to the goods done to church and commonwealth through their own contributions to reproduction. Yet, it is notable that seventeenth-century treatises on marriage define married women as the recipients of a good and not as participants in doing good. Divines urged men to marry as a form of public service but, because they believed women clearly benefited from marriage while providing only limited public service, they did not bother urging women (from whom, furthermore, the option of a convent was taken). Once married, moreover, women were expressly limited to what the clergy termed "private callings," callings whose value was far below that of public callings. Ministers informed women that what they did as housewives had no bearing whatever on their salvation and provided little or nothing of benefit either to church or to commonwealth.[14]

Some contemporaries protested women's exclusion from public callings—those skilled vocations which affirmed the practitioner's moral worth. William Gouge, the popular Puritan minister, took note of these protests in 1623, observing that, "Certain weak consciences . . . think if they have no public calling, they have no calling at all," strongly implying that those weak consciences were female. If it were true, he asked, "what comfort in spending their time should most women have, who are not admitted to any public function in Church or Commonwealth?" Therefore, he assured women that, "Private callings in a family [are] sufficient callings."[15]

These callings, however, seem to have been sufficient in the same way that all men were equal, that is, sufficient in God's eyes but not in the eyes of this world. For Gouge concurred with the newly articulated view that clothes should represent *callings*, and he stipulated that the calling to be represented by a woman's clothes was her husband's. Whatever a woman's own birth or (inherited) wealth, Gouge agreed, her apparel must "be neither for costliness above [her husband's] ability to pay nor for curiousness unbeseeming *his* calling" (emphasis added).[16] The woman's calling, in other words, was not quite sufficient to be an element in determining or displaying her status. Apparel, that prime index for distinguishing between "sorts" and, now, "callings," shed no light on the female wearer's own birth or achievement, serving only to reflect on the status and calling of the wearer's husband. According to the popular manual *Bathsheba's Instructions,* a wife "trims herself not so much for her own as much as for her husband's delight and credit."[17] Interestingly enough, once a woman's apparel was seen as a label of her husband's status and achievement instead of her own, women were permitted an extravagance their grandmothers never knew. The scorn with which the sixteenth-century men looked at women's fashion consciousness, excoriating it as "vanity" and "one of the worms that wastes . . . the commonwealth,"[18] disappeared in the seventeenth century when vanity was turned toward flaunting the husband's success. Thus, Margaret Cavendish, Duchess of NewCastle, could proudly recall that she "took great delight in attiring, fine dressing and fashions," and she characterized this delight as "lawful, honest, honourable and *modest*" (emphasis added).[19]

The elevation of the prestigious public calling—to which "most" women were not admitted—over the "sufficient" private calling gained height when the clergy considered the characteristics of the woman's private calling: women's labor was viewed primarily as a means of preventing women's "natural" sinfulness from harming themselves and others. While (male) public callings benefited others, that is, (female) private callings succeeded only in not hurting others. And recall that sixteenth- and seventeenth-century English people firmly believed in the chastening effects of labor: idleness was the devil's playground/helper; regular work reduced opportunities to behave sinfully. The "regulating" effects of work were a major reason for the call to employ men preferentially over women: the general social benefits of providing men with employment presumably outweighed the particular economic advantages an employer might have attained from hiring women.[20] Poor men needed the discipline of work and masters to prevent them from threatening the status quo. Women, too, needed the discipline of work—as will be seen, they already had masters. But, in the case of women, the need was felt in every "degree," the threat was to their own salvation—and, because sinfulness was so contagious, to morals everywhere—and, finally, women were generally unable, said the clergy, to turn their labor into some greater social good. *Bathesheba's Instructions* put it plainly:

> It is commonly known and grown to be a proverb that women by nature are more talkative, so as greater care is to be had. . . . Whereunto it is a great help that a woman be constant and continuing in her labour. . . . Continuance in labour is a singular remedy against rashness and forwardness of the tongue.[21]

One minister warned that women must be kept busy lest, "for want of employment," they grow lazy and "heartless." Labor in women's private callings, said another, was necessary to avoid "these pestilences" to which women with leisure were subject.[22]

Because what was important about women's labor was that it restrain women's vice, preventing them from infecting men, it was evaluated by its process, not its product. It was not terribly important what a woman did, so long as she "persist[ed] and persevere[d] constantly in her work,"[23] and "exhibited a constant and painful endeavour of doing something,"[24] although one minister insisted she was "always to work some *good* thing" (emphasis added).[25] A man's labor in his calling could "make his election more certain unto [him]self."[26] A woman's labor in her calling was unrewarded by material success or clear social benefit: hence, it could provide no such assurance. Rather than a stepping stone to improved status and salvation, labor for women was characterized as "no discredit nor discommendation at all."[27]

   Thus, the new emphasis on calling as a determinant of social status, while theoretically gender-indifferent, actually operated to devalue women both absolutely and relative to men. Public and private callings were newly defined and then contrasted with each other. The contrasts were to women's disadvantage: public callings provided social benefits—which women received; private callings prevented social ills—which women caused. Women were restricted to private callings, which granted no public status, just as more men, through their callings, were exercising control over their own status. As what men did began to identify their moral and social worth, what women did began to lose social meaning. As men were freed from bonds to particular places, women were restricted to their homes. In the sixteenth and seventeenth centuries, men grasped new tools to achieve status; not only were women denied use of the new tools but also they lost use of the old tools.

JUST LIKE A WOMAN

Fragile or Vicious Beauty: Gender Reassessments

   The restriction of women to private callings and the characterization of these callings as tools to constrain women's natural sinfulness was, of course, part of the broader reassessment of values and ideas occurring throughout English society during the transition to capitalism. More specifically, it was an aspect of the reassessment of woman's rightful place in society. Because, for the sixteenth- and seventeenth-century English, one's place in society was but a reflection of one's place in the moral hierarchy or of one's "worth," this reassessment involved a new consideration of woman's worth. To understand this fully it is useful to examine shifts in ideas about woman's nature and suggest how these contributed to women's decline.

Women had never been regarded as men's equals in England. England may have been a paradise for married women, but the paradise was structured along the same lines as the rest of God's creation: it was hierarchical or, in this context, patriarchal.[28] Conventionally, women in England as elsewhere in Christian Europe were described as "the weaker vessel." In the mid-sixteenth century, the English understood this in the traditional sense that women did not quite measure up to men; the woman was "more weak in body and mind than the man." As John Aylmer put it, in the course of defending Elizabeth's right to rule, "In a woman is wit, understanding and as Aristotle says the same virtues that be in a man, saving that they differ . . . that is, are more in the man than in the woman."[29]

In the course of the sixteenth and seventeenth centuries, however, this notion that women were essentially the same—albeit inferior in degree—was changing. To the seventeenth-century eye, quantitative differences between men and women loomed so large as to be qualitative: women were seen as fundamentally different from men. Thus, as already seen, Gervase Markham in his popular early seventeenth-century manual on housewifery wrote that the understanding of women was so far inferior to that of men that women could not possibly grasp the principles of physic necessary for high-quality medical care—and this was despite his acknowledgment that women had traditionally been entrusted with its provision.[30] Sir Kenelm Digby, a member of Charles's court, claimed that women's minds were so inferior to men's that women were unable to form genuine friendships—they simply could not attain the notion "so high and elevated as men's"[31] necessary to sustain friendship.

Ideas *like* these were not new; women had been labled men's inferiors and castigated for particular inferiorities since before the birth of Christ. Because studies which would quantify and measure shifts in the tone and content of the attacks on women do not yet exist, it is difficult to pinpoint exactly the changes which occurred in England during the seventeenth century. Yet the general trend is clear: men were claiming that women's inferiority essentially separated them from men, and they were ignoring or denying traditional ideas and practices which cast doubt on this notion. Digby's assertion, for example, flew in the face of tradition. Such expressions of popular attitudes as lay dramatic productions expound the view that women's friendships were deep and abiding.

The plays of the Flood, part of a cycle of biblical tales annually presented by craft guilds throughout the fifteenth and sixteenth centuries in England, called attention to Mrs. Noah's deep attachment to her women friends. She relied on them to help her when she needed help and, when faced with a choice between dying with them or surviving without them, she chose to die rather than abandon them. In the version of the play produced by the guilds of Chester, Mrs. Noah's loyalty to her friends is a focal point of the play. Mrs. Noah had organized a group of her women friends, her "gossips," to help Noah construct his ark and she refused to desert these friends to save herself. When Noah urges her to come aboard, she points to her friends and says,

> They shall not drown by St. John
> and I may save their life.
> They loved me full well by Christ;
> But thou will let them in thy chest
> Else row forth Noah, whether thou list
> and get thee a new wife.[32]

Other traditional ideas about women were undergoing similar reassessments. What the sixteenth-century eye had seen to be prudent caution on women's parts, the seventeenth-century eye saw more negatively as cowardice. No longer did women's "natural" caution fit her to be a guardian of children, as Castiglione had argued in *The Courtier*; now it labeled her a being unable to care for herself, much less young children.[33]

The playwrights Francis Beaumont and John Fletcher wrote of women that they were "tender and full of fears."[34] Dorothy Osborne in the mid-seventeenth century told her lover that, though among women she was considered brave, in fact, even thunderstorms terrified her.[35]

Edmund Spenser, in his late sixteenth-century *Faerie Queene*, took aim at another traditional female virtue, their courtesy or tact. One of the few female virtues that Castiglione in his famous handbook, *The Courtier*, had unequivocally praised, women's ability to give pleasure to all kinds—a useful skill in a society peopled by all sorts—Spenser condemned as a pliancy "ready ripe to ill" and contrasted with the unyielding dogmatism of (male) knights who did not—and need not—resort to "womanish" guile in order to "please the minds of good and ill."[36] The influential Protestant minister William Perkins showed his agreement with this new assessment of woman's "pliancy" by noting, "The more women, the more witches" with the explanation that men's resolution gave them greater protection against the temptations of the devil.[37]

Robert Cawdrey, compiler of the first English dictionary, printed in 1604, demonstrated the extent to which women's inferiority was now marking them as qualitatively different from men in his definition of wanton as "womanish." The great debate occurring during the late middle ages over which sex was more lustful had been decided "in favor" of women, and women were so clearly identified with sensual vices that each could be defined and explained in terms of the other. The dramatist John Fletcher in 1621 wrote of a female character, "Because you are a woman, you are lawless,"[38] using "lawless" in its conventional connotation of lustful. This belief that women were the embodiment of sensual vices had the added benefit for men of allowing them to believe that women welcomed rape. The man who raped was not sinfully taking advantage of woman's smaller stature, he was participating in a sport initiated by the woman.[39]

The source of woman's excessive lust, timidity, and other vice was, of course, her nature. Writers in both the six-

teenth and the seventeenth century (and indeed before the sixteenth century and after the seventeenth) agreed that woman's
nature was restless and constantly mobile. The inconstancy
was manifest in specific vices like lust and ambition which, if
not repressed, posed a threat to society. Seventeenth-century
writers, however, do seem to have focused on the ill effects of
mobility with more vehemence, consistency, and outright
alarm than their predecessors. Writing in the mid-seventeenth
century, for example, Thomas Hobbes expressed the prevailing
view that restlessness and mobility would make "the life of
man . . . poor, nasty, brutish and short." Hobbes seems to be
unique in viewing restlessness and mobility as basic *human*
characteristics. His contemporaries, despite evident male social
mobility, identified natural mobility as specifically female, derived from woman's uterus or what physicians called her
"besettment by a succession of foul and vain humors."[40] The
clergy attributed such characteristics to women's descent from
Eve, mother of all humankind but model for and forerunner of
only half of humankind. As William Harrison wrote in the mid-
sixteenth century, "Eve will be Eve, though Adam would say
nay."[41] In the mid-seventeenth century, the minister Daniel
Rogers added a specific twist to this general lament, telling his
female congregants, "Remember, thy sex is crazy, ever since
Eve sinned."[42]

For sixteenth- and seventeenth-century writers alike,
then, woman's nature put her at a disadvantage relative to
man. But, for sixteenth-century writers, the disadvantage was
not disabling, while for seventeenth-century writers it put
women into an entirely different court, as it were, denying
women opportunities to participate—much less successfully
compete—in the (male) world. The seventeenth-century view
of women held that women's nature was so fundamentally different from men's that it justified and, indeed, required placing
severe restrictions on women.

Some of these restrictions, of course, were traditional—part of England's traditional patriarchal structure. But
traditionally, they had been recognized as conventions, artifi-

cial devices designed by men essentially to benefit men. In the new world of the seventeenth century, they were described as natural and necessary, beneficial to women as well as men. A look at how men regarded some of the traditional restrictions illuminates the change. In his mid-sixteenth-century treatise on the laws of England, the lawyer Thomas Smith noted that women lost their maiden names when they married.[43] He mentioned this as part of his illustration of the extent of the legal power of husbands over their wives, and he made no reference to Nature or to women's nature as requiring this convention. Forty years later, when the clergyman Gervase Babington took up the same topic, "the wife [being] called by her husband's name," he used it to illustrate the natural base of law, explaining that law was a social reflection of natural hierarchy. Marriage meant, he said, that the husband and wife were one social unit and, "the man is the worthier person . . . *therefore* by his name shall [they] both be called" (emphasis added).[44]

Also in the late sixteenth century, another popular minister, Henry Smith, took up the topic of women's legal rights—or lacks thereof—over property. Again, Smith the lawyer had discussed this simply as part of a convenient legal structure which placed wives and all their property in the power of husbands—now, forty years later, the minister pointed to it as a legal principle clearly derived from natural hierarchy: women could not own property, he said, because they were "unskillful" in their handling of it, and the law simply recognized this natural fact.[45] Smith the lawyer, on the contrary, had expressed confidence in women's capacity to handle property, commenting that many wives did so even while their husbands lived and citing the frequency with which husbands named wives as executors of their wills and guardians of the children as evidence of women's success in so doing. For Smith the lawyer, the husband's power was a legal device generally convenient for men by often ignored because it lacked a compelling natural basis.[46] For Smith the clergyman, forty years later, it was so natural and necessary a phenomenon that it was to be preserved through the subordination of the widow to a male executor.

Social Roles by Gender

The new view that men and women were by nature different rather than the same but in different degrees explains why Smith the minister would not allow husbands and wives to share control over property. The view that women were like men, albeit not as good, had permitted women many of the same opportunities as men: they were permitted to perform the same social roles, although it was understood that they generally would not perform them as well as men. The view that women were fundamentally different from men called into question any sharing of social roles and opportunities, suggesting, instead, that women were naturally fit for some roles and men for other roles and never the twain should meet. Men, the main espousers of this new view, already had something of a lock on the socially esteemed roles, and the new view helped them to maintain it. The new view implied, for example, that gender should be a determining element in the division of labor, which, as we have seen, was itself gaining in importance as a determinant of status.

The general contours of a division of labor by gender had always been present in English society but were often unenforced. Hence, men and women usually—but not always—performed complementary household roles; guilds were rarely composed of equal numbers of men and women, but guilds did have members of both sexes; most skills were associated with either males or females, but which gender was associated with a given skill might vary over time. Men did receive higher wages than women, for the same work, and men almost always had more opportunities than women to earn wages outside the home.[47] Natural or biological differences, however, could explain directly many of the divisions which were upheld: men were, on the average, stronger than women and, thus, on the average, harvested more. A landlord who was paid in labor services rather than money rent would, therefore, prefer a male tenant to a female tenant and a male representative of the tenant family to a female. A family in which only one adult could be spared from household responsibilities or presence to earn a money income would prefer to send out the adult who could earn the most money. The family preference would be buttressed by the likelihood that the mother, who could breastfeed, could handle infants and young children more effectively than the father. These preferences could—and generally were—hardening into the custom of men going out to work and women remaining at home; and the custom, essentially a gender division of labor by place—women working in the home, men outside the home—appeared natural even as it was becoming second nature.

But other factors with far less clear connections to nature and far more clear connections to the traditional patriarchal structure of English society also contributed to the gender division of labor. These factors were increasing in importance in the seventeenth century—and they, too, were seen as "natural." The dominance of men in late medieval guilds, for example, seems to have owed little to nature. All masters were paid the same price for their products: families of masters received little benefit from any strict gender division of labor.[48] But achieving mastery required a considerable investment for apprentice fees and entry fees and it was a *social* custom that families made their investments in sons. Daughters were viewed as likely to take their profits to their husbands' families, of which, by convention, they became part, while sons presumably repaid the investment to the investing family by either taking care of aging parents or continuing the family business. Male dominance of the guilds, based on age-old social customs, made easier and more "natural" the exclusion of women from crafts and professions requiring special training and education and conferring special prestige and rewards. As, in the seventeenth century, the exclusion hardened into custom and sometimes law, it too was seen as based on nature—specifically, the inferior nature of women, which prevented them from benefiting from training and education and required their subordination to their husbands.

The new view that men and women were fitted by nature for different social roles also encouraged a more extensive and forceful gender division of participation in society itself, or what contemporaries called the political nation of England. The traditional view of society was that it was divinely created to remedy the sinfulness of human nature and to perfect human sociability. Society, or the state, provided the conditions under which the good could live virtuously and the evil could be repressed.[49] It was traditional to assert that women, the weaker vessel, required more repression than men. But, over the course of the sixteenth and seventeenth centuries, the new view that woman's nature was so far inferior to man's as to make her different led to assertions that society was an inadequate and inappropriate remedy for woman's nature. In their natural state, ambitious, lustful—restless—women threatened not only property but society itself. Men feared that women aspired to equality with their husbands, and the men argued (with some basis) that this equality would overthrow the very hierarchical foundations of society.

William Gouge wrote of the ambitious wives who refused to be subject to their husbands:

> Let them think as they list, assuredly, herein they thwart God's ordinance, pervert the order of nature, deface the image of Christ, overthrow the ground of all duty, hinder the good of the family, become an ill pattern to children and servants, lay themselves open to Satan and incur many other mischiefs.[50]

Lustful wives could be even worse. The consequences of adultery, after all, as all Europe knew, were appalling.

> Great inheritances are altered and the right heirs disinherited . . . whereby the father loses his honour, his kindred, his goods. The adulterous wife lades first her honest poor husband with great shame, great travail, great labour, sorrow and pain in . . . bring-[ing] up those adulterous children which are not his own and then dishonours her father, her mother and kindred.[51]

Chaste, subject women were, thus, necessary for the smooth functioning of society. Yet, such women were not easy to find. As Solomon had said of old and minister upon minister repeated in the seventeenth century, it was hard to find a good man but it was well-nigh unto impossible to find a good woman.[52]

Because society was evidently an inadequate means to repress woman's unruly nature, and because woman's nature posed such severe threats to society, men began to argue that women were unfit to participate in society themselves and that their participation must be mediated through their husbands. In the mid-seventeenth century, Daniel Rogers stated that the only perfect woman was a subject woman, and he explained that, in order for subjection to make women perfect, it must be total.[53] A woman who was totally subordinated to her husband posed no more threat to society. Yet, the victory over nature gained the woman no access to society because the victory was won through the surrender of her autonomy—always, and in the seventeenth century more than ever, an essential criterion for political participation. The perfect woman was like the servant "whose lesson," said the clergy, "she must sometime observe":[54] her subjection denied her any ability to threaten or to *contribute* to the common good. Subjection rendered the wife a social and political nullity, a part of her husband, through whom she was "involved" in the commonwealth and who, of course, "lays claim to all."[55] Women's nature required a special society—the family—and once ensconced in this society, they had no need of or rights in any other.

The idea that women were unfit to exercise political power was clearly no seventeenth-century novelty. In England as elsewhere in Europe, the idea had a long and respectable lineage.[56] Elizabeth's very successful and lengthy occupation of the throne probably reduced overt English antipathy to women rulers for a time, but the antipathy was deeply rooted and her reign did not eradicate it. Nor did Elizabeth attempt to do so. She frequently invoked her "manly" courage and "princely"

determination in order to emphasize her divine right to rule. In herself, she admitted, she was but a paltry woman, going on to exult that God had made her a prince and he had given her the royal traits necessary to perform her calling, including the ability to appoint competent counselors and the wisdom to listen to them.[57] Elizabeth's own presentation of her rule was not so different from that of Lucy Hutchinson, fifty years after Elizabeth's death. According to Hutchinson,

> Never is any place happy where the hands that are made only for distaffs affect the management of Sceptres. If anyone object the fresh example of Queen Elizabeth, let them remember that the felicity of her reign was the effect of her submission to her masculine and wise counsellors.[58]

But, in Elizabeth's world, the hands that held distaffs held much else besides, while in Lucy Hutchinson's world some were finding it difficult to hold on to the distaffs.

Is Being a Man the Whole Point?

The changes described in these pages did not occur abruptly or dramatically. The new views that women were different from men and, therefore, fit for different things were recognizable descendants of the old views that women were somehow less than men and should, perhaps, leave some things to men. Thomas Smith proved the ability of women to handle property in the context of explaining the legal impediments to their doing so. One reason guilds were so easily able to exclude women was that the guilds were already so dominated by men. Nonetheless, the changes were significant: men were able to do more with property in the seventeenth century than ever before, and women were able to do less; guilds were conferring greater benefits on men, and they were limiting benefits to women; more male hands were "affecting management" of government, and fewer female hands were "affecting manage-

ment" of their families. And the new views that women were so far inferior to men that they could not do the same work or achieve the same attainments or make the same contributions to society justified and perpetuated their lack of opportunity to try and their subordination to the men who would do it for them.

In the context of changing social and economic circumstances, late sixteenth- and seventeenth-century Englishmen drew upon ideas and practices which already existed but which had rarely been considered as a coherent whole. They brought together and reconsidered disparate ideas in an effort to reestablish social stability and reconstruct its hierarchical structure ever more firmly. In the process of adjusting to the new world opened up by capitalism, they effectively closed off large parts of that world to women. In some cases, this seemed to be the consequences of "natural" causes; in other cases, it was more obviously the consequence of human design. As the next chapters show, the clergy, especially the Puritan clergy, seized upon the family as a key instrument in their effort to reform society. They developed an ideal family whose pattern they urged on their congregants. Their descriptions of woman's nature and her role in the family were colored by the kind of family they wanted their congregants to achieve.

CHAPTER FOUR

The Woman
Had the Keys:
The Housewife
in the Domestic Economy

It was within their families that sixteenth-century English-women are supposed to have found paradise. Sixteenth-century wits claimed England was a paradise for *married* women, and historians have long argued that, within families, "a rough and ready equality" existed between husbands and wives.[1] This equality was disappearing in sixteenth- and seventeenth-century England, as both economic changes and the reformers' renewed demands for a family based on divine precept undermined the wife's position within her family as well as women's position within society.[2]

The Domestic Economy:
Housewifery and Mastery

At the beginning of the sixteenth century, the English believed that housewives did almost everything husbands did as well as everything necessary for family subsistence that husbands did not do. Popular drama portrayed wives as the mainstays of their families. In *The Deluge*, for example, Mrs. Noah worked to feed her family while her husband Noah drifted about waiting for messages from the Lord. Another popular play, *The Second Shepherd's Play*, illustrates even more forcefully the general conception that housewives ensured the survival of their households. Popular in the late fifteenth and early sixteenth centuries, *The Second Shepherd's Play* presents a husband whose labor is unable to support his family. This husband, like Noah, complains about his wife's behavior but, again like Noah, he relies on her to feed the family and to get him out of scrapes. In the play, the wife is continually at work. Even when her husband appears suddenly in the dead of night to get her help in hiding the sheep he has stolen, Mrs. Mak is awake and spinning. As Mrs. Noah had rescued Noah from his inability to complete his planned ark by organizing a team of laborers to build it, so Mrs. Mak rescues her husband from his ill-considered theft by devising a scheme to hide the sheep. Mrs. Mak fails in the end—just as did Mrs. Noah's attempt to save her friends—but the play makes plain that her wit is the family's source of support.

Although unable to prevent detection of her husband's theft, she does succeed in keeping the family fed, if not very prosperous, and she evidently does so with very little help from the husband. As he continues to carp on her pushiness, she asks, "Why, who wanders? Who wakes? Who comes? Who goes? / Who brews? Who bakes? Who makes us our hose?" Mak has no answer. The audience is left to nod agreement as Mrs. Mak answers her own question, observing, "It is sad to behold, / Now in hot, now in cold / Full woefull is the household that lacks a woman" (ll. 415–21).

Writers of technical manuals on the management of family farms shared this conception of the importance and omnipresence of the wife's labor. Anthony FitzHerbert's *Book of Husbandry*, first printed in 1525 and reprinted, with revisions, throughout the century, for example, laid out the basic tasks of the housewife:

It is a wife's occupation to winnow all manner of corn, to make malt, to wash and wring, to make hay, shear corn, and, in time of need, to help her husband to fill the much-wayne or dung-cart, drive the plow, to load corn and such other [tasks] . . . to go to market to sell butter, cheese, milk, eggs, chickens, capons, hens, pigs, geese and all manner of corn, and also to buy all manner of necessary things belonging to the household.[3]

FitzHerbert saw the household as basically self-sufficient: husband and wife divided the chores between them and together produced what was necessary to keep the family going. Although the 1597 and later editions clearly assume the presence of servants in the household, the earlier editions seem to consider only the husband and wife as the producers. The husband's tasks are directly related to heavy farming: preparing the ground for planting, sowing, and harvesting; the wife's to feeding the family and making useful to the family the products of farming. But as the above citation shows, FitzHerbert clearly regarded the husband and wife as a team and required that the proper housewife be able to perform all the tasks usually done by the husband.

Sir Thomas Eliot, writing in the mid-sixteenth century, distinguished between the tasks of husband and wife in a similar way. The husband, he said, prepared while the wife "kept" what the husband prepared. Eliot observed that without the wife's transformation of the husband's products, all the husband's labor was pointless: "In preparing is labour and study; of keeping comes use and commodity."[4] Thomas Tusser's *Points of Husbandry*, written in mid-sixteenth century and reprinted frequently over the next century, made the same point succinctly: "Housewives must husband, as well as the man, or farewell thy husbandry, do what thou can."[5]

The general theoretical distinction between the work of the husband and the wife was that the husband worked outdoors or abroad while the wife remained within, at home. In Tusser's words,

Good husbands abroad, seeketh all well to have:
Good housewives at home, seeketh all well to save.
Thus having and saving, in place where they meet,
make profit with pleasure such couples to greet.[6]

The clergy made this distinction more rigid, especially in the sixteenth century, than did the laity. Miles Coverdale in 1545 published a translation of the treatise of the famous continental reformer, Henry Bullinger, on *The Christian State of Matrimony.*
Coverdale thus brought to English audiences Bullinger's decree
that "Whatsoever is done without the house, that belongs to
the man, and the woman [is] to study for things within to be
done."[7]

In the 1550s, Thomas Becon, one of England's own famous reformers, tried to reconcile this strict continental division
with the looser English customs. In his *Goldē Booke of Christen
Matrimonye,* he, too, decreed that "All provision and whatsoever is to be done without the house belongs to the man: and
the woman ought to take charge within."[8] Yet Becon's text acknowledged that this division of labor was not maintained in English practice. Marketing, for example, belonged to the housewife although it took place outside the house and could bring in
money and provisions,[9] and English women were traditionally
trained in skills which, as Becon put it, made them "more able
to live and to defend the needy life from poverty and beggary."[10]
Becon himself praised women who could "get at least some part
of their living, if necessity should require."[11]

The obstacle Becon and his fellow clergymen encoun-
tered in their effort to uphold a rigid "within/without" division
of labor was that the English believed that women were better
at some "without" tasks than men. The English traditionally
maintained the division of labor they believed to be "natural":
women performed all tasks—inside or out—for which they
were best fitted by nature. Women went out to do the marketing, for example, because the English believed that women
were more shrewd at marketing than men. Traditional English

notions held that women were naturally more shrewish and sharp than men and, because they were weaker than men, more circumspect in spending and more concerned with saving. Men, because they were more likely than women to find casual paid labor, could afford to be what contemporaries called "spending," but women, weaker of limb and less likely to find casual labor, had to develop their mental resources and rely on their wits to survive. Moreover, the English believed that their customs reinforced nature, and that the general division of labor between within and without increased the natural advantages of England's specific deviations from it. Because women were customarily more at home than men and customarily were engaged in meeting their family's subsistence needs, they developed a greater knowledge of what these needs were and more expertise in how best to meet them.[12] Custom, in other words, increased women's natural superiority to men in some outdoor skills, such as marketing, and the English used nature and custom to their advantage.

In the mid-sixteenth century, however, the clerics were becoming less willing to adjust their theories to English fact. Becon and his fellow clerics pressed home the indoor/outdoor division of labor and they prescribed behavior for women which upheld this division. When listing the skills "maidens" should learn, for example, Becon enjoined that they should learn all skills which "become maidens," not all skills which could bring in an income.[13] He warned that women who left their homes were likely to behave unbecomingly, "to meddle with other folks' business, to tattle and prattle." The housewife ought to remain becomingly within—unless, he allowed, "urgent, weighty and necessary causes compel her to go out."[14] In the sixteenth century, even the clergy recognized marketing as just such a cause. Becon and other English clerics conceded that the housewife could leave her home "to go to market to buy things necessary for her household."[15] In contrast to sixteenth-century lay writers and, in view of later developments, significantly, Becon did not believe women should go to markets to sell except as representatives of their families.

The greater leeway sixteenth-century lay writers allowed in the way tasks were assigned within the household reflected their recognition that housewives needed leeway in order to fill their difficult and complex role adequately.[16] Many of the lay writers, who wrote, as they saw it, how-to manuals, not moral prescriptions, were well aware of the effort and skill involved in housewifery. Anthony FitzHerbert, for example, observing that, "It may fortune sometime that [the housewife] shal have so many things to do that [she] shal not well know where is best to begin," proposed a method by which housewives would determine which task had priority. He did not set forth a work plan for the housewife; instead, he proposed a formula through which she could develop her own work plan. FitzHerbert told the housewife to

> take heed, which thing shall be the greatest loss, if it were not done and in what space it would be done. Then think what is the greatest loss and there begin. But, in case that thing which is of the greatest loss will be long in the doing and thou might do three or four other things in the meanwhile [add them together and recalculate].[17]

The traditional tasks of the housewife included providing her family with food, drink, clothing, and "home furnishings" through her own labor. Many of these tasks required lengthy and tedious preparation, shrewd foresight, and a compendium of skills. Breadbaking and brewing, for instance, involved planting one year to sow and use throughout the next; meat-preserving required an ability to forecast whether animals could be fed through the winter or were utilized more efficiently by themselves being food; preparation of medicines involved gardening skills as well as knowledge of herbal and other folk remedies.

Yet, although sixteenth-century works on husbandry and housewifery acknowledge the complexity of these tasks, they rarely offer instruction in the skills required. Tusser told men what general criteria should be used in selecting cattle but broke off the discussion by telling husbands to follow their wives' advice: "Good housewives know best all the rest how to guide."[18] FitzHerbert commented that he "needeth not" tell housewives how to perform their tasks, "for they be wise enough."[19] The skills necessary to perform these tasks were, in fact, passed from mother to daughter and from lady of the manor to maidservant or maid. Poor girls were sometimes apprenticed or hired out to learn specialized domestic skills such as dairying, useful in earning money and in feeding their own families. Wealthier girls were "placed out" in the homes of patrons where, interspersed with lessons in "breeding" or social graces they learned the practical skills necessary for them successfully to manage large households of their own.[20] Margaret Hoby, a gentlewoman of the late sixteenth century, epitomizes the competent housewife who was, in the words of Nicholas Breton, a popular pamphleteer, the

> world of wealth . . . the hand of labour . . . an exercise of patience and an example of experience . . . she is the kitchen physician . . . the dairy's neatness, the brewhouse's wholesomeness . . . the gardner's provision and the garden's plantation . . . poverty's prayer and charity's praise . . . a course of thrift and, in sum, God's blessing and man's happiness, earth's honour and heaven's creature.[21]

Hoby was educated in the traditional manner of the sixteenth-century gentlewoman, "placed out" in the homes of ladies who ensured she learned housewifely skills. Her diary, spanning the years 1595–1601, reveals the broad use to which she put her training. Living for the most part on her own country estate, she performed the multitudinous tasks enumerated by Tusser and FitzHerbert as the work of the housewife. While her husband was engaged in other business, she managed both her own and his estates. She collected the rents due them, paid the servants' wages and the household's bills, hired and supervised additional workers to perform specific tasks. She went to courts of law herself on estate business and, while she did not herself do the marketing for her very large household, she drew up the marketing order before delegating the shopping to her steward. She supervised the cooking and preserving of bread, pastries, meat, poultry, and fruits, sometimes participating in the actual work. She served as the physician for both her own household and those of her neighbors less skillful or well-read in physic than she, also acting as companion or midwife's assistant when relatives and friends were brought to childbed.

She sowed and reaped both herb and flower gardens, using the herbs in cooking and physic and the flowers in preparing cosmetic and medicinal waters. She tended to the provision of malt and ale, hemp, flax, rushes (the floor covering) and the sowing, letting, and distribution of corn and wheat. The honey she used in preserving was from her own apiary; the candles she used for lights (wax, as befitted a woman of her exalted rank) were made by her maidservants and herself. A model of thrift, she discarded neither clothes nor linen when they became torn or outmoded; instead, she dyed and mended them, showing herself to be, despite her rank, what Thomas Tusser termed more a good housewife than a lady.[22]

Margaret Hoby's record as a housewife in her country home was almost without reproach. At home, she was a paragon of industriousness and thrift. In London, however, and the other cities in which she spent a goodly amount of time each year, Lady Hoby was not quite so industrious. The tasks she performed in her country residence were apparently irrational or redundant in the city. There, she spent much of her time reading, attending sermons, visiting friends and relatives. She relied on markets to supply her household needs and even, like many other gentlefolk, her house—she rented lodgings. The men, who by the turn of the seventeenth century were complaining that "spending too much time and leisure in London . . . alienate[d]" women from domestic skills "more necessary and virtuous" and chastising women for their lack of industry in London,[23] could have been referring to her. The epitome of industry in the country and nearly the epitome of its absence in the city, Hoby testifies to the eroding effect of urbanization and the growth of markets on the productive role of the housewife. That her city habits were the object of great and vociferous criticism testifies to the extent that changes in ideas about the role of the housewife lagged behind changes in reality.

In the country, too, however, Hoby was not quite the perfect housewife. In an age when maternity was seen as an essential element of housewifery, Hoby had no children. Among her own social stratum, the mother's role was so highly esteemed that Baldesar Castiglione, in his handbook for aspiring aristocrats, *The Courtier*, wrote, "The world finds no usefulness in women except the bearing of children."[24] This viewpoint, articulated frequently by clerics and scholars throughout the middle ages, was echoed in England even by that flower of the English Renaissance, Sir Phillip Sidney. Sidney, in his *Arcadia*, wondered whether giving birth might not be "the message for which [woman] was sent into the world."[25] Cornelius Agrippa, the noted humanist, wrote a treatise in defense of the excellency of women in which he asserted that their greatest excellency lay in their ability to bear children and called maternity "the greatest and chiefest office of a woman."[26]

Maternity, of course, was important for all social classes, not just the aristocracy. The aspect of maternity that all classes most valued was fertility—the ability to conceive and give birth to live infants. Because of the high infant and child mortality rate, over which few families could exercise control, families had to provide many offspring in order to raise any to maturity, and the family member who did this providing was the wife. Giving birth was a duty like thrift: in the same way that housewives were praised for saving large amounts of barley or money, so they were praised for giving birth to large numbers of children.[27] The popular minister Henry Smith lauded fertility as one of the first blessings and "chiefest treasures,"[28] and other clergymen claimed that women, damned through Eve, could be redeemed by bearing children.[29]

There were, to be sure, differences in the ways the aristocracy and the other social classes regarded motherhood. The wealthy could afford to view children as their parents' "chief jewel and riches . . . comfort against care and heaviness."[30]

Most people had to see their children in more utilitarian terms: to most people, children were not so much jewels as they were hedges against poverty in the future. Children were a form of old-age insurance and part of a general strategy for providing for the married couple. As the housewife produced enough ale to get the family through the month, so she produced enough children to get her and her husband through old age.

In his influential works, Thomas Tusser treated maternity as one among the myriad tasks of housewifery, considering it an element of domestic work, not a specialized or separate vocation. In the sixteenth century, housewives juggled tasks connected to maternity with those connected to managing the domestic economy, of which children were a part. Tusser put the whole issue of the housewife's reproductivity in clear economic terms, seeing children as an economic resource and their care as a subject for tactical consideration. Children, he added, were "profitable" to their parents or, if not, were "better . . . unborn."[31]

Thomas Becon, the clergyman, saw maternity in the same light: he believed that housewives "ought" to reproduce just as they "ought" to manage their households. In Becon's words, "The woman ought to take charge within, to see all things conveniently spent or saved as it ought to be, and to bring forth and nourish her children, and to have the whole doing of her daughters and womanservants."[32]

The issue of nourishing children sheds light on traditional attitudes toward housewifery and motherhood. Tusser encouraged women to breastfeed their own children, noting that good housewives (not mothers) "count it good luck to make their own breasts their own child to give suck." He echoed the well-founded belief that maternally nursed babies had the greatest chance of survival.[33] But he advised women that there were circumstances which warranted sending infants out to nurse and proposed guidelines for selecting nurses in these circumstances. Although Tusser shared the clergy's preference for maternal breastfeeding, he warned that wives must not permit breastfeeding or the "noisome" needs of the one infant to distract them from their primary responsibility of attending to the needs of the entire family. In effect, Tusser dealt with the issue as if decisions about it were to be made on economic grounds. On the one hand, wealthy women who could afford servants to take over their household work were to breastfeed and, on the other hand, poor women who could not afford wet-nurses—and, indeed, might be forced to hire themselves out as nurses—were to breastfeed. In between these two groups, women engaged in substantial productive activities were to decide on the basis of what was more vital to the *family* at a given moment: their own production; the cost of the nurse; their ability to hire someone satisfactory; all these factors were to be weighed and the housewife was to choose. Tusser's advice appears to reflect sixteenth-century practice.[34]

Throughout the sixteenth century, then, the role of the housewife included that of mother and, for most English families, motherhood was subordinate to housewifery. The tasks which mothers performed were those which they would normally perform in the course of being housewives. They attended, for example, to their children's material wants, both because that was an element of housewifery itself and because they were more likely than fathers to be able to forecast those wants accurately. As women developed expertise in marketing through their presence at home, so also they developed expertise in childrearing through their presence near the children.

Mothers also attended to their children's early education. According to Tusser, this duty, too, arose from its economic necessity. Mothers, that is, had to "break" children into profitability or suffer the unpleasant consequences of undisciplined, untrained offspring who would deplete rather than add to the domestic economy.[35] All who wrote on the subject agreed that the earlier one began to discipline the child—or, to put it more positively, to inculcate Christian principles—the likelier the principles were to take. Most writers did phrase this early education in the positive form of "instructing children with precept."[36] But it is evident that they saw this as having worldly as well as otherworldly benefits. Children disciplined

and "christianized" at early ages were more likely to be "profitable" children.

Gervase Markham, for example, the writer of seventeenth-century tracts on housewifery, explicitly advocated religion as a means for ensuring that men pay "more faithful [atten-
tion] on all their businesses."[37] Dorothy Leigh, in her popular
Mother's Blessing, advised mothers to instruct their children and
housewives to instruct their servants in basic English literacy. In
this way, she said, they could guarantee pious and productive
workers.[38] Children should be taught young, she added, because, until they were ten or so, they "were not able to do any
good in the commonwealth" and therefore might as well "learn
how to serve God, their king and country by reading."[39] If parents were to obtain the best results from their children, they had
to begin educating those children early, both to overlay unruly
nature with the second nature of Christian discipline and to be
able to evaluate their children's attitudes so that they could be directed most aptly in their callings.[40] Because the housewife/
mother was the adult who, in the performance of other duties,
was most generally present, it fell to her, as Tusser explained, to
undertake this early education, either by overt instruction in
skills such as reading and writing or by implicit example.

For the performance of all their duties, of course,
housewives required certain "liberties." To go to market, for example, required the freedom to move abroad in society. To
make the best deals at the market required the freedom to negotiate and to allocate household resources. Wives had to be able
to direct the labor of servants and, if they could not be coequal
in determining, at least they had to be conversant in, the over-
all strategy for the family's economy in order to implement it.

Sixteenth-century women, considered responsible for
the domestic economy, possessed those liberties necessary to
fulfill their responsibilities. Some English men believed wom-
en's responsibilities were so great that women might require
power over even their husbands to perform their tasks credi-
tably. The household, Thomas Smith explained in 1545, was
best likened to an aristocracy, not a monarchy. In the family,

"not one [governs] always: but some time and in some thing one, and sometimes and in some things another does bear the rule."[41] Authority and obedience within the household, he went on, should be assigned on the basis of skill, not gender. Thomas Becon, who, as was seen, had divided family responsibilities into within and without, observed that the skills exercised within as part of housewifery developed women's business sense and made of them worthy partners without. He reminded men, "Women also many times can give better counsel than men and are able to determine what is good and what is otherwise, no less than their husbands. Their counsells, therefore, are not to be neglected."[42] Other clergy reminded their congregants that Solomon himself had asserted that women should "rule" their spheres, their homes, without interference from husbands.[43]

So widespread was the belief that women could and should exercise authority within their households that some Englishmen explicitly criticized husbands who attempted to gather all the reins of government in their own hands. In the late sixteenth century Thomas Bentley, a mild and moderate cleric, wrote that this amounted to an abuse of legitimate authority, constituting "tyranny" rather than husbandly rule.[44] Gervase Babington, himself no feminist, excoriated those husbands whose

> wives must be syphers to fill up a place or make the numbers thus or so; but have any rule, disposition or government of such things as yet belongs properly to their place or sex, or to be acquainted with their husbands' purposes, strangers, cheer or anything, they may not.[45]

Babington warned those husbands that they were missing opportunities for profit by denying their wives their "proper" sphere. The adage, "To thrive, you must wive," was devoid of meaning if wives were deprived of the ability or power to make and execute their own plans.

Yet, this is exactly what was happening over the sixteenth and seventeenth centuries. The change was neither abrupt nor total: it affected the various classes differentially and was itself affected by other social changes. Still, what women did as housewives in 1650 was different from what they had done in 1500 and, whatever the cause(s), the effects were to contribute to the decline in the social esteem accorded women.

Contemporary acknowledgment of their failure was swift, so swift that, in many cases, it preceded the failure itself and helped to bring it about. The attacks on wealthy and gentry women like Margaret Hoby for their urban idleness, for example, spread the notion that idleness was the general condition of the gentlewoman. In families which aspired to gentility, therefore, the wife was often thrust out of productive activity so that her idleness could testify to the family's high status. Other attacks on the gentry's way of life had the same effect of marking out a particular pattern of action (or inaction) as genteel, and thus encouraging amid the social aspirants the very behavior condemned. Some social critics attacked women for their "frivolous" desire to live in cities where they had neither to spin nor to toil,[46] and others for their "ambitious" idleness and abundant employment of servants.[47] But these critics were only partially accurate; men were engaged as fiercely as women in the struggle for status. Husbands were as eager as wives to employ servants—and husbands who did so were praised for providing employment to the poor—in order to demonstrate their own worldly success through their wives' lack of productivity.

Babington, for example, directed criticism at men he believed to be social climbers for trying to raise their status by denying their wives their still necessary household roles. Babington conceded that some wives ought to have no role in their domestic economies. There were households, he said, in which, by reason "of height of estate in the community," wives were properly ciphers.[48] For Babington, too, the wife's idleness was the mark of the husband's success, proof that the family was in no way dependent on any contributions from the wife. He looked benignly on men who hired servants to take over the tasks of their wives if those men had achieved the social and economic heights entitling them to cipher-wives. Indeed, Babington was among those who noted that such men were performing a social service and contributing to the public good by providing employment to the poor.

The diary of Lady Grace Mildmay, wife of one of Elizabeth's counselors, illustrates the problem inherent for women in these transitional circumstances. Although of a very high social station, Lady Grace was like many sixteenth-century housewives whose traditional work was becoming redundant and/or socially demeaning. Their labor was not necessary to their family's economy, and increasingly, traditional housewifely tasks were perceived as "beneath the dignity" of prosperous women of yeoman status, much less of gentry. Yet the idleness of these women was at the same time an abomination to zealous men and to themselves. Lady Grace's diary shows her to be a virtuous and pious woman, fervent in her efforts to live in accordance with God's will—as that was interpreted by the clergy. It also shows that she was casting about, searching for something to occupy virtuously her time and mind. She scrupulously observed instructions to remain within, shunning, as she put it, "all opportunities to remove into company, lest I might be enticed and drawn away by evil." When invited out, she replied, "God had placed me in the world in this house; and if I found no comfort here, I would never seek it out of this house."

The problem was that she did find no comfort. She saw, for instance, idleness as the gravest threat—next to the evil suggested by bad company, that is—to her religious salvation. But she had nothing she had to do. She and her husband employed servants, as befitted his high station, and purchased what the servants did not make, practicing, as did all those late sixteenth- and early seventeenth-century courtiers who could, "conspicuous consumption."[49] Lady Grace spent hours engaged in busywork, honing, albeit never to razor's edge, "accomplishments" in lute playing, singing, and embroidery. She acknowledged that she was "but meanly furnished to be excellent in any of those exercises." Her main motivation for continuing them seems to have been that they provided indoor diversion from idleness and boredom. They produced nothing but "recreation." Yet, because she had nothing otherwise to do, the traditional tasks of the housewife being either below her station in life or beyond her training, she claimed "They did me good."[50]

Lady Grace is an early example of the housewife whose housewifery was unnecessary. At this early stage, the options of such women were limited, indeed. As Richard Braithwait put it in his early seventeenth-century work *The English Gentlewoman*, directed precisely at such women, they had to "choose rather with Penelope to weave and unweave than to give idleness the least leave."[51]

Braithwait himself offered no solutions to this dilemma other than country residence. Many of his contemporaries, however, offered more constructive suggestions. Sir Hugh Plat, for example, wrote several works aimed at "ladies" in which he suggested time-consuming activities in which they could busy themselves. He heartily commended, as an instance, the making of comfits, a sweet, noting that, "with good speed," a lady could produce three pounds in three hours[52]—hardly the activity for FitzHerbert's overburdened housewife but singularly appropriate as a substitute for weaving and unweaving.

Plat's books and other such works written to the newly emerging industrious middle sorts and minor gentry who aspired to social success redefined the tasks of the housewife, redirecting her industry. The housewife prescribed in these works no longer devoted herself to producing all that was necessary for the family's subsistence; instead, she supervised the purchase and distribution of goods and devoted her main efforts to her husband's reputation, best defended, apparently, by her quiet residence inside and slight activity.[53]

The view that the primary responsibility of the housewife is maintaining the "credit" of the husband clearly prescribes a very different type of work for the housewife from the traditional, although the description often sounded the same. The Marquis of Halifax, for example, who in the mid-seventeenth century told his daughter that her husband's credit was her primary concern, began by stating, "The government of your house, family and children . . . is the province allotted to your sex."[54] So far, traditional. Halifax departed from tradition, however, by defining this government as delegated from the husband. The wife, he explained, governed her province as the lieutenant of her general/husband, or, as the minister Henry Smith put it at the turn of the seventeenth century, the "underofficer in his commonwealth."[55] Halifax told his daughter that her husband's "mind must be your chief direction," not, that is, her own judgment.[56]

Moreover, busy as she was with her husband's reputation, she could not be bothered manufacturing—producing of her own—household needs. Rather, Halifax said, "Expense . . . the art of laying out money wisely" was to be the focus of her study. In this as in all else it was her husband's reputation she must consider: the wife was "accountable to her husband" for her performance and must remember "it is not only his money, his credit too is at stake."[57] Halifax described his daughter's duties as wife in general terms; others dealt with these in more detail.

William Perkins, for example, one of the most influential Puritan ministers, laid out the wife's duties in his turn-of-the-century *Christian Oeconomy*. The wife, he said, was responsible for "ordering her children and servants in wisdom. [She was] to give the portion of food or cause it to be given in due season." If possible, she was to "exercise herself in some profitable employment."[58] The *basic* tasks, in other words, were not profitable or productive. As Halifax told his daughter, so Perkins told his congregants and fellow ministers, the tasks of the wife involved disbursing the provisions made by the husband. Perkins stated explicitly—and in contrast to tradition—that it was the duty of the *husband*, whom he called the *paterfamilias*, "to provide for his family meat, drink and clothing."[59]

Other ministers followed Perkins' lead. William Gouge, for example, in his own treatises on *Domesticall Duties*, assigned to the housewife the tasks of "nourishing and instructing children when they are young, adorning the house, ordering the provision brought into the house, ruling maidservants, with the like."[60] Thomas Gataker, another cleric, said in 1624 that the wife was to ensure "the provident and faithful keeping and preserving of provisions made and brought in by the man, that they not be imbeciled or made away, that no waste be made of them." He echoed Perkins in advising that, "as ability, leisure and opportunity shall give leave, [the wife ought to engage in] some profitable activity"—clearly not housewifery.[61]

Dod and Hind, the clerical authors of the popular *Bathesheba's Instructions,* observed that families no longer expected (nor did they get) very much from housewives. Noting that "It is thought that the wife has sufficiently performed her duty if she do safely preserve and keep those things her husband brought in," they denied that this negative activity was sufficient and declared that housewives should work at some tasks which would bring in "something" on its own account.[62] While they criticized the wives who did not do so, however, they also did not suggest any "profitable" tasks.

In contrast to FitzHerbert's recognition that the housewife's time was overburdened, the general assumption at this point in the early seventeenth century seems to have been that housewives surely had the leisure to engage in profitable activity (ability was a different question altogether). Indeed, the "wise housewife" would have as much time on her hands as Lady Grace. Daniel Rogers told his congregation, "A wise housewife will contrive and dispose as well by sitting still, and using her brain as some other by bending the force both of soul and body."[63] Her wisest action, of course, would have been marrying a man who could afford both the servants to whom she could "contrive" to delegate the work and the products her servants could turn into food and clothing for her to distribute.

Still, like Lady Grace, this wise housewife might yearn for something to do while those around her worked, and many of the seventeenth-century housewifery books addressed this yearning. Like Hugh Plat's works, for example, Gervase Markham's *The English Housewife* and *The Country Housewife's Garden* were replete with ideas for occupying time in decorative ways. Markham's works provide detailed instructions for basic household tasks such as brewing and baking and also for what appear to be less essential works, such as selecting wines, making paper flowers and perfumes and skin lotions.[64] And for those still eager for work more vitally connected to the family's maintenance, there was always motherhood.

Motherhood

Motherhood, in fact, was increasingly presented by ministers, and accepted by the laity, as so vital—and time-consuming—a chore that it was a "special vocation." As fertility was the woman's religious salvation, so nurturance of what she had conceived could prove her secular and social salvation. Motherhood was a visible means of contributing to the family's welfare and, for women otherwise excluded from such contributions, a godsend. The clerical apotheosis of motherhood and nurturance was as close as the clergy came toward recognizing the potentiality of women finding "callings."

Changing attitudes toward "nourishing" the children illuminate the transformation of maternity. As mentioned, both laity and clergy traditionally urged women to breastfeed. Men cited the biblical example of Sarah and Mary, warned families of the high mortality rates for children sent out to nurse, told parents that nursing milk contained character traits as well as nutrients (i.e., nurses would transmit propensities to vice and coarseness of thought as well as nourishment), and excoriated women who were frustrating divine will by refusing to use their breasts as He had intended. Yet, men had traditionally excepted some women from breastfeeding. Tusser had required housewives to direct their attention to the needs of the wider family first; ministers had conceded that "want of health or ability or any other just impediment" overrode the mother's duty to nurse her own child.[65] Gervase Babington said outright that social circumstances were a "just impediment": addressing mothers, he wrote, "Judge of this thing in a godly feeling, *according to your place* and other true circumstance . . . I leave it to you."[66] By the early seventeenth century, however, clergy were not so tolerant, and aristocratic women themselves had joined in the debate, urging all women as "true mothers" to nurse their children as God ordained.

The injunctions did not go unheeded. There is some evidence of an increase of maternal breastfeeding among the aristocracy and middle layers of English society in the seventeenth century.[67] This evidence is testimony to the increasing numbers of women who could afford to breastfeed. William Gouge was one of the ministers who insisted that mothers nurse their children, but in his discussion of the issue, he acknowledged the "hindrances" to maternal nursing: "a mother that hath a trade or that hath the care of an house will neglect much business by nursing her child: and her husband will save more by giving half a crown a week to nurse, than if his wife gave the child suck."[68] For Tusser in the mid-sixteenth century, it had been exactly these calculations which had determined whether a housewife breastfed or not and, with the acquiescence of the clergy, he had dispensed women who had the care of a house or other responsibilities from nursing. Gouge gave no such dispensation.

Instead, Gouge asserted that this task was the one most vital and "acceptable to God" of all the tasks a housewife could legitimately perform and that, in performing it, she was manifesting "her special calling." He concluded, "Therefore, other business must give place to this and this must not be left for any other business."[69] Gouge considered maternal nursing to be so important that he advised wives to disobey their husbands' instructions, should their husbands tell them to hire a nurse, and to refuse payment of the "marital debt" should the husbands' advances interfere with nursing. The famed Protestant elevation of marriage as "mutual society" stuck at this insistence that women's biological capacity to nurse must take precedence over their psychological capacity to provide help, comfort, and companionship.

Contemporary dramatists did not overlook the disabling effects of the new insistence on breastfeeding on women. Dekker and Webster, in their seventeenth-century play *Westward Ho,* claimed that the insistence on maternal nursing was a means by which husbands could more strongly impose control over their wives. One female character said to another, "I heard say that [your husband] would have thee nurse thy child thyself. . . . There's the policy of husbands to keep thy wives in."[70]

Women seem to have displayed less awareness of this element of the more rigid demand for breastfeeding than did Dekker and Webster. Indeed, many women of the prospering middle strata may have welcomed the task. It gave men a ground to keep women home but it also provided women who were restricted there anyway with some acceptable rationale for their restricted movements and with something to do at home. The increase in breastfeeding is likely to have occurred because these middling strata were prospering, and their prosperity meant that the mistress of the household was being defeated as a housewife and turning to motherhood as a source of activity and esteem. For those families who still depended on the housewife's skills and labor, breastfeeding remained in the seventeenth century as in the sixteenth the subject of economic calculation, and despite the clergy and the Countess of Lincoln, who published a tome praising maternal nursing, women devoted themselves to maternal nursing only when redundant as housewives, when in need, that is, of a "special vocation."

Alice Thornton, for example, was a pious woman of the middle strata in mid-seventeenth-century England. Her particular circumstance was prosperous but not exactly prospering—her husband was not a very sharp businessman. Nonetheless, she did nurse her own children and lavishly praised herself for doing so. Yet in her autobiography she praised her mother, who did not nurse, handsomely for both piety and housewifery and regretted that she was not nearly so competent a housewife as her mother (nor was her husband nearly so competent a provider as her father). She offered not one word of reproach for her mother's failure to nurse, apparently recognizing this failure as part of her mother's success as a housewife. Instead of faulting her mother for neglect of her duty or vanity, Alice praised her mother for discrimination in the selection of nurses:

> My father and mother living at Kirlington where I was born, and my brother Christopher also, the same maidservant attended upon him . . . which kept me after I was weaned, being likewise both nursed by one wet-nurse (though upon having fresh milk, she had a child between the nursing of my brother and myself) and having been very good and careful of the first child, my parents saw it fit she should nurse the second, too.[71]

Lady Anne Fanshawe's depictions of her relationships with her mother and her children further demonstrate that, for women, maternal nursing remained but one element of house-wifery so long as housewifery was an essential factor of the domestic economy. Early in the seventeenth century, Lady Anne's mother nursed her until, as Anne put it, her mother grew "sick to death of a fever" and could nurse her no longer. When Anne described what else her mother did, she named some decorative accomplishments but no productive achievements. When Lady Anne herself gave birth, she had to take up the management of her husband's estates while he went off to war. Despite her mother's example, Lady Anne did not consider nursing her own child, leaving him when he was but two months old "with a nurse" under the care of "another Lady," herself but a recent acquaintance of Anne's. Lady Anne's only comment about her rather casual child-care arrangements was that she left her child to take up her "first manage[ment] of business"[72]—clearly, a task of more importance for a housewife than infant care or breastfeeding. Preserving the heir came second to preserving the inheritance.

The memoirs of the Verney family also demonstrate clearly that the new ideology of motherhood triumphed only in particular economic circumstances. Lady Verney, in the early seventeenth century, managed the affairs of her family and estate with little participation by and no help from her impractical husband, who was busy trying to achieve political success. Lady Verney gave her husband the financial wherewithal with which to pursue his elusive place in court by devoting herself to tasks of housewifery and husbandry. She paid scant attention to her nurslings, other than to replenish their number, giving birth almost every year for more than a decade.

Her eldest son Ralph took over the management of the family property at a young age. His letters show that he accepted wholeheartedly the new ideas about the housewife's role. In his view, the male ran things and the female carried out the instructions of whatever male functioned as *paterfamilias*. The civil war forced him to flee to France and to return the administration of the estate to female hands. His wife administered the Verney property during the war. She also gave birth during the early years of the war and sought hard for a wet-nurse for the infant. While convinced of the importance of proper nursing, she does not appear convinced that it was proper only to do it herself. She devoted considerable thought and effort to finding a "suitable" wet-nurse. Not surprisingly, only poor women offered this service—and not many poor women, at that. Although Lady Verney complained to Ralph that "nurses are much dearer than they ever were," the wages of wet-nurses were too low to support families without help, and many potential wet-nurses were compelled to do other work.[73] Mary's time remained valuable enough to the family that the relative cost of paying a wet-nurse was negative: it freed Mary to perform tasks she and her husband valued more than maternal nursing. Despite the Countess of Lincoln's encouragement of maternal nursing and the Verneys' very evident desire to conform to the new conventions of sex-gender roles, then, Lady Verney did not work at her "special calling"— because her housewifery was more vital to her family than this new and exalted aspect of maternity. Fortunately for her family, Lady Verney proved to be a shrewd housewife of the old style. With Ralph's guidance from afar, she did salvage some of their property from sequestration and the ills of war.

Education: Knowledge Is Power

Ladies Verney and Fanshawe both felt keenly their lack of experience and training in managerial skills when the "managerie" of their estates fell on their shoulders. This lack stemmed from prevailing notions about education. Throughout the sixteenth and seventeenth centuries, the English generally provided and evaluated education with reference to the lives the students would live when grown. In the sixteenth century, Richard Mulcaster, one of the foremost educators of Elizabethan England, and an advocate of educations geared to social class and gender, claimed that the educational program he set forth conformed entirely to English custom. Boys' education must be broad, he said, because men's "employ is so general in all things." Women, on the other hand, were employed "within limit [and] so must their train be." Nonetheless, he encouraged wealthy parents to observe the aptitudes of all their children, for, he said, there were women "of rare excellencies" who could reach the same educational heights as men and, in view of the benefits provided by educated persons of either sex to church, commonwealth, and family, these women should be allowed to climb.[74]

He noted that there were, for example, women in English public life and, even, women of great political power. Some women had been born to this power but some women had achieved it, through their own efforts and/or marriage. In all cases, he warned, if women were to use this power benevolently and so benefit country, church, and family, they needed a sound classical education—just as did males who exercised power.

For women of most strata, Mulcaster conceded, marriage was the main goal. The education of girls had, obviously, to take this into account, teaching obedience, housewifery, and skills of husbandry. But there were exceptions, he explained,

If a young maiden be trained in respect of marriage, obedience to her head, and the qualities which look that way must needs be her best way; if in regard of necessity to learn how to live, *artificial train must furnish her out her trade;* if in respect of ornament to beautify her birth and honour her place, rarities in that kind and seemly for that kind do best beseem. [Emphasis added.][75]

Mulcaster did caution parents against "overeducating" their daughters. Women, he commented, usually married "to their lowest station" or down the social scale. The social graces and rarities beseeming gentlewomen were not very helpful to yeoman wives whose time was better spent baking than translating. Furthermore, while Mulcaster believed ladies should understand what was involved in basic housewifery that they could effectively supervise their servants, he conceded that their housewifely skills need not be highly developed. And he admitted that women without servants or with few servants needed expertise that academic learning could not provide.[76]

However, because girls were to be educated to be the wives of men, he recommended that all girls develop their skills in areas other than domestic arts alone. The clergy concurred: as Henry Smith, the minister, suggested, "As a pair of gloves or a pair of hose are alike, so a man and wife should be alike, because they are a pair. . . . If thou be learned, choose one that loves knowledge . . . if thou must live by thy labour, choose one that loves husbandry."[77]

Smith was not implying that the wife of a classical scholar had to know Latin and Greek in order to be a good wife. Yet he did mean that a wife, even of the upper class, should know something of her husband's occupation and be able to help the husband move forward in that occupation. Thus, Smith and Mulcaster would have disapproved of Grace Mildmay's limited education. Mulcaster held up as models for women of Lady Grace's position women who could converse in the "universal language" of Latin and contribute to their husbands' advantage—and their family's advancement—by providing intelligent understanding of their husbands' concerns and colleagues. The models he pointed to were real women, his own contemporaries. Although later generations have dismissed the educational attainments of these women as un-seemly and tended rather to excuse than laud their attain-ments, Mulcaster and many of his peers saw the intellectual achievement of these women as helpful to their souls and their families.

The Cooke sisters, daughters of a noted scholar and pedagogue who practiced his educational theories at home, all married very well, were highly praised for their intellectual ca-pabilities, and were sought as patronesses by writers, clergy, and hopeful parents of unmarried daughters. Mary Sidney, sis-ter of the famous knight-poet, shared in her brother's literary work and continued it, to great praise, after his death. Queen Elizabeth herself took great and justified pride in her educa-tional attainments, seeing them not as tied directly to her office and, therefore, excusable, if unconventional, in a woman but more as the necessary intellectual equipment of the lady who moved in the highest society. During Elizabeth's reign, more-over, there were even some (few) women at lower levels in so-ciety who used intellectual skills as means of moving up.[78]

Mulcaster and Smith represented the sixteenth-cen-tury humanist position on the education of women which held that a rigorous education was of positive benefit to women and their families, because it taught women virtue, religion, and even commercial skills. Less enlightened men also saw educa-tion as helpful in keeping wives virtuously engaged. Lady Grace practiced the lute; Nicholas Breton, the popular pamphle-teer, suggested translation as an activity more satisfactory to the average housewife. He told husbands to persuade their wives to take up the translation of works from foreign lan-guages to English: "It will keep her from idleness and it is a cun-ning, kind task."[79] The large numbers of sixteenth-century translations of pious works done by women attest to the accep-tance of this suggestion and to the large numbers of women in the sixteenth century proficient enough in foreign languages to do the work of translating.[80]

This practice of providing girls with an academic edu-cation was short-lived.[81] At the turn of the century, Ben Jonson and other dramatists were already attacking "overeducated" women or "Learned Ladies." However, their grounds were startlingly different from those of Mulcaster, who had limited academic education to those with "skill and time to read without hindering housewifery."[82] Ben Jonson denied all women this education, arguing that it turned them into show-offs and parrots, provided no useful activity and, on the contrary, contributed to wives' idleness.[83] John Marston, another dramatist, wondered whether perhaps it might be better if women learned nothing but housewifery, that is, not even how to read and write English.[84]

On the whole, Marston's advice was not followed. Clergy and lay educators continued to encourage families to teach their daughters to read English. There is a clear shift in the education of girls from the sixteenth to the seventeenth century. But, contrary to Marston's wishes, the trend was not toward reinstituting training in domestic skills. Instead, continuing to train up their daughters with an eye to their future, families shifted their emphasis from teaching housewifery to teaching daughters how to catch a man and raise his children. While Mulcaster in the sixteenth century saw literacy as a source of "great contentments, many and sound comforts, many and manifold delights," seventeenth-century educators commended it as the most effective means of Christian socialization of children. It was essential for mothers of young children to read; it was not so essential for women to read.

Education in basic domestic skills once deemed necessary for housewives was limited as the role of the housewife was limited. Women who did not brew their own beer or bake their own bread or help their husbands to farm their land could not pass these skills along to their daughters. For daughters married "to their lowest station," of course, this was something of a problem. The new kind of housewifery books which proliferated in this period were an apparent consequence of this. Earlier writers like Tusser and FitzHerbert had listed necessary tasks and given rules for determining priorities among them; seventeenth-century writers provided detailed instructions for even the most elementary of tasks. Sixteenth-century writers wrote to women who "knew best"; seventeenth-century writers addressed themselves to ignoramae. Thus, Gervase Markham, one of the most popular of seventeenth-century writers on housewifery, gave lengthy descriptions not merely of how to set up a brewery but also of how to brew, not merely of the uses of honey but also of how to collect it.[85] Knowledge once almost ingrained in women was being lost, and for those women who yet needed it, the loss was sorely felt. Women not trained in the traditional domestic arts were at a clear disadvantage if they married men who expected them to perform traditional housewifely tasks. Markham helped these women as well as helping women without traditional housewifery to occupy their time.

Women untrained in caring for families were not, however, at such a disadvantage in obtaining those families. Indeed, their education was geared to the objective of finding husbands and, presumably, fitted them to do so. As early as the turn of the seventeenth century, a new consensus was forming on the best type of education to be provided for girls and was being implemented through the creation of boarding schools. This consensus emphasized "accomplishments" as the surest way to attract husbands. It made only modest concessions to social position, once past the barrier of dependency on wages. Lady Grace might almost have served as a model for all women above the husbandman or journeyman status. The core curriculum consisted of English literacy, singing, dancing, playing a musical instrument, a smattering of French, and fine needlework. The boarding schools for girls, a new phenomenon in seventeenth-century England, provided this basic curriculum for daughters of yeoman and gentry alike.

For daughters educated at home, there remained the possibility of additional instruction in some domestic or academic skills, but this depended on the ability of the mother and the temperament of the father. One of the concessions to social standing seems to have been the delicacy of the sewing skills taught to girls. The higher the social position, the less likely the girl to be trained in any useful sewing crafts. Alice Thornton, a gentlewoman educated in the second quarter of the seventeenth century, shared the education of the daughters of the duke of Strafford. The daughters of the duke learned only "fine works" of the needle: Alice's mother supplemented this education with what Alice called "working skills"[86] for making clothes.

The daughters of the duke were precisely those women whom Mulcaster in the sixteenth century had believed should learn Latin and Greek. By the second quarter of the seventeenth century, however, the English approach to female education had so altered that these skills would have hindered rather than helped them to entice husbands. The cleric Daniel Rogers in 1642 claimed that such knowledge was "unseemly," and "ill-bestowed upon a woman."[87] Richard Braithwait stated the new approach plainly when he told his aspiring English gentleladies in 1630 that the lady did not desire "to have the esteem of any she-clarkes; she had rather be approved by her *living* than *learning*."[88] The mother's role in the education of children, after all, was to provide them with a model, a pattern for living, not the intellectual or practical skills with which to earn a living or assess one's life.[89] As mothers they needed no intellectual skills, and because they could occupy their time with the new tasks of motherhood, they no longer needed intellectual skills to provide them with recreations of the mind or cunning tasks of busywork.

The increasing numbers and visibility of women who did not know how to meet their families' needs without resort to the market and deployment of servants did mean that there were positions available for maidservants. But poorer women were not necessarily able to fill them, for the daughters of the poor also faced a restriction of their available educational opportunities in the early seventeenth century. First, they were not taught to read. The results of the spread of literacy had been somewhat frightening to male ideologues.[90] Although the Puritans made haste to publish their English commentaries of the Bible, they no longer were quite so eager to provide women (or poor men) with the skill to read the Bible themselves. Thus, wealthier women were denied the Latin or Greek or Hebrew to read the Bible unaided by Protestant marginal notes, and poorer women were denied education in anything above rudimentary reading skill. Second, just as the daughters of the elite no longer learned domestic skills at mothers' knees, so also the daughters of the poor had to go outside their ill-equipped homes to learn housewifery. Those who sought to learn the housewifery at which their grandmothers had excelled had to be apprenticed to it. Housewifery, in fact, was the only trade in which the numbers of female apprentices continued to grow in the seventeenth century.[91] But its growth as a commodity reflected a declining number of women able to practice it in their own homes, outside the market, and probably enforced different standards of performance. It is unlikely that females raised in poor households could have learned to meet the new standards at their mothers' knees, since their mothers had only meaner equipment and daughters were sent out young to earn their livings.

Seventeenth-century English women appear to have been unaware that their grandmothers enjoyed wider opportunities. Among the upper strata, contemporaries even had the erroneous impression that female education had substantively improved from the sixteenth to the seventeenth century. In their memoirs, both Alice Thornton and Lady Anne Fanshawe described their mothers' educations as the best available "at the time" and both list their accomplishments in gentle skills and quiet piety; neither shows any awareness that Greek, Latin, and physic had been accessible, albeit often refused by parents as unsuitable for their children.[92] The apprehension of Thornton and Fanshawe that their own educations were superior to what had been available in the past was correct only insofar as their education included more subjects more superficially studied. Lady Margaret Hoby, for example, had more English commentaries on the Bible than had her mother-in-law, Lady Russell, but Lady Russell had been able to read the Latin version of scripture and to make her own sense of the Word.

On the whole, the seventeenth-century English tended to see and color the past through their own narrow(ed) conceptions of decorum. Gervase Holles, for example, was the son of an intellectually accomplished woman who had devoted herself to managing the family economy. But, what Holles praised in his mother was not her sound management or her successful fulfillment of her obligation to provide for her family. Instead, he praised her for the accomplishments prominent and valued in women of his own day. Noting that his mother had "judgement beyond most of her sex," he praised her education as "the best and choicest" in that it made her (despite her good judgment), "equally accomplished with the best of [her sex] . . . She played excellently well upon a lute (according to the way of music in those times) and sang as excellently."[93]

Lucy Hutchinson provides an even more telling example of the extent to which the intellectual education of women had been discounted and devalued in the seventeenth century. The daughter of the commander of the Tower of London, she and her mother had in the early seventeenth century both been instructed in physic by men such as Sir Walter Raleigh and Lord Francis Bacon during their confinements in the Tower. Lucy herself had been educated quite beyond the usual limits of girls, showing herself to be more eager for and adept at the study of Latin than her brothers. Nevertheless, while very proud of her own scholarship, she assumed (correctly) it to be singular in her own time and never allowed it to interfere with her unquestioning deference to her slower-witted husband. Moreover, she expressed ambivalence, with a tilt toward condemnation, about more widespread intellectual education for women. In her biography of her husband, Hutchinson told the story of a female relative of her husband. This relative apparently had posed an intellectual threat to her own husband. Educated in the mid-sixteenth century, she had been well-tutored in languages, translation, and literature, writing her own verse composition. For these achievements, Hutchinson damned her with faint praise. She did give unequivocal praise to the lady's

skills as an "incomparable mother." However, before she ful-
filled the role of mother so admirably, the lady had had a nervous breakdown or, as Hutchinson put it, "her most excellent
understanding [was alienated] in a difficult childbirth" and she
never regained mental competency.

Hutchinson expressed unequivocal admiration for the
lady's life after her breakdown. In a revealing statement, Hutchinson characterized her "ravings [as] more delightful than
other women's most rational discourse." Hutchinson noted
with approval that the lady continued to serve as her husband's
wife after her breakdown, giving birth to and raising several
children, despite her mental disorder. Her breakdown ensured
that her intellectual aspirations ceased to interfere with her primary function of breeding. Although her vacuity of mind compelled her husband to move her into retirement in a country estate, it did not prevent him from cohabitating with her—more
happily than before—or leaving the custody and education of
young children in her now questionably competent hands.[94] As
Braithwait would have it, this lady ended by being certainly
more approved for her living than her learning.

These examples illustrate the decline in esteem suffered by housewives in the seventeenth century. Hutchinson's
praise for her distraught ancestor, for example, condemns intellectual pretensions by women but also very notably calls attention to the lack of intellectual prowess necessary for housewifery. Her ravings may have been more delightful than other
women's most rational discourses—after all, rational discourses,
like Latin, were ill-bestowed on women—but they were ravings
and that they made her a more rather than a less fit housewife
and mother suggests that housewives and mothers were viewed
with some disdain within their families.

Other seventeenth-century characterizations of wives
and mothers confirm this suggestion. Lady Anne Fanshawe, for
one, wrote disparagingly of her stepmother that "She was a
very good housewife, but not else qualified extraordinary in
anything."[95] William Gouge told mothers that they should not

be surprised by their children's ill-treatment of them; on the contrary, he said, it was a wonder that mothers, "though they seem contemptible to others, yet not to their children."[96]

The scorn experienced by women within their families is in some measure attributable to their declining productive activity, for fewer numbers of women were playing vital productive roles within their families' economies. Nonetheless, there remained many women who continued to play vital roles in their families' economies, and they shared in the opprobrium. The question of how the shifts in the tasks of housewifery effected such a debasement of women's place must be answered by examining the way contemporaries perceived the shift.

The Domestic Sphere: Housewifery and Drudgery

One of the most significant changes in contemporary perceptions about housewifery centered on the issue of who bore ultimate responsibility for the family's basic economic survival. The person responsible for the family welfare was, conventionally, granted the authority to make and implement all the decisions and plans necessary to achieve prosperity. That person received all the esteem and gratitude given to the person to whom one owed one's own survival and comfort. In the sixteenth century, husbands and wives, as was seen above, very clearly shared this responsibility and the power and esteem deriving from it. "Husbands abroad . . . housewives at home," the married *couple* provided for themselves and their family.[97] When determining whether one had the economic resources to marry and support a family, ministers encouraged men to consider the economic contributions of their future wives and mothers to raise up daughters who could "get their living."[98] Household government was an aristocracy in which "each obeyeth and commandeth other and they two together rule the house."[99] Writers on husbandry reminded farmers that to thrive, they must wive, and clergy reminded parishioners that, without a wife, a man, "be he never so rich, hath almost nothing that is his."[100]

Seventeenth-century ideologues conceived of the household structure very differently. Richard Braithwait called the family "a domestic kingdom, a monarchy,"[101] and the clergy defined the family by its monarchical features. "The family was a natural society of such persons as have mutual relations, either to the other, under the government of one,"[102] where "one is always higher and beareth rule, the other is always lower and yieldeth subjection."[103] The husband ruled, the wife yielded. In this little monarchy, the wife "helped" the husband, "for he is the prince and chief ruler; she is the associate,"[104] or, as seen above, her husband's "lieutenant" or underofficer.

Far from husbands and wives sharing responsibility for the domestic economy, "the burden," claimed Daniel Rogers, "lies all upon [the husband's] shoulders."[105] In determining whether one had the wherewithal to marry, the potential husband considered his ability to afford his wife allowance of all necessary comforts. The wife of a poor man, of course, was to do all she could to help him, but that all was understood not to amount to very much,[107] while wives of the wealthier sort might try but, as Gouge commented, "question might be made of" the value of the wife's efforts, "at least for the greater sort of number of wives."[108]

Even granting that wives of the wealthier sorts were doing less than they had done and that wives of poor men were failing as miserably as their husbands to upgrade their standard of living, many wives were still doing quite a lot. Gouge, for one, acknowledged that many wives had the care of the household (no little burden) and/or pursued trades. But, in marked contrast to the practice of sixteenth-century writers, Gouge and his seventeenth-century contemporaries considered the wife's achievement of household management actually to be the husband's. Because they defined the husband as the undisputed head of the household, whatever the qualifications or lack thereof of the individual husband, and the wife as his lieutenant, his underofficer, his instrument, everything she did—not simply her goods or her income but the very fruit of her labor—was credited to him. The minister Henry Smith encouraged the wife to "help [her husband] in his business"[109] and William Whately allowed her to "rejoice in his prosperity,"[110] but the business was his, whatever her help; the prosperity was his, whatever her gladness. In 1642, Daniel Rogers put it very plainly. He told wives that, whatever they did, whatever help they provided, the fruits of their labor and even the very right to order the labor belonged to the husband: "Thy helpfulness is not thine, it's thy husband's. . . . He lays claim to all."[111] Wives might work as hard and as productively as ever they did, in other words, but either question would be made of the value or the value would be attributed to the husband.

The change in perceptions thus involved both the assessment of domestic labor and the assignment of authority for labor. Neither of these revolutionary changes passed entirely unnoticed. Gouge's female parishioners, for example, protested his denigration of their labor, insisted that the domestic economy depended on the *housewife's* skills, and claimed that this dependence gave them authority over the family property. Responding to these vehement protests, Gouge did concede that some wives might be mainstays of their households and more wives might strive to be, but he defended his denial of all authority to wives by reference to scripture.[112] Gouge and his contemporaries alleged that the definition of the husband as the head of the family and the wife as his "help" was straight from the mouth of God: God created Eve to be a help to Adam and so all wives were to be the helps of their husbands. The Puritan minister Thomas Gataker asked forthrightly, "What is a wife, but a woman given to a man to be an help and a comfort to him?"[113]

Generations of literature maintaining the theoretical superiority of the husband over his housewife buttressed these definitions. Even as Thomas Becon, for instance, urged women to "work and take pain to get their own livings," he had urged husbands to take up callings profitable enough so that wives need not get their own livings.[114] The new element in the seventeenth century—one which eased the acceptance of the new family division of labor—was that seventeenth-century husbands were able to heed this call: more men could provide for their families without the aid of their wives. Becon's indoor/outdoor division of labor had been impossible for most families to achieve in his own time; throughout the course of the seventeenth century, not only were more and more families finding their subsistence totally dependent on what the husband "got"—but also many of these families were enjoying great prosperity and status. To be sure, the prosperity was often nurtured by the wife's efficient spending, but to the untutored eye, the wife's contribution of shrewd spending what the husband got was not quite equal to the husband's contribution of getting.

And to the tutored eye, the wife's contribution was markedly lower in value. As noted, ministers were quick to deny the economic value of what women did within the home. They also underlined the increasing difficulty women faced trying to get their own livings. Daniel Rogers, for example, attempted to discourage husbands from leaving their wives by pointing out how helpless women were. As he put it, the wife's "subsisting is imperfect in her self; it's wholly substantive and real . . . [only in her husband]." So, he asked husbands, "if thou desert thy poor shiftless wife, and leave her mends in her hands, how great is the desertion?"[115] William Whately told husbands they must provide for their wives and not rely on women to get their own living. To those who criticized the wife's failure to maintain the family, he asked, "Is she not sickly, is she not weak? Has she not breeding and bearing and looking to thy children to employ her? . . . Must she over and above earn her own living?"[116]

Moreover, seventeenth-century men consistently denigrated what they left to women of their traditional work. As already mentioned, William Perkins, who transferred responsibility for household maintenance to the *paterfamilias*, suggested that wives might engage "in some profitable employments" in addition to whatever they did as part of their regular domestic work. Perkins thus distinguished, as sixteenth-century writers had not, housewifery from other occupations by its lack of market value. Perkins's successors, more enmeshed than he in a market economy, exaggerated his distinction. Daniel Rogers, for example, divided the work of supporting the household into the "deeper and higher kind," the "great and weighty" belonging to the husband and the trivial drudgery, "less, but very needful," belonging to the wife.[117] The wife was necessary, said William Whately, to attend to those matters "too mean and trivial" for the greater dignity of the husband.[118] Rogers warned wives to be humble about their meager household contributions; wives should not swell, he said, as if they were props of the house.[119]

When men actually enumerated the tasks they left to wives, they were even more explicit about relative values of the wife's and the husband's work. William Gouge, as seen above, assigned women the tasks of "nourishing and instructing children when they are young, adorning the house, ordering the provision brought into the house, ruling the maidservants, with the like."[120] Adorning the house is less weighty than providing it; ordering the provision less needful than furnishing it.

On a close examination, Thomas Gataker's already cited description of the housewife's duty makes a sharp contrast to sixteenth-century descriptions. According to Gataker, one recalls, the wife was to ensure "provident and faithful keeping and preserving of provision made and brought in by the man, that they not be *imbeciled* or made away, that no waste be made of them" (emphasis added).[121] One of the striking characteristics of this statement is that, on the surface, it is so traditional. It almost echoes Sir Thomas Smith's sixteenth-century description of the work of the wife. Yet Smith had seen housewifery as the process of turning raw materials into useful materials, while Gataker saw it as not "imbeciling" or wasting the fruits of the husband's labor. For Smith, the husband's provision was meaningless without the wife's labor; for Gataker, the work of the wife was almost meaningless. The surface similarity masked a profound change in content and eased acceptance of that change in content. Because seventeenth-century men did not announce the revolutionary nature of their prescriptions but presented them as if a refinement or continuation or purification of past practice and hallowed tradition, the revolution occurred in almost an evolutionary way. Women experienced a slippage in prestige rather than an abrupt end and unmistakable fall.

These clergy, for instance, did not denude women of all authority within the household: they simply placed the woman's household authority in a broader context. The wife's authority was a delegation from the husband and exercised under his oversight. William Perkins called for the wife to exercise authority "as much as concerneth her in her place" and observed that her place was "assistant" to the husband, "the prince and chief ruler."[122]

Again, upon close examination, this denigrated and stripped away the traditional authority of the wife. William Whately, as an instance, encouraged husbands to allow their wives (depending, of course, on individual capacity) some discretion in household decisions. On the surface, this would reinforce the wife's prestige. Yet Whately justified this discretion by explaining that those household decisions the husband should delegate were of such "trifling" importance that the delegation was in order "that [the husband's] authority not be undervalued,"[123] not because wives had any particular expertise or skills. When the list of affairs over which the wife's authority was said to be dependent on the husband's express consent is read, Whately's characterization of the matters to be left to the wife's discretion as trifling appears singularly accurate.

Seventeenth-century housewives, for example, "responsible" for adorning the house were responsible in the same way that they were responsible for distributing the husband's provisions. Seventeenth-century men insisted that wives should obtain their husbands' consents before meeting their responsibilities. Husbands should exercise not only "ultimate oversight" but also tight control over their wives' "fashions, attire, company and expenses."[124] Provider of all comforts, his was to be the determining voice in what those comforts were. Neither the choice of wall-hangings nor the clothing of the children was so trifling as to allow the housewife discretion over it.[125] Indeed, Gerald Winstanley, famed political radical, "Digger," believed the very distribution of food at mealtimes to be the husband's province, done by the wife only under his guidance.[126] That wives, too, were to answer to their husbands for what appear to be exceedingly trifling matters explains why the housewife was beginning to depend on the husband's constant support as the only means to ensure, as William Gouge put it, "that she is not despised nor lightly esteemed."[127]

The effects of the debasement of the housewife's work and circumscription of her authority were felt by women of all social classes. A woman who continued to perform traditional housewifery did so in a changed environment, one which denigrated her labor rather than elevating it. Did she continue to cook, to clean, as Mrs. Noah had said, to come and to go? Well, answered the dramatist Ben Jonson, "Wife . . . I have a cook, a laundress, a house drudge that serves my turns and goes under that name."[128] Did the poor housewife attempt to earn money for her family? Well, Daniel Rogers told her that "It be little . . . which a poor woman can add to the estate of her husband."[129] Did the wife of an artisan or craftsman attempt to join him in the practice of his trade or learn one of her own? Well, the ministers would then ask, was she neglecting that other burden of family (mothering) in order to ply it?[130] Did she attempt to direct household finances? Well, why was she "so curiously prying" and intermeddling about how much income she had to spend?[131] Her husband would give her what money he was willing to have spent, and she was to lay it out "for his credit" under his direction.[132] Did the wife, as counseled, devote herself to maternity? Well she might: who else but a mother could "endure that clamour, annoyance, clutter, . . . clothing, feeding, dressing and undressing, pecking and cleansing?"[133]

In essence, then, seventeenth-century housewives were no longer seen as doing everything—or even anything—that husbands did, and since husbands provided, housewives were, by definition, if not yet by fact, excluded from this role. Women who continued to view household maintenance as a joint endeavor and sought to contribute equally found themselves disadvantaged by the new economic conditions outside the home and by the new perceptions of the housewife's role within and without their homes. Men and women alike were beginning to express scorn for the domestic work women performed in their families and to deny that this work entitled women to prestige or to power. The rough and ready equality between husbands and wives which was the basis of the English paradise was collapsing in the face of women's dependence on men.

Where once men had married as the first step on the ladder of thrift, now women married as the only way to escape servitude or, as Dorothy Osborne put it, avoid "depend[ing] upon kindred that are not friends."[134] The help given by the wife was overmatched by the help given by the husband. As the minister William Whately explained, "Doubtless the man was to give help as well as receive it, and to do more good, by how much he was endowed with more strength and set in the higher place."[135] Women, set in the lower place, were forced to find new ways to give what (little) help they could.

CHAPTER FIVE

Legendary Hearts:
Women in the Family

Just how low the Protestant reformers placed women has been the subject of debate among historians. Some historians have argued that, because the reformers raised the prestige of marriage and made it into the central unit of Christian society, they raised the status of women. In this view, the acceptance of marriage as a godly way of life, rather than only a not-quite-pious alternative to purgatory, entailed a higher estimation of women as necessary partners in this life rather than threats to male piety (temptresses) or superfluous and unproductive not-quite-members of society—nuns.[1] But did this conception of marriage offer women new roles which could serve as routes to power and prestige in their families? If women lost as housewives, did they yet gain as wives or mothers? What was happening to women within the "new model" family, to wives "as they should be"?[2]

The Social Functions of the Family

From as early as the time of Aristotle, philosophers pointed to the family as the base, model, and microcosm of civil and political society.[3] Relations in political society supposedly mirrored those within the family, and the behavior learned within the family mirrored that exhibited in the larger community. The Protestant reformers shared this belief: the family, as the preacher Thomas Becon put it in the mid-sixteenth century, served almost as a school, wherein were learned the principles of authority and subjection.[4] William Perkins described the family as "the foundation and seminary of all other sorts and kinds of life in the Commonwealth and the Church."[5] William Gouge expressed a widespread consensus when he observed in his *Domesticall Duties* that on the one hand there was but "little hope that a disobedient child will prove a profitable member in Church or Commonwealth,"[6] while on the other hand, obedient children, properly trained, were "like to do much . . . good in Church [and] Commonwealth."[7]

The "well-ordered family," wrote the cleric Matthew Griffith, was God's building block for a well-ordered society.[8] In fine, the family created, replenished, and set the pattern for society, and at the heart of the family, responsible for the replenishment and behavior molding, were the husband and wife. They were the hub: if relations between husband and wife were "distempered" or not in accordance with God's plan as set forth in scripture and interpreted by the clergy, then society itself would totter—"children unruly, servants ungoverned and all out of frame."[9] The correct temper of this hub was patriarchal; the husband/father was to rule, the wife/mother to obey. In part, as discussed in chapter 3, this was simply part of the general hierarchical ordering of society. The family, a little society, required hierarchy as surely as did larger society so that tranquillity and concord could emerge.[10] Ministers and their lay male counterparts claimed the wife was the person "meet" to bear subjection, for God not only had formed woman inferior to man but also had expressly ordered her subjection.[11]

The distinctively Protestant elements of this view of marriage had been foreshadowed by earlier writers. They lay in the insistence that marriage was an honorable, pious institution, capable of engendering good as well as repressing sin. The Protestants believed that God created marriage and blessed it, for positive as well as negative reasons: not only that men could direct their lust into legitimate channels but also so that men could have an opportunity to live in a godly way and to do good.[12] The celebrated Protestant elevation of marriage essentially consisted of raising marital chastity to a state of holiness comparable to that of celibacy and persuading that, through marriage, a *public good,* one manifested selfless virtue, while the celibate exhibited a more egoistic virtue.

However, in framing their definition of the public good of marriage, the English reformers undercut the position of women, reinforcing the power and prestige of men at the expense of women. They claimed that it was the *man's* contribution to the commonweal which made marriage so socially beneficial. Matthew Griffith, for example, while he praised marriage as "good generally for mankind," and asked, "who prefers not a common good before a private?", defined men as the doers of the common good and women as the recipients. As noted above, he and others argued that a primary social benefit of marriage was that it gave women, who otherwise, he implied strongly, would become a public charge, protectors.[13] Women's role in begetting the seed with which to replenish church and commonwealth, the other primary social benefit of marriage, was, in this view, passive: women carried the seed implanted by men.

Women, therefore, were debased rather than elevated by this conception of marriage. Marriage rose in social esteem partly because women fell, and the new articulation of women's place in marriage and the behavior suitable to that place assumed this fall. The first social good of marriage required wives to be subordinate to their husbands, that is, both because God so ordered it and because they depended on their husbands, sometimes for their daily bread. As William Gouge put it, "The Apostle requireth [humility] of all Christians . . . [it is] needful for inferiors: most of all for wives"—those who received so much help.[14]

The second social good of marriage—the replenishing of church and commonwealth—also required women's strict subordination to husbands. For producing "profitable" members of church and commonwealth meant training children in authority and obedience or, more generally, Christian virtue, and thus, the woman's "humility" was necessary as an example to the children. Mothers were required to demonstrate their humble gratitude in order to instruct the children (and servants) in the obedience and submission due from inferiors to their bountiful superiors—the fathers who provided for and protected wives and children.[15] The family which best instructed in authority and obedience was the family in which the lines of authority and obedience were most clearly drawn. The woman's place in this family was that of exemplary "inferior." As a wife, her dependence provided her husband with the opportunity to do good; as a mother, her submission provided her offspring with instruction in acceptance of social place.

THE MARITAL UNIT:
WHAT GOD HATH JOINED TOGETHER

Seventeenth-century men were not unaware that this view of the family as it should be had devastating implications for women. Thomas Middleton, the dramatist, for one, noted, "The best condition is but bad enough. . . . No misery surmounts a woman's. Men buy their slaves but women buy their masters."[16] Even the cleric William Gouge conceded that the domestic structure he prescribed left women entirely under the power of their husbands. Yet, Middleton's female characters, with few exceptions, "adapt" to their misery and Gouge defended his structure by arguing that it was designed by God and its purpose was to ensure household and social stability, not specifically to oppress women. Lay and clerical writers agreed that men must "rule as becomes a husband" and women must submit in order for marriage to serve society, and to deserve high status.[17] According to Gouge, unless the husband somehow acted the "tyrant," the wife could have no just cause for complaint over her subjection.[18] It was, after all, ordained by God, conducive to social order and, increasingly more to the point, a just consequence of total dependence on her husband. Who preferred not the common good of wifely subordination over the private good of marital equality?

Seventeenth-century ministers hammered home the last point, repeating again and again that the wife's base position relative to her husband was, in some measure, a function of her abject dependence on him. Significantly, they did so in an almost flattering fashion. Where, in other contexts, for example, they taunted *women* for being "incompetent" to earn their own livings, they came close to praising *wives* who depended on their husbands, and they wholly encouraged this as appropriate wifely behavior. Gouge explained why: the wife, "being in subjection under [her husband] cannot without him provide for herself." Indeed, he went on, the husband "has taken [the wife] from her parents and friends [who] will take no further care of her. . . . Who then shall provide for her, if he do not, whose wholly and only she is?"[19]

As the description of the changing economy of England makes evident, women provided for themselves less and less frequently these days. What seventeenth-century ministers were doing was legitimating the condition to which so many seventeenth-century women were being reduced by social and economic changes anyway. They presented wifely dependence as a natural condition, divinely ordained and therefore an inappropriate focus for resentment or rebellion; it was even a condition to which all women should aspire. Moreover, they accelerated the reduction of women to this dependent status, presenting as "correct" the removal of all the props by which Englishwomen had traditionally maintained their position relative to their husbands.

The possession of property, for example, had enabled women of the wealthy classes to oppose their own desires to those of their husbands. Lady Anne Clifford, at the turn of the seventeenth century, recalled of her husband that, "Sometimes I had fair words from him and sometimes foul," but that the security she felt in the possession of a landed estate allowed her to tolerate the foul words without changing her own demeanor.[20] Sixty years later Lady Elizabeth Hatton, of the same socioeconomic stratum but without her own property, appears scarcely to have drawn a breath without considering its effect on her husband. She wrote to her son, "He is pleased to speak kindly to me and is more cheerful than he was. . . . I shall be . . . careful not to say anything that may displease him, which puts me at a great stand in respect of other necessaries."[21]

Men believed that women with some means of subsistence of their own were unlikely to accept quietly the debased place in the family men assigned them. Thus, they denied that women could have any means of subsistence of their own. The dramatist Phillip Massinger, for example, dismissed traditional warnings that poor(er) men should not marry the daughters of the wealthy, claiming that the daughters themselves were penniless. Large dowries would "add much" to a prospective bride's attractions but would belong, he said, to her husband. Everything a wife had, he declared, "was borrowed from [her] husband."[22] This claim was upheld by the clergy who, as shown in chapter 4, advised wives that everything they had and, especially pertinent to poor women and women of the prospering middle strata, everything they *earned* rightfully belonged to their husbands.[23]

Writers readily admitted that they denied women property rights partly to convince women to exhibit suitable submission, to play the part of Lady Hatton. They believed that only women convinced of the need to submit would do so in the "meek and quiet spirit" men demanded of them. What greater need—outside conformity to God's will—could women have than their own survival?[24] At the same time, the insistence by ideologues that wives should not have their own property and should rely on their husbands for all comforts and necessaries sanctioned the novel phenomenon experienced by so many seventeenth-century wives of total dependence on their husbands. It was the case, as the clergy kept saying, that fewer and fewer women were able to subsist independently of their husbands. But the presentation of this as providential, part of God's plan for married women, helped convince women quietly and meekly to accept their dependence. After all, it allowed that women might still be capable of independence; the individual woman might even be superior to her husband and still it required her as a wife to resign her superiority. The husband was "surperior in place and power to [his wife, even if] he is inferior in gifts and sufficiencies."[25]

Another traditional prop which had permitted the wife some independence was her natural family. The Protestant elevation of marriage sanctioned the removal of this prop, too. The unit the reformers elevated was the marital couple; the exemplum they held up was Ruth who went where Naomi went and lodged where Naomi lodged despite the distance from her own family.[26] Again, the extended family which had sheltered abused wives and supported alienated ones was already disintegrating: the reformers gave moral acceptability to this phenomenon, they did not initiate it.

The clerical insistence that the married couple forsake mother and father and cleave only to each other legitimated a disinheritance and effectual abandonment of daughters. The Marquis of Halifax described the effects on women of the new emphasis on the nuclear family unit when he told his daughter that she was to be "grafted" onto her husband's family and advised her

> like a stranger in a foreign country, you should conform to their methods. . . . Endeavour to forget the indulgence you have found at home. . . . The tenderness we have had for you, my dear, is of another nature, peculiar to kind parents, and differing from that which you will meet with first in any family into which you shall be transplanted.[27]

Alice Thornton's experience of the transplantation was not atypical. She wrote that, as the marquis forecast to his daughter, her marriage placed her "so remote from all my own relatives and friends [that] I was exposed as a stranger."[28]

The clergy believed, logically enough, that this experience would add to the wife's submissiveness. They did urge the husband to "tender [his wife] as much as all her friends, because he has taken her from her friends,"[29] but, in cases where husbands did not or exercised unconscionable behavior, the clergy offered wives no real recourse. Thus when, early in the seventeenth century, the Earl of Clare believed his son-in-law to be abusing his daughter, the earl could see no remedy other than resentment of his son-in-law. Even this he manifested only after his daughter's death, for fear that, during her life, her husband may have seized on it as an excuse for further harsh treatment. When the daughter of the Earl of Leicester asked her father for help with her abusive husband, that earl, too, praised the sanctity of marriage and suggested naming her son after her husband in order to assuage the husband's temper.[30] These powerful fathers believed themselves impotent to help their daughters. How many fathers seized upon the excuse offered by the clergy to abandon their daughters and how many only reluctantly accepted the limitations on their ability to aid their daughters is unclear. It is clear, however, that "ex-daughters" were increasingly at the mercy of current husbands and that, far from propping up wives, the Protestant doctrine of marriage encouraged total wifely dependence on husbands as the surest foundation for godly marriages.

Finally, the very "elevation" of marriage itself undermined women's social place. The Protestants physically shut down nunneries. And in claiming that marriage was the most godly and estimable way of life, they were ideologically closing off the option of the single life for women. The economic and ideological conjucture here was different for men than for women, for whom, again, it was becoming increasingly difficult to maintain themselves as single women, anyway. The legal, social, and economic structure of England all pushed even wealthy and quite resourceful women into marriage.

A central message of even early sixteenth-century drama, for example, of *Ralph Roister Doister*, was woman's need for male protection. This early play made it apparent exactly why women needed men—not because women are naturally incapable of providing for themselves or leading morally upright lives but because society was dominated by men and only men could protect women from other men.

In *Ralph Roister Doister*, the female protagonist, Christian, is a widow and, as befits her name, an exemplum of industry, piety, and submission to men. Engaged to marry someone else, she is, nevertheless, "courted," over her persistent and vehement objections, by the objectionable Ralph of the title. Ralph is a blustery fool whose greatest skill seems to be that of spotting (albeit, not successfully exploiting) a good economic prospect. Christian, a successful entrepreneur and employer of labor, is just such a good economic prospect for Ralph. Unfazed by her rejection of him, Ralph continues to woo (or harass) Christian. His continued pursuit damages Christian's reputation, causing her fiancé to break their engagement because he and his fellows (males) believe Christian must have encouraged Ralph (i.e., she was asking for it).

Christian is unable to stop either Ralph or the gossip and laments, "Have I so many years lived a sober life and showed myself honest, maid, widow and wife, and now to be abused in such vile sort. Ye see how poor widows live void of all comfort" (IV, v).

Ralph almost succeeds in ruining Christian's well-planned life. Luckily, she finally manages to convince her fiancé of her good faith, and he threatens Ralph with physical violence. Ralph *is* fazed by this and leaves Christian in peace—a peace restored by the good offices of a male.

The picture presented in *Ralph Roister Doister* was true to the real lives of sixteenth- and seventeenth-century women who needed men in order to negotiate successfully with the male world. Lady Anne Halkett, for example, a gentlewoman who had inherited an estate sufficient to maintain her, in 1644 expressed a desire to remain single, having, as she put it, "no inclination to marry." She found herself, however, in need of male protection of her reputation and male help in getting her legal rights recognized—in gaining for her the use of her inheritance. Before marrying, Anne had displayed considerable intelligence, courage, and ingenuity in serving the royalist cause. She also displayed considerable passion, falling in love with a married man. She married, in 1655, a man greatly devoted to her. In her recollections of her decision to marry, she made no mention of any passionate attachment to James Halkett. Instead, she described her relief in being able to rely on a man to take charge of her legal and financial affairs. Lady Anne appears to have married because, even for a woman of her strength, wit, and wealth, the single life was too difficult.[31]

For women with fewer resources, the material benefits of marriage more immediately outweighed any desires to remain single. Alice Thornton, for example, wrote that she did not want to marry but that marriage presented "so general a benefit to my family" that she had no real choice. Her widowed mother and siblings needed a male to protect their interests, and Alice married, despite her "great unwillingness" to do so, in order to provide them with one.[32] Alice did not find so effective a protector as did Lady Anne, but then again, neither could she manage as well as Lady Anne herself. She was matched to her level of competence: her need to marry was immediate and she had few financial assets with which to attract a husband. She took what she could get and her entire family was grateful.

Many women clearly felt compelled to marry in order to escape dependence on brothers or other unwilling relatives.[33] Ralph Verney, as an instance, had five sisters and he begrudged every penny he spent on them, despite the provenance of his money, a bequest from their common parents. When his sisters married, they were well aware they could not look homeward for help against or with their husbands. Yet they married in haste, as soon as the opportunity arose, one without even consulting her brother Ralph, for fear of losing the opportunity to escape dependence on him.[34] The wealthy entrepreneur John Evelyn advised his grandson that it was acceptable to "dispose" of his daughters "meanly"; those daughters might well have found dependence on a husband in a house of their (or his) own preferable to dependence on a father who, seeing in them no profit, refused to invest in training them or on relatives who were not particularly close. Marriage did not provide independence but it did raise women from the ranks of dependents: the woman of the lower economic strata who did not marry was lucky to remain a paid domestic servant; the woman of higher economic strata who did not marry was likely to remain an unpaid domestic servant. The place of the wife was low but it existed: outside marriage, women had no place at all and depended upon the comfort of distant kindred.[35]

In praising marriage, seventeenth-century ministers added moral and religious incentives to marry to the already present social and economic ones. The clergy claimed that there was no place or use for women outside marriage. They excoriated the Catholic convent, the institution by which Catholics provided for single women, and argued that woman was created for man. Henry Smith, at the turn of the seventeenth century, told his audience in a typical fashion, "Beasts are ordained for food and clothes for warmth and flowers for pleasure, but the wife is ordained for man."[36] The distinction between the woman and the wife was that the wife was fulfilling the office for which God created woman. Thomas Gataker, for example, asked, "What is a wife but a woman given unto man?" and answered, "A wife is a woman joined to a man to be a help unto him."[37] Only by becoming a wife could a woman do what William Whately, the cleric, called "the one principal thing which the Lord did aim at in making the woman."[38] In the poet Milton's words, he for God alone, she for God in him.

It is, of course, unlikely that many women married simply to fill God's purpose in creating them. Most found, as has been shown, many more compelling reasons. Nevertheless, in insisting that the proper role of woman was that of dependent wife, moralists clearly justified and reinforced the closing off of other options for women and the denial of civil and politi-

cal rights to them. This definition of women and their role undermined women's ability to play any other role. Women who
were provided for by their husbands did not have the same
need as men for jobs or decent wages—and they did not get
them. Women who were part of a marital unit did not need special representation of their own political rights—and they did
not get them. Married women "shared" the wages of their husbands and, through their husbands, they were represented in
the state and at law.[39] The definition of marriage as woman's
proper state and the married woman as the inferior part of her
husband allowed men to ignore the rights and needs of those
unnatural women who remained single. For the most part,
women who remained single did so through no choice of their
own and were invisible, unrealized women, often too busy
struggling to survive, too downcast by their social failure, and
too isolated from one another to unite in defense of their common interests. The men who could have helped them by influ-
encing legislation or raising wages to take into account the
needs of single women were the same men busily defining
women as wives and, therefore, without these needs. Far from
making special provision for unmarried women, these men
sought to convince women that marriage was their natural des-
tiny and that the bonds of matrimony tied women inextricably
and subordinately to their husbands, making independent action by women as unnecessary as it was undesirable. As Gervase Babington told his congregants, "Whatever befalls the husband, either to weal or woe, reaches also in the same sort to the
wife, as a partaker with him in the same."[40]

Few of the men who defined women as wives and
wives as passive partakers in the lives and achievements of
their husbands appear to have done so out of a plain hostility to
women or a conscious desire to elevate men over women.
Most, of course, believed that God had already raised men
above women.[41] But, when pressed (as they sometimes were
by their congregants), even those men who criticized women
most sharply for their "imbecility" acknowledged that women
were not so very inferior to men. Richard Hooker, for example,

while claiming that women were subject to men because of the imbecility of their nature, observed that the difference between men and women was "in so due and sweet proportion as being presented before our eyes might sooner be perceived than defined."[42] William Gouge, who gave husbands almost absolute authority over wives, conceded, "If man and woman be compared together, we shall find a near equality." When asked, "What is then the preference of malekind? What is the excellency of an husband?" he answered, "Only outward and momentary. Outward, in the things of this world only . . . momentary, for the time of this life only."[43] For a less pious person, this might be "eternity enow," but Gouge did believe this life and this world to be of momentary duration while the hereafter would last forever.

Indeed, the sharp insistence on the wife's dependency on her husband and the sharpness of the criticism of her intellectual capacities and her worldly incompetence may have sprung in part from the very close equality evident between men and women and the recognition that wives *could* be better than their husbands—better Christians, better parents, better husbands.[44] Such female superiority was an affront to the very fiber of divinely ordained hierarchy (not to mention male egos). If wives were better than husbands, might not paupers be better than kings or servants better than masters? "What," asked the minister Daniel Rogers, "is more unwomanly than a mannish heart and stomach in a woman?"[45] Such a monstrosity might be compared to lordly airs in peasants. And, in the intimately connected chain of being created by God, if one existed, so could the other. Thus the ministers explained that the wife who appeared superior to her husband was actually inferior—contaminated by that awful vice of pride—and declared that the only perfect woman was a subject woman, "one that walks in a due and daily sense of her infirmities."[46] Thus the highlighting of women's weaknesses and, perhaps, the apparent joy felt when women did evince inferiority and did, in fact, depend "wholly on their husbands."

Seventeenth-century ministers so feared that an incorrect tempering of relations between husbands and wives would lead to social chaos that they attempted to buttress husbands' powers by assigning to husbands powers they themselves refused to exercise as clergy. Protestant ministers, for example, refused the title "priest" and condemned the notions that Christians needed a mediator between themselves and God. Except for wives. William Gouge, who rejected the title priest for himself, declared that the husband is "as a Priest unto his wife and ought to be her mouth to God when they are together."[47] Daniel Rogers asserted that the wife is

with an awful and singular eye, and honouring heart to behold in her husband the gifts of God, as namely, that ability God has given him to be in God's stead unto her in all things pertaining unto her soul [and to] exhort inferiors to the duties of their order and condition, wife, children, sojourners, servants.[48]

Henry Smith reminded the husband that it was his duty to "rule like a King and teach like a Prophet and pray like a Priest."[49]

Where all other subjects were counseled to obey only "in the lord," wives were counseled to obey. The husband's word was as God's. Thomas Gataker encouraged wives to obey their husbands even against their own consciences. He said,

God has applied the husband's will to be the rule of and square of the husband's will, not the wife's of his . . . so here though the husband's will be crooked, so if it be not wicked, the wife's will is not straight in God's sight, if it be not pliable to his.[50]

It must have been a great comfort to the wife that, should she "die in her sins," though her husband's default, God would require her blood at his hands.[51] They could burn together in Hell.

Affectionate Marriage

The wife's increased dependency on her husband, for everything from soup to salvation, obviously changed relations within marriages. One of the most notable effects was the strong stimulus it gave wives—as, for example, Lady Hatton— to attempt to engage the affections of their husbands. Marriage among the highest strata had been and often continued to be a means of forging political alliances, and, as was shown earlier, English men and women of all strata traditionally recognized that marriage was a union with economic aspects.[52] Of course, neither of these phenomena precluded affection between spouses.[53] On the contrary, the sixteenth-century English believed affection to be a necessary element in realizing the economic benefits of marriage. Thomas Tusser, for example, had observed that "rancor" between spouses prevented them from achieving prosperity.[54] Walter Raleigh advised his son to work at being "beloved of your wife" because a wife who felt affection toward her husband would work diligently at preserving his estate while an alienated wife might ruin it.[55]

The traditional notion that marriage was an economic partnership from which both husband and wife would derive benefits according to the efforts of each encouraged both husbands and wives to seek to develop affection in the other. The popular writers on domestic economy frequently spoke of the reciprocal need for married love. Thomas Tusser counseled wives that they could achieve greater power in marriage through securing their husbands' affection than by argument or contests for power: "What wrestling may lose thee, that win with a kiss"; while FitzHerbert told husbands that they could achieve greater prosperity in marriage through securing their wives' affection than by asserting their own dominance. As FitzHerbert noted, "Seldom doth the husband thrive, without leave of his wife."[56]

But, neither FitzHerbert nor Tusser considered affection to be a necessary element in choosing a spouse. They and their contemporaries relied on its evident necessity after marriage as sufficient surety that it would develop. One writer, Edmund Tilney, observed that it was simple prudence on the wife's part to love her husband. "For," he explained, "reason does bind us to love them with whom we must eat and drink . . . of whose joys and sorrows, wealth and woe we must partakers be."[57]

Reason bound seventeenth-century women more straitly than it had their mothers to strive to love their husbands and, more important, to strive to make their husbands love them. The Marquis of Halifax, that kind parent, told his daughter that it was "one of the disadvantages belonging to your sex" that women had no choice but to "endeavour" to love their husbands and, "by wise use of everything they may dislike in a husband, turn that by degrees to be very supportable, which, if neglected, might in time beget an aversion."[58] But in the seventeenth century, reason no longer had quite the same binding effect on men.

In the first place, the insistence that men were "the" providers in the family coupled with women's diminishing productivity to make men less consciously dependent on the "leave" of their wives to thrive. In the second place, fewer men were restricted to the company of their wives. Greater numbers of men were leaving their wives' society, in search of wage-earning positions, to work at such positions, or, at the higher levels of society, to take part in court or legal activities. Wives continued to share in the weal or woe of their husbands in the sense that their subsistence was a "gift" from their husbands and their social status and economic prosperity directly depended upon his, but proportionately fewer wives were sharing in the achievement of weal and woe. Men were finding fellowship and solace outside their homes; women were losing the aid of propinquity in the spurring of conjugal affection. Poor men traveled the country looking for work; wealthier men tended to remain in urban areas which offered increasing amenities and opportunities. Both sorts of men were free from dependence on their wives for society.

Indeed, the practice of men establishing separate residences or somehow dwelling apart from their wives was becoming so common that ministers and government officials began to condemn it. William Gouge, for one, attacked the "many men, who living themselves at one place (suppose at London) send their wives unto some country house and there mew them up, as hawks." The attacks on wage-earning men who left their wives in search of economic advancement or relief from responsibility were more virulent: the men might find labor to subsist; the abandoned women were likely to require poor relief.[59]

Thus, the forces compelling husbands to love their wives were diminishing just as wives were becoming more dependent on that love. It is in this context that the new emphasis on marriage as a source of "mutual society" and "earthly delight" and on training women to please their husbands should be set. Ministers urged husbands to look on their wives as a source of "all content"; clergy and laity alike urged women to provide content.[60] The clergy denied the economic motives enforcing affection between husbands and wives, but they reiterated both the spiritual necessity and the psychological benefits of spousal affection. William Whately, for example, denigrated the wife's economic role in the household but reminded husbands that "The Lord of heaven and earth . . . has said, 'husbands, love your wives.' " It would not, he conceded, hurt if the wife was "beautiful, witty, housewifely, dutiful, loving and every way well conditioned."[61]

Chastity

The ways in which the new ideas about and emphasis on affection in marriage differed from traditional notions and practice are clearly visible in discussions of chastity and the perfect wife. In the case of chastity, the new ideas strongly reinforced the double standard. Chastity had been traditionally venerated by upper-class men as the one indispensable virtue in women, necessary for men to "be certain of their offspring."[62] In the seventeenth century, as men of the industrious middle strata accumulated wealth and honor to leave their off-spring, their demands for certainty became as insistent as the aristocracy's. Where popular literature in the sixteenth century had occasionally allowed the possibility that an adulterous wife could be forgiven and restored to the bosom of her family,[63] by the seventeenth century, even the suspicion of a lack of chastity was punished by social opprobrium and, for the unmarried woman, permanent spinsterhood. "Chastity is an enclos'd garden," wrote Richard Braithwait in 1630, and "it should not be so much as assaulted, lest the report of her spotless beauty become soiled."[64]

Seventeenth-century men and women equated chastity with wealth: it was women's capital. According to Dorothy Osborne, chastity was "all a woman's wealth"; it was her only "saleable" commodity. Dramatists observed that only the wealthy woman could afford to maintain it:

> Distressed needle-women and tradefallen wives
> fish that must needs bite or themselves be bitten.
> Such hungry things as these may soon be took
> easy targets of wealthy seducers.[65]

The transformation of chastity into a commodity allowed wealthy men to buy both chaste wives and unchaste mistresses. Secure in their own wives' possession of chastity, the men could revel in the lack of chastity among poor women.

The new ideas about affection in marriage—and the wife's role in maintaining it—prevented women from imposing on their husbands the same strict standards their husbands were imposing on them. Men argued that wives should accept the adultery of their husbands. The Marquis of Halifax was quite frank. He told his daughter, "Next to the danger of committing adultery yourself, the greatest danger is that of seeing it in your husband. An affected ignorance is a great virtue here."[66]

The reason that wives were to ignore their husbands'

infidelities was that a confrontation between husbands and wives over adultery would disturb the concord and tranquillity of the home. Only when adultery tainted the honor of the patrimony—i.e., when it was the wife who was adulterous—was adultery sufficiently troublesome to risk domestic discord. Halifax urged his daughter to keep quiet and try to win her husband back, regaining his affection through fulfilling the wifely role of guarantor of household harmony.

The minister William Gouge, despite his claim to oppose the double standard, in effect prescribed the same behavior as did Halifax. Gouge observed that the temporal "inconveniences" attendant on a wife's adultery far outweighed those of an adulterous husband.[67] His discussion of the damage wrought by the husband's adultery suggests that wives could limit it. Gouge seems to have viewed the begetting of bastards as the only irreparable consequence of adultery. Thus, since male adulterers escaped pregnancy, the "fruits," as he called them, of adultery by husbands might be minimized or avoided. According to him, these fruits were the alienation of affection, the maintenance of an "harlot" at the expense of the family, the hatred engendered between the betraying husband and the betrayed wife, and the bad conscience of the adulterer. The wife could not quite solve the problem of the adulterer's bad conscience, but Gouge believed that the good wife could reclaim affection—indeed, he and other ministers cautiously suggested that continuing marital relations with the errant husband might be one means of doing so—and the continued exhibition of wifely virtues could prevent hatred from festering.[68] Wealth, that boon to the seducer, could provide for the maintenance of both harlot and family. As Gouge laid it out, the husband's failure to remain faithful only increased the need for the wife to work at creating a harmonious, pleasing home atmosphere, one capable of weaning the husband away from his vice and restoring the godly affection between spouses.

In essence, then, more husbands, particularly of the growing upper and middle strata, were in a position to demand chastity of their wives but fewer wives, again particularly of these upper and middle classes, were in a position to demand it of their husbands. For wives who depended on their husbands for their very subsistence, the dangers of (further) alienating those husbands by accusing them of adultery were great, as the case of Elizabeth Stafford early in the sixteenth century attested and warned. Far better to keep quiet, affect ignorance, and study how to please one's husband so well that he would not want to stray. Far better, that is, to be a perfect wife.

The Perfect Wife

Seventeenth-century discussions of the perfect wife contain unmistakable implications about the new attitudes toward affection in marriage. Seventeenth-century men and women alike recognized that wives were far more dependent than husbands on the affections of their spouse, and that this inequality undermined the traditional guarantor of marital affection: reciprocal dependence—the need to work and live together. They assigned to wives the task of taking up the new slack: it was the wife's duty, they said, to ensure that a comfortable level of affection was maintained with the domestic economy. Wives were supposed to elicit affection from their husbands and to endeavor, as Halifax put it, to feel affection toward their husbands. To help them in their new task, men set about identifying those characteristics most likely to win a husband's heart.

Seventeenth-century discussions of marriage accordingly made more frequent mention of premarital affection than did earlier discussions, which had tended to rely on the husband's need of and gratitude for his wife's domestic management as the spur to marital affection. This new emphasis on premarital affection was a consequence not of a new desire for marital affection but rather of a failure of old ways of attaining it. Writers, for example, paid scant attention to informing men how to make themselves attractive to women or telling women how to choose lovable husbands. Their focus was on identifying the qualities which would arouse and maintain a *husband's* love and on instructing women in how to cultivate those qualities. Lay and clerical writers presented the perfect wife—and ideal woman—as the woman who catered to her husband's emotional needs.[69]

Writers advised their readers that a pleasant submissiveness was a woman's most important characteristic. Daniel Rogers, as noted above, forthrightly defined the only perfect woman as "a subject woman."[70] Thomas Gataker advised men to seek a wife with a "kind and courteous disposition," which, he said, would derive from "a meek and quiet spirit." Neck and neck with chastity, then, and even perhaps overtaking it because it guaranteed it, "lowliness" was a woman's primary virtue, the *sine qua non* for wifely adequacy.[71] As William Gouge put it, "Till she be fully instructed . . . and persuaded" in her due sense of inferiority to a husband, no other quality mattered.[72] William Whately frankly discounted traditional criteria for judging wives. He denigrated housewifely skills, intelligence, and shrewdness, claiming "a mean capacity and slow wit," a more acceptable standard for a wife, "since that encouraged her to put on her the spirit of subjection" which was a quality far more necessary than shrewdness.[73]

Lay writers, equally insistent on the requirement of submissiveness, usually described it in positive terms, calling for women to display "a sweet disposition" and "cheerful countenance."[74] Lay writers also praised other—more immediately appealing—qualities whose value the clergy denied. The clergy generally condemned any emphasis on beauty, money, or "bodily pleasure," because these were but transitory qualities,[75] while the laity, admitting the transitory nature of these qualities, claimed that while present they created an initial base of affection on which submissiveness could build. Lay writers wanted submissiveness *plus*. William Wentworth, for example, believed a "slow wit" to be a hindrance to marital success. He called for humility as surely as did Whately but advised his son to find a woman "of healthy body . . . good complexion, humble and virtuous, some years younger than yourself and *not* a

simple wit" (emphasis added).[76] A quarter of a century later,
Sir Kenelm Digby said the perfect wife was "beautiful to please
[her husband], well-formed to bear children, of *good* wit, a
sweet disposition" (emphasis added).[77]

Writers who upheld the traditional requirement that
husbands and wives should have similar backgrounds or a "par-
ity of estates," did so expressly to ensure that husbands and
wives had similar, if not mutual, interests.[78] Wives who were to
be, as Francis Bacon put it in his turn-of-the-century description of the wife's role, "young men's mistresses, companions
for middle age and old men's nurses,"[79] or, as the cleric
Thomas Gataker put it in his, "playfellow, or a bedfellow, or
tablemate," needed to exhibit some greater allure along with
submissiveness.[80] Even most ministers conceded that, if a marriage were to function as it should, wives had to offer more
than either Jonson's drudge or Whately's care-worn reproducer. The good wife, they acknowledged, possessed those possibly transitory qualities which enabled her to provide "many
singular comforts."[81] Daniel Rogers asked his congregation,
"Who will deny but that a virtuous wife may sometime come
short of an exact housewife?"[82]

Education

The education necessary to raise up virtuous wives capable of being playfellow, mistress, and companion was of a
very different order from that commended by Mulcaster or
Becon in the mid-sixteenth century. Training in academic
skills, always restricted to a very narrow social stratum, would
be limited further since men declared these skills inappropriate and unbecoming in women. Education which prepared
seventeenth-century females for their life roles trained them in
those accomplishments which would attract a husband and,
once married, to "stud[y] nothing but to please" their husbands.[83] For perfect wives of the seventeenth century, skills in
the art of conversation were more important than domestic or

commercial skills. Seventeenth-century women needed to develop the ability to make of the husband's home "an earthly paradise," where a paradise meant the husband could forget his material cares, rather than a refuge in which he could lighten his load by sharing it.[84]

In fact, the kind of education described above as the new standard for female education was exactly suited to the task of creating submissive and attractive wives. The decline in vocational training helped to produce the dependent wife so esteemed by the clergy. The focus on dancing, modern languages, and music helped to produce the accomplished wife so entertaining for her husband and so incapable of challenging her husband's rule. The very obviousness of the inferiority of their education to male education helped to produce, with some rare and notable exceptions, wives convinced of their own inferiority. One of the rare exceptions, Margaret Cavendish, the Duchess of NewCastle, embarked in adulthood on an eclectic course of self-education because she believed her education, which had been, she said, "according to my birth and the nature of my sex," prevented her from achieving her full potential or even from expressing her thoughts "so well as otherwise I might have done."[85]

Another exception, the uncommonly well-educated Bathsua Makin, tutored the daughters of Charles I. She complained that the level of education available to most English women was so low that it created in women a more debauched inferiority than nature alone could have done.[86] She did not question, she said, woman's inferiority to man but, on the contrary, believed, as had sixteenth-century humanists, that this very inferiority required better education than was offered. "Crutches," she added, "are for infirm persons."[87] Her description of contemporary female education suggested that women were fit for better things, but she acknowledged that few men or women agreed with her and that she could point to no contemporary English woman to prove her case, although she blamed this lack on the inferior education currently available to females. The most common objection to her proposal, as she herself admitted, was that highly educated women would be unable to find husbands.[88] Makin attempted to answer this objection, but she seems to have convinced few parents.

Indeed, the new type of education took hold because more and more parents were focusing their educational efforts on making their daughters "ornaments to [their] sex" rather than partners to their husbands—if they concerned themselves at all with the education of daughters.[89] Kind, affectionate parents may have done so for the reason Richard Braithwait cited, in order "to enforce motives of affection," recognizing that a woman's surest way to economic security was to marry and gain the affection of a prosperous man. Less affectionate parents may have done so because they were reluctant to invest money in education which would benefit only the nuclear family of husband and wife.[90] In fact, of course, this continual study to please one's husband was an impossible subject to master: few women were wealthy enough to ignore housewifely skills in favor of bed-fellowing; declining numbers of women were learning sufficient housewifely skills to provide their husbands with the ample and peaceful meals in which tablemating could achieve real value; and finally, even those women without financial problems were sometimes so involved in the duties of maternity that they fell short of the arbitrary standards by which each husband would judge his playfellow.

The woman aiming to give all content to her husband might have succeeded better had she been able intelligently to discuss with him his political troubles as Margaret Cavendish did or effectually to remove cares from her husband's shoulders as Lady Verney did rather than simply and prettily distracting his mind from cares as did her sister-in-law, whose inability to provide for herself greatly added to her husband's cares. But Lady Verney herself assessed this somewhat flighty woman as "the best wife" of all her sisters-in-law, and even Bathsua Makin acknowledged that men were not generally attracted to equal women. Mothers told their daughters, "Be careful, whatsoever you do, to love and obey your husband in all things fitting for a reasonable creature. . . . let no respect be wanting to your husband"; they did not encourage them to take care to develop intellectual or commercial skills.[91] To seventeenth-century English men and women, the perfect wife was clearly inferior to and dependent on her husband, and her role was to provide him with respite from care, not alleviation of care. Perfect wives gave moments of relief and joy; they did not help to build enterprises.

Motherhood Reprised

Most of the skills of the perfect wife also held English women in good stead in the new role of mother. The education which placed her at so clear a disadvantage to men in economic and political society worked to her advantage in the nursery. The same slight musical skills which "stirred" men into proposing could lull infants to sleep; the slight proficiency in modern languages which displayed a woman's breeding could beguile small children; the literacy devoted to pious readings increased both the woman's exemplary traits and her proficiency in catechizing her children. Women untrained to participate in intellectual or economic society may not have missed its stimulation, and may not have resented, as men believed they themselves would, the "constant company" of nurslings experienced by women aspiring to meet the new obligations of motherhood.

These new obligations only began with the duty to breastfeed. Seventeenth-century ideologues, as indicated in chapter 4, made motherhood a "special vocation" and exalted it as a woman's most important—possibly her single—contribution to her family and to society. The vocation, of course, involved much more than fertility: mothers were enjoined to take up nursery duties and devote themselves to child care and early childhood education. Mothers themselves, said William Gouge, were to "feed and clothe their children." He reminded "mothers especially to note this point of timely nurture, as a point in peculiar appertaining to them. . . . Mothers should teach their children, especially when they are young."[92] Dod

and Hind told mothers it was their duty "to bring up and instruct their children, even their sons, in the fear of God and to
endue them with lessons and precepts for the whole course of
their life."[93]

The way Dod and Hind described it, this special vocation appeared to be one which would grant women much
power and prestige—giving them, for example, authority to instruct even their sons! Yet, upon close examination, the glory
of motherhood fades somewhat. Ministers, after all, explained
that God assigned women the role of the infant care—as was
evident in his making "the clamour, annoyance and complaint
among poor nurslings" such that only a woman could tolerate
it.[94] And the primary task the ministers laid out for mothers
was that of exemplifying social inferiority: mothers were to instill Christian acceptance of social hierarchy, place, and discipline and they were to do so by embodying appropriately passive acceptance of their own inferior place.

Moreover, the clerical insistence on maternal breastfeeding eroded the powers and prestige women had accrued
through their role in household production. As shown above
the clergy demanded that mothers nurse no matter what the
economic cost to the family of their housewifely skills. Although mothers did not always accede to this demand, their
failure to do so probably caused many mothers—and fathers—
distress, increased family tensions, sharpened the woman's
awareness of her relative impotence, and encouraged the devaluation of housewifely work. The memoirs of Simonds D'Ewes
are revealing in showing some of the processes involved here.
In the early seventeenth century, his pious mother earnestly desired to breastfeed him while his father demanded that she give
her attention, energy, and time to household management.
Lady D'Ewes struggled with her husband for some weeks over
the issue but ultimately surrendered and never again attempted
to nurse any of her children. D'Ewes's memoirs show his—and
his mother's—awareness that nursing was, as the clergy put it,
her "bounden duty"; they also show his firm conviction—and
his mother's more reluctant acceptance—of his father's author-

ity to make all decisions affecting his wife and children. D'Ewes appreciated his mother's futile effort, but he approved of his father's success in putting his mother in her place and, like his father, valued the place of housewife more than that of mother.[95]

The D'Ewes memoir thus further confirms the low place of the mother in the family hierarchy. Despite the theoretical exaltation of motherhood, women's role as reproducer took center stage in English families only once women were no longer necessary or valued as producers, and women did not attain through motherhood the same power and prestige they had achieved through housewifery. Mothers had no equality at all with fathers.

On the contrary, both laity and clergy denigrated the role of mothers relative to that of fathers. As shown above, women were losing the power to make and implement decisions within their families. They did not regain as mothers what they lost as housewives. All decisions mothers made and actions they took, including whether to breastfeed or how to clothe children, came under the oversight of the husband/father, whose agent the mother was considered. Significantly, mothers lost even their delegated powers over their children as the children approached the "age of reason." Once, that is, the child was old enough to realize s/he owed gratitude and/or respect to the person who cared for it, the child was removed from the exclusive care of the mother. Among the upper classes, children were often removed even from the physical presence of the mother, and among the lower classes, the children may have been sent out to other families as servants. Just as the child grew able to appreciate that, as the Marquis of Halifax put it, "No respect is lasting but that which is produced by our being in some degree useful to those who pay it,"[96] the mother lost her usefulness to the child.

When Thomas Hobbes claimed mothers deserved power over their children because mothers gave and protected the lives of their children, his contemporaries reacted with horror at the idea that mothers could have had equal, much less more, power than fathers. Seventeenth-century men both denied power to mothers and derided mothers' usefulness to their children. Men argued, first, that the mother's usefulness, like all woman's usefulness, belonged to her husband, and second, that the work of the mother, like all "women's work," was base and contemptible and productive of only a base and contemptible usefulness.[97] They emphasized that it was the father who provided the child with the training and/or capital necessary to allow the child to escape from dependence and said plainly that the father alone had "power to reward or revenge."[98] Mothers cleaned infants; fathers set up sons in businesses and daughters in marriage. As William Gouge commented, the wonder was not that mothers were scorned relative to fathers: the wonder was that mothers were not contemptible to their children.[90] In a case where the demands of the parents conflicted, seventeenth-century ideologues agreed that there was no question but that the "father must be obeyed, yet so as the child no way show any contempt to his mother, but with all reverence and humility make it known to her that it is best for both, for herself and himself, that the father be obeyed."[100] Mothers who raised children so politic as to achieve this diplomatic feat were rewarded by not receiving opprobrium at the hands of the objects of the mothers' own unbounded affections, their offspring.

None of this means that children, even grown children, fully conscious of to whom they owed what and who controlled the purse strings, did not love their mothers. It does, however, suggest that mothers were rated differently from fathers and received different, probably less deferential, treatment from their offspring than fathers. The available evidence bears this out.

Dorothy Osborne, for example, shows that the *power* possessed by fathers made even the fathers' reliance on the "ties" of affection far more sure than such a reliance by mothers. She told her suitor that her father was giving her the freedom to choose her husband, but that his liberality increased her resolve not to oppose his wishes. She wrote, "Though he has left [the decision] more in my power than almost anybody leaves a daughter, yet, certainly, I were the worst person in the world if his kindness were not a greater tie upon me than any advantage he could have reserved."[101]

The Marquis of Halifax bluntly told his daughter that, "when a father lays aside his authority and persuades only by his kindness, you will never answer it to good nature, if it has not weight with you."[102] Mothers had no authority to lay aside.

The very abundance of the mother's kindness, her "unbounded affection," diminished its power to compel filial affection and respect in return. The English believed great parental affection was natural, and both laity and clergy traditionally worried lest parental fondness turn into an overfondness, breeding spoiled children and undisciplined adults.[103] Loving parents were believed to be reluctant to "press" their children against the children's desires and eager to provide their children with all possible material comforts. Cleric and layman alike warned that loving parents could go too far; overfondness threatened the stability of the state through its production of ungrateful and insubordinate offspring and the salvation of the parents and children as parents risked their own and, by example, their children's souls to achieve worldly prosperity for their children. In the seventeenth century, fathers were apparently escaping from this bind while mothers were becoming more deeply mired in it. Seventeenth-century clergymen who, in one breath, commended breastfeeding as a means to increase maternal affection, in the next breath chastised the mother's tendency to "dote" on her children.[104] Women themselves described mother-love as "unbounded" and warned their children of the ill effects of such intense feelings. Said one gentlewoman at the turn of the seventeenth century, the mother's love was "hardly contained within the bound of reason."[105] The remedy to the mother's unrestrained affection was the father's more reasonable fondness. Seventeenth-century men thus called for the subjection of the mother's passion to the father's reason—or, put another way, they subjected mothers very definitely to fathers. They described the father's love, traditionally compared to God's love for humanity, as the source of "a loving fear or a fearing love," which William Gouge declared to be "the ground of children's duties."[106] The father, then, through his power over mother and child, produced the profitable member of the commonwealth that doting mothers might have tainted.

The psychological contrasts between the mother's doting and the father's rational affection tended further to erode the mother's place in the family. The portrayal of mother love as all-embracing, unswerving, and mothers as deeply attached to their children from day one (with breastfeeding but deepening their obsession)[107] encouraged children to take their mothers and the love their mothers felt for them for granted. The portrayal of father love as measured, rational, and godly encouraged children to strive to "earn" their fathers' love.[108] The father, therefore, enjoyed not only the esteem due the parent useful to the child but also the esteem granted by the English to that which was harder to get. The mother, on the other hand, suffered the ignominy of familiarity which bred contempt.[109]

Women possessed of a strong sense of their own self-worth and proud of their contribution to their domestic economy, to their husbands and their children, might have found such ignominy bitter. Perfect wives convinced of their inferiority and humbly submissive to their husbands might not have noticed the contempt. Secure in the knowledge that their dependence was part of God's plan, seventeenth-century women were made so insecure by that very dependence about everything else that the familiarity of their children may well have been welcome. At least temporarily, motherhood gave the new model women, the emblems of social inferiority, someone over whom they were superior. The familiarity which preceded contempt from children was, however, a far cry from the rough and ready equality with husbands traditionally enjoyed by English women.

CHAPTER SIX

Putting the Pieces Together

The metamorphosis of the English woman from help-meet into dependent or from housewife into wife and mother was, as the last five chapters have shown, a complex process. The transformation had material and ideological causes; it had material and ideological consequences. And it occurred unevenly: ideological change sometimes preceded material change, easing it; material change sometimes preceded—and forced—ideological change. The metamorphosis occurred in different ways at different rates in the different social strata, different geographic locations, and different age groups. But the process was at work in all strata and every geographic location, and all females felt its effects. Every woman's fall diminished women and left other women less able, as Thomas Becon had put it in 1550, "to defend herself against the needy life." This chapter looks more closely at the complex process of transformation, examining first how one facet of change—a new rigidity in divisions between "within" and "without"—altered many facets of a woman's life and, second, the impact of the new social divisions of strata and geography on rates and effects of change.

Ideas and Influences: Within and Without

The increasing rigidity with which late sixteenth- and seventeenth-century ideologues viewed the distinction between what they called "within" and "without"—today, often equated with the "public" and "private" spheres—was a change with significant implications for women. As previously shown, the English had always made some distinctions between within the home and without and had generally placed women within. Yet, as has also been indicated, the English had always permitted women some liberty without, for example, going to market. Even the clergy, who early urged the English to heed the distinctions more carefully, had allowed women some freedom without. Clerics likened the housewife to the turtle: when she went beyond her doors in pursuit of her housewifely duties, she carried her house about her like a shell, "without" which she never stepped.[1] Sixteenth-century laymen expected wives to participate in public banquets, christenings, and other spectacles, criticizing women who remained enclosed within for exhibiting "contempt and disdain of others" rather than praising them for their appropriate modesty.[2] By the seventeenth century, men, doubting that any profit came through the wife's attendance at public events, began to complain of the frivolity, the "liberty and looseness" of women who sought companionship or entertainment beyond their own doors and spent their husbands' money making themselves presentable for society.[3] Seventeenth-century men encouraged women to remain within, protecting their chastity—and, as important, their reputations for chastity and their husbands' purses. Without, men claimed, was a world women could not (and should not) understand and, indeed, a world in which they were not safe. In the late sixteenth century, the cleric Gervase Babington warned women of the rapes just waiting for them without their doors and told them it was their own "needless getting abroad" that provoked rapes.[4] By the late seventeenth century, laymen, particularly of the middle strata of society, were hard put to find any "need" at all for a woman to be without. So far were seventeenth-century men from disapproving of women like Mrs. Stubbes who "shunned the outside world," as Lady Grace Mildmay had put it, that, instead of praising the clerical wife who organized poor relief in her husband's parish, they condemned her as a meddler.[5]

Two important processes were coalescing here: first, the distinction between inside and out was losing its traditional flexibility, and second, women, whose sphere had always been within, were losing their traditional right to define the tasks entailed in their work and themselves establish boundaries between within and without. The fruition of these processes was, of course, more drawn out than the stark contrasts presented here indicate. Some men of the sixteenth century had urged women to remain at home regardless of housewifery, and some men of the seventeenth century defended their rights to stray outside their doors.[6] But the processes were clearly occurring: distinctions between within and without were becoming more rigid, and new descriptions of the wife's role as a private calling were reinforcing traditional restrictions on women's participation in the society without their doors. The coalescence of these processes meant that "within," the world of women—who, one recalls, were being *defined* as unproductive—was defined as a sphere in which no productive activity occurred, while "without," the male public world, was defined as the sphere in which productive activity occurred.[7] The distinction between within and without was, as yet, more conceptual than physical: women who stayed in their proper sphere may well have performed tasks of use to their families, even tasks which brought in money, and men may well have performed "productive" tasks, such as weaving or tool-making, within their houses. But the conceptual distinction between within and without seemed to be based on natural, physical grounds and did justify the failure to instruct women in the skills necessary to negotiate successfully or productively in public society, thereby accelerating the decline in their ability to subsist, within or without, on their own.

Managerie

Alice Thornton is an exemplum of the new demarcations between within and without, leaving women without either the productive or the social skills acquired through participation in society. Though quite aware that her mother had been "much oppressed and injured through the bad managerie" of the executors her father appointed, she was equally aware that her own lack of experience would make her a worse manager of her husband's estate than even neglectful male executors. She urged her husband to appoint executors and, when he died without having done so, she scurried about looking for a male to "take administration . . . and . . . order and pay things according to the law."

She recognized that her own interest would make her a more concerned administrator than a hired man would be and did not doubt her own intelligence; she also recognized that her decorous reside within had made her less than fit to deal with society without—to handle, for instance, workmen and wage negotiations with the same aplomb as her husband or as Lady Margaret Hoby had done 60 years earlier.[8] Clerics such as William Gouge presented it as a flat rule that husbands should not name their wives as executors of their estates. He doubted both women's natural ability to manage property and their social skills, insisting that women were too inexperienced in the ways of the world to succeed in so worldly an endeavor. Whatever natural business acumen a woman might have had, he implied strongly, disuse had stultified.[9]

The "advices" left by key fathers to sons concurred with the clerics. Upper- and middle-strata fathers advised their sons to keep tight reins on their wives' spending, warning that sons should be liberal only with those (rare) women who had first demonstrated thrift.[10] Sir William Wentworth, at the turn of the seventeenth century, explaining his insistence that wives under no circumstances be made executrixes of their husbands' wills, noted that they had no opportunity to develop managerial skills. "Though she be wise and well-given," he went on, she was not likely to get experience soon enough to develop skill: rich widows were likely to remarry soon and place all their affairs in the hands of another man.[11]

Charity

The effects of this novel and clear-cut differentiation between within and without reverberated beyond the domestic economic sphere. The new differentiation, for example, interacted with the reappraisal of the Christian duty of charity undertaken by Protestant reformers and altered women's role in philanthropy. Reformers denounced the traditional practice of giving money to the church in exchange for masses and decried the practice of dispensing alms to whomever asked for them and distributing "extras" to neighboring poor. According to Puritan theory, this charity provided no real help to the recipient and it allowed undeserving idlers to continue their reprehensible ways. Reformers called for an institutionalization of charity, wherein the parish, rather than the individual or the family, would be the responsible unit, and the parish could establish workhouses or similar programs to ensure that only the "deserving poor" received charity.[12] The indiscriminate charity condemned by reformers was largely the work of women. The selective charity the reformers commended was the province of men. Women who had "constantly" given "the offal of the table . . . to the poor," as did the mothers of Lady Fanshawe and Gervase Holles, were discouraged from performing such indiscriminate acts,[13] and by the seventeenth century they were discouraged from providing charity at all, except under the direction of their husbands.

William Gouge was one of the ministers who directly addressed the issue of women's role in charity. He denied women the right to give gifts of charity without their husbands' consent. His explanation for this was of a piece with the denial to women of property rights, but it was not derived alone from this denial. Instead, it derived also from the rigid division he made between within and without or, as he also termed them, the public and the private spheres. Gouge asserted that a genuinely charitable act required a knowledge of society women could and did not possess. True charity involved judging who deserved help and how best to provide it, and the wife who remained within, he said, had no basis for judging. Gouge acknowledged that she might know "what may in the house be best spared" to give and said she should give this information to her husband. The husband would then, on the basis of his knowledge of society, determine to whom and how to be charitable.[14] He and his fellow clerics urged those women without husbands to guide their philanthropical efforts to make institutional endowments so that the male-headed institution could direct the dispersal of charity.[15]

Charity remained an obligation incumbent on all Christians.[16] But women's ability to fulfill the obligation properly was restricted: women were declared dependent on male help. Such an idea—that women were dependent on their husbands if they were properly to perform their Christian duties—was part of the new approach to marriage and family relations. In the instance of charity, new approaches to old problems of how to give in the most Christian way coupled with the newly clarified differentiations between male and female activities and reinforced the dependence of wives on their husbands.

Chastity II

The reevaluation of celibacy and continence which was part of the new approach to marriage also reinforced the dependence of wives on husbands and also did so partly through the newly rigid differentiation of spheres. As was noted elsewhere, marital chastity rose in public esteem and celibacy fell. Marital chastity rose much farther, of course, than celibacy fell: men did not begin to criticize other men who were celibate, and many still referred to the ability to remain celibate (without burning) as a special gift from God.[17] But, there was increasing talk, in the seventeenth century, of the selfishness of celibacy and much praise of the apparently less demanding virtue of marital chastity.[18] Daniel Rogers in 1642 called chastity "the fairest flower . . . the richest jewel . . . the crown of marriage." It was, he said, "one of the chiefest ornaments of the married and so of all, in either sex."[19]

No longer connoting only virginity, chastity was now seen as what Matthew Griffith, the seventeenth-century pastor, called, "unspottedness of the flesh." Although presumably less difficult to achieve than celibacy, this chastity surpassed celibacy in godliness, for it involved performance of the "holy" act of intercourse. Married intercourse, undertaken in the proper spirit and, "providing always that the man is to maintain his superiority and the woman to observe that modesty which beseems her towards the man," was, according to William Perkins, "a figure of the conjunction between Christ and the faithful," and, therefore, a positive good, not simply a means of avoiding evil.[20] Marital intercourse could be abused: Perkins reminded his congregation that, "even in wedlock, excess in lust is no better than plain adultery before God" and "immoderate" desire turned lawful intercourse into fornication.[21] But the seventeenth-century clergy conceded that the sex act was useful "for linking the affections" and urged that the act be performed with "good will and delight"; pleasure did not diminish its godliness.[22]

The divines were, however, quick to point out that the path to marital chastity was thorny. It required, first, that sexuality be considered a duty and obligation between husbands and wives. Each was obliged to meet the sexual needs of the other with what the clergy called, in traditional terms, "due benevolence." Second, it required that the chastity of each be measured by the chastity of the other: adultery by either husband or wife destroyed the chastity of both.[23]

This latter aspect of the new notion of chastity had severe implications for women. First, it denigrated female virginity as a sign of spiritual salvation or source of social prestige, and placed women in greater dependence than before on men. Chaste women—the best women—were now married women.

Moreover, they were married women who were somehow managing to keep their husbands sexually faithful. Second, because this new notion supplemented but did not replace traditional notions of female chastity and broad strata of men were beginning to demand strict observance of traditional dicta about female chastity in order to guarantee the "honor" of their patrimony, it reinforced the men's efforts to control the movement and behavior of their wives.[24]

As Dod and Hind explained, "It is not sufficient that women do keep themselves chaste and untouched of vicious men, unless also they be of that integrity and uprightness, that they minister not so much as the least occasion for suspicion."[25]

Since the seventeenth century was a time when, as the dramatists Beaumont and Fletcher observed, "People in this age are prone to credit / They'll let fall nothing that may brand a woman,"[26] and as Margaret Cavendish fifty years later echoed, the "world was apt to lay aspersions even on the innocent," few women could hope to avoid "the least occasion" for suspicion.[27] The new doctrine of marital chastity meant that this suspicion cast aspersions on the husband's spiritual estate as well as the wife's, thereby giving added impetus to the husband's drive to make his wife's chastity the "enclosed garden" prescribed by Richard Braithwait—the garden which sustained no male assaults. This, many were pleased to believe, was best accomplished through enclosing the wife herself, or as Gouge had put it, "mewing her up" away from the temptations and attacks of other men.[28] Needless to say, mewed up wives had few tools by which to ensure the chastity of their husbands and, thus, their own "marital chastity." The new doctrine of marital chastity, despite its apparent contradiction of the traditional double standard, in fact increased both male insistence on traditional chastity and women's difficulty in achieving chastity. It bound women tightly within as insurance of the chastity men required from them and dependent on men for the chastity God required of them. Given that the double standard still exists today, women's reliance on male fidelity for their own chastity placed obstacles insurmountable for many women to their godliness.

Social Structure, Ideology, and Economic Change

Of course, not all women in seventeenth- or even eighteenth-century England were so wholly dependent on their husbands, and even of those who were, not all were so harshly subordinated. Indeed, the very vehemence with which seventeenth-century men proclaimed the husband to be the sole support of and only real contributor to the family economy contrasts with the silence of sixteenth-century men on this same point, suggests the novelty of such claims, and casts doubt on their validity. Their very novelty suggests in turn that they could not have been universally applicable: in other words, the claims were not only suspect, they were clearly inappropriate for some families. Women collectively may have fallen in status and been more subject to men, but one hundred years is quite a short time for all women to have surrendered their autonomy to men, and no evidence suggests that such a shocking phenomenon occurred. Evidence does suggest that some women did so, and that many more men and women were expecting that women would do so. But the new claims of patriarchal power to wifely dependence had varying applicability to real women—class, status, and geographic location all had significant impact.

All available evidence suggests that it was in the upper and middle strata of late sixteenth- and early seventeenth-century English society that the model of the dependent wife first came to life. By the turn of the seventeenth century, men of these strata quite evidently believed that wives were economic burdens rather than helpmeets. At the turn of the century, Lord Burleigh, primary counselor to Queen Elizabeth, penned an "advice" to his son, telling him how to derive the most advantage from marriage. According to Burleigh, the only opportunity for gain through marriage came before marriage; the strategy he commended involved the "portion" brought to marriage by the wife. He told his son, "If your estate be good, marry near at home and at leisure; if weak, then far off and quickly."[29] If his son was in good economic shape, in other words, he should take the time to consider the effect of merging his property with his wife's property in deciding whom to marry. He should look for a woman whose property could be easily and successfully integrated into his own estate, for, after all, he would manage both. If, on the contrary, his son was economically distressed, the object of marriage must be an immediate infusion of capital, a portion which could put the son back on his feet again, and he must marry quickly, perhaps before word had spread of his distress. Burleigh cautioned against expecting any benefit from a wife other than the property conveyed in the portion, arguing that even noble blood must be accompanied by a sizable portion. No blue blood himself, Burleigh commented, "a man can buy nothing in the market with gentility," expecting that consideration to dissuade his son from a disadvantageous marriage with a poor aristocrat.[30]

Burleigh's peers, Sir Walter Raleigh and Sir William Wentworth, expressed a similar view of the economic role of the wife in marriage. Wentworth told his son to hold out for a large portion; no matter what attributes a wife might bring to marriage, he said, "a good portion makes her the better."[31] Both Raleigh and Wentworth expected wives to be financial drains on husbands, requiring husbands to provide them with incomes to live and not contributing to that income. Both urged their sons to exercise careful control over their wives' spending. Wentworth suggested keeping a wife on a very small allowance until she had provided heirs. Then, he conceded, "If you think she deserve and need it, enlarge her jointure."[32]

These men were writing from their own experience: Wentworth had something of an ax to grind in that he believed his mother had dissipated his own inheritance through ill administration and favoritism to his sister; but Raleigh, who had married for love at some cost to his career, simply did not believe women could manage large households profitably. A loving wife such as his own would try to help, but he placed no confidence in her skills and warned his son against doing so. Burleigh's evident unwillingness to rely on women as economic helpmeets is particularly interesting, for two reasons. First, his own wife was one of the famous Cooke sisters—regarded as among the best-educated and brilliant of all sixteenth-century Englishwomen. Surely, if any woman could help, Burleigh's could. Yet Burleigh thinks of wives as emotional and intellectual supports; he does not credit his own nor his son's potential wife with superior—helpful—domestic skills. Second, Burleigh was the uncle-in-law of Margaret Hoby who, as has been seen, was an extremely capable administrator of property. Yet Burleigh's experience with Lady Hoby was mainly limited to the city, and in the city, Lady Hoby spent. She was not yet dependent on her husband, but women like her were to be on the road to it, and her own husband had attempted (unsuccessfully) to rein in her independent habits. It was only her successful housewifery in the country which ensured her of some independence.[33]

Thus, paradoxically, the first caveat to the general picture of women's declining status and increasing subjection was exactly in the strata where the picture was most generally true. Some country wives and, especially, middle- and upper-strata rural wives whose husbands resided elsewhere while leaving the property in their hands, fared well throughout the seventeenth century. The woman who met her own and her family's needs "more from the provision of her yard, than the furniture of the markets," as Gervase Markham put it, was free from abject material dependence on her husband and the necessity of receiving an allowance from him.[34] In rural areas, moreover, the new attitudes toward philanthropy only slowly took hold, so, throughout the seventeenth century, many housewives continued to appoint themselves, in Richard Braithwait's words, "overseer[s] for the poor," dispensing charity without the mediatorship of their husbands[35] and playing significant roles in community relief. Wives whose husbands exercised authority from afar were more likely than wives with resident husbands to be able to exercise freedom of choice in directing their own and their servants' activities. Granted, the country housewife's choice of ministers was more limited than the city woman's because there were fewer ministers in the country parishes, but she often remained free to conduct the household worship according to her own preference. The distinction between within and without remained somewhat blurred for the country housewife, who continued to perform important tasks beyond the physical boundaries of her home and whose virtue was not attacked each time she stepped forth from her doors.

However, as seventeenth-century men continually pointed out, this self-sufficient country housewife was a rare phenomenon. Already by the early seventeenth century, few women living in the country could aspire to such a paradisical existence: self-sufficiency required considerable land in which to grow food and graze animals, considerable skill through which to turn the crops into household consumables, and considerable freedom with which to exploit these. Even women with the first two requisites were often hard put to maintain the third.[36]

Women without the first requisite, land, were compelled to depend on their husbands' wage and/or to do work for wages themselves. The literary works of the upper classes mocked poor women for their failure to achieve the desired self-sufficiency and for the paucity of their earning, but the effect of these failures on the status of women within the poor families is unclear. Poor men, after all, were not doing much better, and may have been doing much worse, at their appointed tasks than women at theirs. Daniel Rogers, for example, who pointed out that poor women could do little to increase their family's wealth, also declared that women *should* do nothing to raise their husbands' estates. According to Rogers, it was God's will that the burden lie all upon the husband's shoulders.[37]

It is therefore possible that poor women enjoyed a freedom of action unknown to their wealthier sisters as the poor women continued to come and to go, to brew and to bake—to share the burden which their husbands were incapable of carry-

ing alone. It is possible that poor women retained a level of esteem lost to the wealthier sisters as poor women continued to
perform the visible day-to-day tasks necessary for basic survival. While their husbands went out to earn wages, the wives
may have been doing wage work at home and very visibly
maintaining the meager earnings of the husband. When both
spouses were failing, perhaps one did not rise at the expense of
the other.

Women with enough land but without the second requisite, the skill to work it, suffered a clear decline in status
within their families. Residence in the country, apart from their
husbands, might be a preferred way of life for these women,
but only to free them from the more oppressive manifestations
of their husbands' power, not as a means of asserting or but-
tressing their own. Lady Margaret Hoby was a country housewife par excellence: when her disagreeable husband came to
their estate, she exerted herself to be pleasant but she did not alter her activities. Lady Hatton sixty years later was a country
housewife with few skills: when her disagreeable husband
came to visit, she feared for her very sustenance. In some ways,
therefore, country residence was a far greater boon to Lady
Hatton than to Lady Hoby, but the boon lay in the distance
from her husband, not in increased status or freedom from subjection, and it was double-edged. City life offered amenities
and "vain pleasures" undreamt of in rural locales.

It was thus the country housewife with the skills and
the wealth to run a country household and the intellectual resources to enjoy doing so who was in the strongest position.
But this country housewife could see her future in the life of
her urban sister, and her future was clearly limited by factors
over which women were denied control. The changes in wom-
en's roles which were only becoming visible in seventeenth-
century rural areas were plainly evident in urban areas, accelerated by sophisticated market economies. Lady Hoby's lack of
housekeeping during her residence in the city testifies to the different roles played by the housewife in the city as contrasted
with the country at the turn of the century. In the city, families

could purchase relatively cheaply and easily products which it yet made sense for rural families to produce themselves, and in cities, social and economic competition was far more intense than in the less crowded countryside, and had higher stakes. While it is probable that many housewives among the industrious middle sort still worked long and hard both to help their husbands in their work and to supply their families' needs in the most efficient manner, it is certain that their work was no longer perceived as the fulcrum of the domestic economy. The burden was falling on the husband.

Ideas, social structure, and economic conditions all played a part in the urban housewife's decline. One way in which they interacted was a lag in perceptions about the economic possibilities open to housewives. Neither the irrationality of the wealthy London lady producing her own beer nor the impossibility of the poor London housewife doing so, for example, relieved either of them of the social stigma of failing in their duty to do so. Despite the profound differences in their own situations and between their lives and the lives of their grandmothers, both women were judged by the traditional, undifferentiated standard applied to their grandmothers, and both were judged failures—by the same men, moreover, who urged them to keep an eye to the times and meet their responsibilities in new ways.

The failure of one generation of housewives then fed the failure of the next, reducing the likelihood that housewives could recoup power and productivity. Women who did not bake their own bread did not pass along to the daughters the skill of bread baking. Nor, importantly, did the mothers pass along the expectation of self-sufficiency or independence. The expertise and responsibilities lost in one generation did not reappear spontaneously in the next.

Finally, each individual failure by a housewife was magnified and refracted into a debilitating collective loss of power and prestige by women. The social power women had traditionally exercised at the market diminished when they came to the market primarily as consumers. Ironically, they lost the production skills which had made them expert consumers and permitted them to set market or fair prices just as their role in consumption grew.

Housewives, moreover, who sent servants to do their marketing, as did increasing number of middle- and upper-strata women, no longer participated in the exchange of skills and information at the market. Because they had few means to judge who was behaving unconscionably, they no longer formed part of a reserve pool of public opinion which could be set off by unfair market behavior. Poorer women who now came to markets only as buyers of goods and sellers of labor power were at the mercy of those who set selling prices—instead of negotiating them—and of those who established hiring practices. Women's powers of negotiation were severely limited by their dependence on the market.

Again, at the lowest levels of the social and economic structure, it is impossible to know how women fared within their families. Obviously, fewer women than men were being apprenticed to trades, and women's work for wages was, generally, low-paying and not prestigious. Yet, the wages of the laundress may have been what fed the laundress's children, and if women could not earn a living by spinning, at least, they qualified by spinning for poor relief. Poor women did remain zealously industrious in the seventeenth century as peddlers, fishwives, seamstresses, domestic servants, and similar occupations. Moreover, since the lower orders as a whole were excluded from society—defined out of the political nation—it is possible that the women of these strata suffered no effective loss by the exclusion of their gender from society and the political nation.

Women of the industrious middling sorts, however, did lose relative to their husbands and brothers. While their brothers received specialized training enabling them to set up in some business or profession, their own education was more often cursory and makeshift.[38] They came to marriage bereft of skills qualifying them to act as responsible partners. What training they received after marriage depended on their husbands' good will and vocation: was the vocation one which required a helper? And must the helper be someone whose presence and attention were constant, or could the husband utilize his wife when she was free from the demands of the household?

Moreover, the higher the social stratum, the less necessary—and the less desirable—the wife's help. Wealthy husbands could do without the aid of their wives in their own industry and could afford to hire substitutes for their wives for household work. Because the ability to do this was an obvious sign of wealth and success, many men promoted their wives out of the domestic economy even when those wives had no interest in leaving. The wives so promoted were dependent on their husbands for their own subsistence and functioned, as Gervase Babington, the minister, put it, as "syphers" in their houses,[39] providing, as well, cipher-like models for their daughters. These daughters grew up with dependent and unskilled mothers and believed that the natural condition of mothers.

The decline of women is thus likely to have been fastest in the upper and middle strata of society and in urban areas. Throughout the seventeenth century, it was spreading out into the country and down into the lower ranks—spurred by the desire of members of lower ranks "to ape" or to show their solidarity with their "betters," by the desire of those betters to master their inferiors, and by the diminishing ability of women to assert themselves. But—and this is important—the seventeenth-century decline was not uncontested. Where they could find openings, women continued to play important social and family roles. During the civil war, for example, women throughout society played significant roles both in the public prosecution of the war and in the private maintenance of their families.

In urban areas and countryside alike, women intervened directly in the political process, presenting petitions to Parliament and fomenting agrarian disturbances.[40] Women played a major role in the development of communications networks and the spread of journals describing, analyzing, and proselytizing for the war effort.[41] They were acknowledged to be a primary source of support for the Levellers, a radical political party. Many women took charge of their family property while their husbands were away fighting or in exile or prison.[42] In public and in private, the efforts of these women were crowned by success. Clearly, when push came to shove, women could pick themselves up and learn the skills—including aggressiveness and intrigue—necessary to provide for and protect their families.

Equally clearly, however, men were not pleased by the success of women. Throughout the war, men attempted to limit the participation of women. John Goodwin, a leader of the Levellers, for example, although not averse to using women to increase the appearance of mass support for the Levellers, was quick to restrict their activities to those directed by men. He preferred to limit women's independent activity to prayer, for, he explained, "Prayer is a service wherein women also may acquit themselves like men, their prayers commonly are as masculine and do as great service and execution as the prayers of men."[43]

Husbands who relied on their wives to salvage the family property attempted to direct their wives' efforts and reminded them of the extraordinary nature of their activities.[44] The men accepted their wives' help, seeing no alternative, but they did so less than gracefully. Ralph Verney, for one, repeatedly complained in letters to his wife about the burden of child care he bore while in exile in France. She was not exactly luxuriating in England: she was trying to remove Parliament's sequestration of the Verney property and to steer clear of the political shoals upon which Ralph had so nearly wrecked the family fortunes.[45]

More ominously, however, men viewed the dislocations of the war as caused in part by the efforts of women to step outside and above their place. Men and women alike saw the civil war as proof of Daniel Rogers's dictum that the "distemper" of husband/wife relations would cause "all others to be distempered, children unruly, servants ungoverned and all out of frame."[46] As William Gouge had warned, women who refused to accept their place had "overthrow[n] the ground of all duty . . . become an ill pattern to children and servants . . . incur[red] many other mischiefs."[47] In this view, the bold perversion of nature, and consequently of society, had begun at the very pinnacle of society, with, that is, the marriage of Henrietta and Charles. It was her interference in public business which had led to war.[48] The excesses of the war had similarly been perpetrated by women or caused by their misguided and perverse attempts to help direct the course of political reformation, abetted in their outrageous activity by men with a like ineptitude for rule, i.e., men of the lower orders.[49] Reestablishment of social peace obviously required putting women back in their place.

The end of the civil war saw women thrust back to their "natural" inferiority with a speed unmatched even by the similar transformation 300 years later of Rosie the Riveter into Hannah the Homemaker at the end of World War II. The Restoration ushered in an era of peace and prosperity in which the new conceptions of woman and her role in society and the family were perceived to have been tested by fire and found good. The economic transformation which had robbed women of the upper strata of their traditional family roles were becoming more deeply rooted and therefore exercising greater impact on women of the lower strata. More women were free to devote themselves to maternity in the same way as more men were free to enter into wage contracts. Women created childhood; men created factories.

There did continue to be significant variations in women's lives, depending on their husbands' or fathers' place in the social hierarchy and the material circumstances of their own lives. But large numbers of women were attending the same schools or otherwise receiving similar educations (or lack thereof). This, as their parents intended, put the women on a par in the developing national marriage mart, although the content of their education also aggravated their need to marry and their dependence on their husbands once married. Trained to attract husbands rather than to be housewives, women of all strata provided their husbands with the opportunity to exercise mastery in their homes. They were harder put to provide their husbands with support and partnership. Richard Braithwait in 1630 declared that a man's home was *his* castle;[50] the husband ruled alone. The wife's role was to create an earthly paradise, a respite from the cares of the world, not to help in alleviating them. The woman fulfilling this role posed no threat to social order, presented no competition to men, and required no independent political voice. Outside society and her own natural family, she would do well to submit to her husband. If he desert her, as Daniel Rogers had said, how great would be the desertion.[51]

CHAPTER SEVEN

Much Remains
to Be Done

A central question emerging from this study of the changing role of women in their families and in society in England during the transition to capitalism is why women submitted so apparently peacefully to their own degradation. Why did women, in some cases, even cooperate in reorienting their activities in directions leading to a debased place in society? For, although there is some evidence that some women objected to the male characterizations of their labor as valueless and their natures depraved, there is more evidence that numbers of women leapt at the opportunities to relinquish their labor onto the market or to immerse themselves in maternity, and that intelligent and well-educated women deprecated the intellectual and moral nature of their sex.[1] This study provides partial answers to these questions, through the examination of the interdependent relationship between ideology and life, and shows that more complete answers may be found only by placing these phenomena in the context of the larger changes occurring in sixteenth- and seventeenth-century England.

The crushing workload of the "typical" sixteenth-century housewife is one reason that women gave up some tasks. Anthony FitzHerbert's early sixteenth-century suggestion on how to choose between tasks when so much had to be done that some things were impossible to do goes to the heart of the matter. The housewife's "provision" for her household involved so much work, so many skills, and so much time that few housewives would have objected to transferring some of this work to the market—to buying candles, for instance, rather than making them, if the money could be spared, to buying beer rather than setting aside the time and space to manufacture beer each month, to hiring servants to perform specific tasks such as sewing or laundering—in order to free the housewife to perform some of the myriad other tasks necessary to ensure her family's survival and increase its prosperity.

The ideology of the household or family as the basic social unit also played a part in women's changing status. The wife's role in this conception was to meet the family's needs, not to shore up her own social or family position. If the money which would have purchased stillery equipment and the space to house it might go toward a family enterprise and offer a visible financial return, so long as the wife could meet the family's beverage need easily, cheaply, and satisfactorily at the market, few wives would have been likely to insist that the money be frozen in brewing equipment so that they could retain their traditional role. The wife's genuine concern for the welfare of the family of which she was ineluctably part could easily have led her to propose more economically rational ways of promoting the welfare, regardless of the effect on her own labor, once these ways appeared.

Moreover, and here the larger social and economic changes directly impinge on the choices women made and the effects of these choices, few women could have foreseen the ultimate effects of their withdrawal from their traditional activities. Women were subject to the same fears and anxieties as men. The same status anxiety, therefore, which may have prompted men to assert their control over and independence of their wives may have led women to cede control and accept their own dependence.[2] When social status was defined as it traditionally had been by degrees of freedom from the need for manual labor, and the wise housewife was newly defined as

the one who sat still and told others what to do, the wife's decision to remove herself from participation in productive activity
is explicable in terms of her own ambition as well as family interest. The wife's leisure suggested the husband's success and
the family's social position, and, possibly, its state of grace.[3]

Even the wife's acceptance of the restriction to "within" is explicable. This restriction did not seem unambiguously
to threaten her power and status within either her family or society. After all, for generations, "within" had been the fulcrum
of society. At a time when so many social, economic, and political activities occurred within the home, when the king's government itself was yet said to be an extension of his household,
what woman could have foreseen that restriction to the home
meant permanent exclusion from society? Ben Jonson might
term the housewife a drudge, but, for generations, the tasks
Ben Jonson scorned had been part of the housewife's duty and
the housewife had received social esteem. Who could have
known that in retaining only the "drudgery," housewives were
giving up the esteem? William Whately might identify the
housewife's sphere of influence as trivial and mean, but for generations, the successful management of her sphere had granted
women its extension: competent housewives participated in all
aspects of their families' lives. What housewife could have believed that the separation between home and society, between
within and without, between private and public would become
so frozen and so significant that it prevented the expertise of
the housewife from finding an outlet in spheres of "importance"? For generations, the home was the world—who could
have seen that the world outside was expanding and the home
would remain as only a haven inside it?

But the larger changes England experienced in these
two hundred years, its transition to a market-oriented capitalist
society, for example, and to a nation-state governed by professionals, made these consequences possible, and women's initial
acquiescence in the changes in their own roles robbed them of
the weapons with which to fight back. This work has tried to
show that women's devaluation was the consequence of the in-

teractions of ideology and material changes, and that in this interaction is found the causes of women's expulsion from their English "paradise." In the sixteenth century, women were not equal to men in access to wealth or education or power, but as England became a capitalist state, the disparity in access both increased and became more meaningful.

In the effort to explain women's place in capitalist society, this study has looked to the dialectical relationship between ideology and practice rather than to nature, technology, or other forces apparently outside human control. It locates women's civil, political, and economic inferiority in the family and in family ideology as both were reshaped in the sixteenth and seventeenth centuries. The added debilities imposed on women by industrialization had little to do with the technological imperatives of industrialization. Women were not disenfranchised or excluded from social and economic acitivity by industrialization: rather, the factory institutionalized outside the home the hierarchy already in place within the home.

Maternal nursing, as an instance, was a factor preventing women from outside work in the nineteenth century—but only because it had been defined in the sixteenth and seventeenth centuries as a private act, one which prevented women from competing with men for outside work or inside power. Prior to this time, nursing and child care had not prevented women from participating in economic production inside or outside their homes. Maternal breast-feeding hindered this participation only when social convention transformed it into a private act, demanded of all women but denied public space.

Maternity itself as defined by late sixteenth- and seventeenth-century ideologues appeared to offer women an opportunity to participate meaningfully within their family life—but, as this book has shown, acceptance of the opportunity was fraught with peril. On the one hand, "motherhood" was exalted as a source of prestige, a contribution to the family, the church, and the commonwealth. It was welcomed particularly and early by women who made no other direct contribution to their family's well-being and had no other independent source of prestige. On the other hand, effective performance of this role hindered women from pursuing other activities, and mothers, so far from accruing power and prestige as the reward of their labors, found themselves but "lightly esteemed" and dependent on their husbands for support against the contempt of their children and servants.

It is not the case that the traditional housewife and mother came into existence with industrialization.[4] The essential elements of this "traditional" housewife, her identification with the private sphere, child care, and dependency on men, predated industrialization and, indeed, her existence was one of the significant factors shaping industrialization. The creation of the private housewife was part of the segmentation of the labor market which fostered competition among various groups of workers rather than between workers and employers. The restriction of women to the private sphere, coupled with women's material dependence on men, has helped to mold women into a conservative social force, promoting of social stability rather than potentially threatening to it.

In its simplest terms, this effect has arisen from women's isolation in their homes, where they had little opportunity to develop a collective or class consciousness. Women's conservatism, however, is also a logical consequence of their private and public impotence. The kinds of labor performed by women in their homes or for wages has, since the sixteenth and seventeenth centuries, provided women even more rarely than men with a sense of power or control over their own lives. On the contrary, a primary goal of the English reformers was to convince women that they had neither right nor ability to control either their own lives or their families. The reformers achieved their goal. When a person believes she is unworthy and unable to win power, modern psychologists claim, she is unlikely to seek it. The conservatism of women is consistent with their own experience of social defeat. As the reformers believed, a woman's inability to survive without a man offers her scarce encouragement to challenge entrenched political and economic powers, either of gender or of class.

Other effects of women's dependence on men also, as the reformers hoped, promoted social stability. The dependence forces women to strive to ameliorate the unpleasant conditions of life faced by men outside the home by providing their husbands with "havens in heartless worlds" or, more to the point in sixteenth- and seventeenth-century England, churches in godless worlds. This striving, however, has been directed into expressive rather than directly productive or political channels. As this study has shown, sixteenth- and seventeenth-century Englishmen urged women to support their husbands emotionally and discouraged them from providing their husbands with material support. This too has had contradictory effects.

On the one hand, it has increased the economic burden on the husband/father.[5] On the other hand, it has given the husband/father a material stake in the status quo. A man might be poor, depraved, trodden upon, bestial—no matter, he retained power over his wife and civil, political, and economic advantages over other women. Moreover, if his wife were successful in providing him with the earthly paradise demanded by seventeenth-century Englishmen, anger or frustration sparked by the world outside the home would be defused inside the home, and husbands and fathers could go forth, refreshed, to work again.

Rather than these phenomena being consequences of industrialization, the argument presented here suggests that these phenomena enabled industrialization to proceed more rapidly and peacefully than might otherwise have been the case. In demonstrating how changing ideas about women affected women's family roles and, through this, their political and economic potential, this study also suggests that changing women's place in modern capitalist society involves more than a restructuring of industrial relations to allow women "equal opportunity" in the workplace. Such a restructuring is impossible without the dismantling of the ideology of the family and women's place in it first articulated in sixteenth- and seventeenth-century England during the transition to capitalism. None of these larger changes of English society and few of the particular changes were inevitably degrading to *women:* motherhood, for example, is not an intrinsically debasing role, nor reproduction of the family and society intrinsically worthless. Neither intrinsically disqualifies one for other social roles. Women's fall must therefore be understood in the light of a society which itself debases these tasks and restricts such functions to "inferior" creatures unfit for other work. Any measurable progress of women toward equality must be through changing such a society—ideologically, socially, and economically.

APPENDIX

Literary Sources: Why and Which

Although many of the changes in the lives of English men and women during the years 1500–1660 can be measured and quantified, their meanings are apparent only through the examination of how contemporaries perceived and adapted to these changes. The discovery that men challenged the female monopoly of midwifery, for example, reveals little in itself about women's status relative to men or their opportunities to earn money and prestige. But the examination of contemporary attitudes toward male and female midwives reveals that men were able to make this challenge successful because male physicians were extending their opportunities to earn money and prestige at the expense of female midwives; that traditional social conventions prohibiting male presence at childbed were being undermined by the disrepute into which female midwives were falling; and that the failure of female midwives to protect their monopoly was one aspect of a more general narrowing of opportunities for women to find prestigious and gainful employment.

This work tries to get at these latter kinds of revelations, to show what the material changes in England's economic and social structure, discussed in chapter 2, meant to women, and why and how these meanings emerged. The major focus, therefore, is on changing ideology: understanding the concepts and ideas by which people made sense of their world and ordered their own actions within it, and how these changed. The book describes probable causes of the changes and illustrates how the changes in perceptions of the world were translated into changed forms of activity in the world, demonstrating the dynamic relationship between ideology and material reality; the way in which we understand the world shapes our response to it, but the world's response to us shapes our understanding.

The evidence used for this study is primarily literary. The kinds of literary sources both useful and available fall into four main categories: popular literature written by laity for a general audience and for a specially segmented female audience; literature written by clergy; diaries, collections of correspondence, and memoirs left by contemporaries; and finally, popular drama.

The validity of literature as a source of historical analysis is, of course, problematic. Until the invention and use of the printing press and the extension of literacy to strata outside the church and aristocracy, literature was aimed at and used by very restricted social strata. Nonetheless, in the sixteenth century, the printing press was in widespread use in England, and England, thanks to the convergence of two major intellectual movements, Protestantism and humanism, was undergoing an "educational revolution," the effects of which were to promote basic English literacy among all social strata and both sexes.[1] Indeed, there was a short period in the mid-sixteenth century during which some women of the upper and middle strata achieved literacy in the "universal" tongues of Greek and Latin. Although this pinnacle was not maintained, basic English literacy was spreading among men and women throughout the sixteenth and early seventeenth centuries.[2] Furthermore, because it became common practice for households to conduct "readings" during prayer and work sessions, even those who did not read gained exposure to popular literary works.[3]

An effect of this extension of literacy and of the

cheapening of books was to broaden the potential audience for literary works. Literary historians characterize the development of the professional author as a sixteenth-century phenomenon.[4] Until the sixteenth century, writers had been dependent on the patronage of the aristocracy or the church. Few writers challenged the values and beliefs of the men from whom they hoped to gain support. The professional author of the sixteenth and subsequent centuries, however, looked at the sales of his work for profits and recognized a large, nonaristocratic audience out there which he hoped to attract. Moreover, professional authors could afford more easily to mock and tease the sensibilities and values of their readers than could writers who lived by patronage because professional authors required from each reader only the purchase price of their book, not subsistence.

Professional writers, nevertheless, did have to appeal to readers if they were to subsist by the mass sales of their works. The nonautobiographical lay literature used in this study is, in the main, the popular works of professional authors, those which succeeded in appealing to what is traditionally described as the "industrious middle sort" of society, the new market for books. Studies of this new market show that these "middling sorts" looked for books that would help them get ahead in this world and, through this world, to heaven. They justified their purchase of books with references to utility, to how, in other words, the books helped them to advance in this world and/or to display the proper behavior in this world which would enable them both to maintain or rise in their place in this world and to achieve salvation.[5]

Writers were very conscious of the desire of their audience for instruction and sought to meet this desire. They frequently called attention to the educational aspects of what appeared to be merely diverting works. One mid-sixteenth-century compiler of prose fiction or "novels" explained the purpose of his work to be providing "rules for avoiding of vice and imitation of virtue to all estates."[6] Phillip Sidney, an aristocrat who did not depend on the sale of his works for subsistence, defended fiction itself on the basis of its pedagogical potential. In his late sixteenth-century "Defense of Poesie," Sidney wrote that the successful poet, or writer of fiction, was he who persuaded his audience of the truth of his vision of good and evil and induced them to act in accord with it:

> the philosopher teaches, but he teaches obscurely, so as the learned only can understand him, that is to say, he teaches them that are already taught, but the poet is the food for the tenderest stomachs, the poet is, indeed, the right popular philosopher, whereof Aesop's fables give good proof. . . . It is not rhymings or versings that make a good poet. . . .

Sidney noted, "It is that feigning notable images of virtues, vices or what else, with that delightful teaching."[7]

This self-conscious goal of improving the character and, sometimes, the economic circumstances of their readership allows the historian to use these literary sources as means of understanding contemporary attitudes toward social structure and family relations. Lay and clerical writers intended their works to be normative: as one seventeenth-century minister declared, he wrote not about families "as they are but as they should be."[8] The problems for the historian lie in assessing, first, the convergence of "how it should be" with how it was and, second, the popular acceptance of the author's version of how it should be.

In the case of lay literature, sales figures provide some index to the reliability of the work. All the works discussed in the preceding pages were reprinted at least once and most more than once. Although purchase of a work does not necessarily mean the purchaser accepted the work's ideology, the continuing outlay of money for particular books suggests that these works were perceived by their purchasers to be at least potentially useful. Additionally, in the cases of technical works on farming and housewifery and of etiquette books, the frequent revisions made by authors and booksellers to bring their works in line with contemporary practice as it changed suggest that the writers or booksellers did make some efforts to ensure the reliability of their guides to living.

Sales figures alone do not attest to the validity of the vision of life embodied in particular lay works or the possibilities for readers actually to do what the works direct them to do. The same or similar visions repeated again and again, however, do indicate some reliability as an index to what larger numbers of people did think. In some cases, the tone of the author makes specific the limitations of his work as a picture of social reality; in other cases, other evidentiary sources such as diaries, correspondence, memoirs, statutes, and data on prices or trade help to give a general sense of the historical use to which particular works may be put.

Lay and clerical literature present somewhat different problems to the historian. The lay literature falls into two broad categories of its own: technical or "how-to" manuals and narrative works. The how-to manuals range from instruction in particular skills, such as managing a dairy or keeping accounts, to expositions on general behavior, such as how a gentlewoman would occupy her time or a lady dress. The general works were directed at women who had not been adequately trained for their current stations in life: either the women had been raised to gentility and found themselves no longer gentry (or poor gentry) or the women had been raised without "breeding" and now found themselves addressed as "worshipful." At the same time that works intended for male audiences assured men that their births need not prevent them from acting with "gentility," works intended for female audiences gave women rules on how to manifest gentility in a genteel way. Narrative works offered idealized pictures of the behaviors of men and women of all estates and strata.

The clerical literature falls into one category, sermon, but offered both technical instruction on the manner in which women should exhibit their skills, if they had any, and more general instruction in apparel and occupying one's time. It also presented, as did lay narratives, a type of idealized picture of proper behavior in the model women it portrayed. While the lay literature was usually directed at a particular segment of society, however, clerical literature was ostensibly applicable to all elements of society. Certainly, the clerical works provided the ideological framework within which debates over issues of social and political significance were set. The clergy occupied a position of unmatched ideological importance in early modern England. As Christopher Hill has put it,

> In the sixteenth and seventeenth centuries, the Church had a monopoly of thought-control and opinion-forming. It controlled education; it censored books. Until 1641 the publication of home news was prohibited. . . . In the absence of other media of communication, sermons were for the majority of Englishmen their main source of political information and political ideas. Men came to church for news and in addition to disseminating news, sermons had replaced the confessional as a source of guidance on moral and economic conduct.[9]

The works of the clergy, whether or not applicable to each English person, touched each English person. The English, under compulsion of law, attended church every Sunday, and many voluntarily attended additional "lectures" throughout the week. In fact, groups of individuals formed associations in order to hire ministers to lecture regularly to supplement— or, possibly, challenge—the official government-sponsored Sunday homilies. It was the clergy's traditional role to interpret both God's word and the world to their parishioners. Despite some "dumb dogs" among them, on the whole, the clergy succeeded in maintaining the prestige and legitimacy associated with the role of interpreters of God's will.[10] Their pronouncements on family structure thus bore not only the weight of the learned in a semiliterate society but also the imprint of divine will in a devout society.

In contrast to lay literature, therefore, there is little problem in determining how successfully these clerical ideas reached the public. The sermons used here were very popular.

They had huge sales, and many had frequent reprints. More significantly still, they are by influential ministers—those who set the tone followed by lesser clerics throughout England—many of whom were hired and rehired by their parishioners rather than appointed by bishops.

Most of the clerical works discussed herein are by prominent Puritan ministers. There are three basic reasons for this. First, Puritans printed their sermons in far greater numbers than did ministers of the established church, since they relied on the sermons to attract and comfort new members. Second, because the Puritans despaired of the ability of the established church—with its pitiful component of adequate preaching ministers—to fulfill its role of religious and moral bulwark successfully, they consciously set up and used other sites to supplement the deficiencies of the established church. One of these sites was the family. Puritans therefore devoted much effort to defining, explaining, and prescribing internal family relations which could best supplement or even substitute for the church. In addition to outnumbering the established church in the production of sermon literature in general, that is, the Puritans outnumbered it even more massively in the production of sermon literature devoted to family relations and the role of women in particular. Third, these works were all extremely popular and even mainstream in their presentation of family life. They were the works of ministers whose popular drawing power was great and whose sermons in general were frequently reprinted. Because Puritans emphasized lively preaching while ministers of the established church did not, popular works by Puritans outnumber those of their conservative counterparts. It is significant, however, that, as will be apparent from the discussion of clerical works, the content of Puritan works on the family and women did not contradict the message of the established church. The clerical literature under review here is not a statistical sampling but it does represent the range of views offered by the clergy, Puritan and Anglican, to their parishioners.[11]

Additionally, because so many of the ministers presented sermons they had already delivered orally, this sampling illustrates changes made by the ministers in response to comments and criticism from auditors. In this way, some answers are provided to the question of the divergence between families as they should be and families as they were. More answers are provided by the comparison of the works of the laity and of the clergy and between the sermons of the clergy and the letters and memoirs of contemporaries. As this book shows, the ideological power of the clergy was so great that the laity often adopted and espoused clerical ideas that they were incapable of practicing, apparently unconscious of the gap between the clerical ideal and their way of living.

The laity's lack of consciousness of the contradictions between their ideals and their practices was not shared by the clergy. The clerical literature early on set forth a full, coherent, and cohesive theory about women's roles in their family and society, a theory which was revolutionary in its implications. Yet, because the clergy would make concessions or "allowances" in response to the complaints of their congregants, these changes were actually experienced in a gradual or evolutionary way. Analysis of the clerical literature reveals an essentially unchanging dogma with, however, changing emphases and changing dispensations from dogma. The clergy were involved in a dialogue of sorts with their parishioners and strove to present their ideas in a lively, engaging, and acceptable way.

The exact relationship of clerical and lay prescription to the way people lived cannot be precisely defined, partially because it was so dynamic. Ministers, for example, responded to the cries of their congregants that they were calling for the impossible and/or debasing women sometimes by modifying their demands, sometimes by explaining them more carefully in what the ministers obviously considered more palatable form, and sometimes by excoriating their congregants. Lay works also were sometimes adapted to make them more practicable, as in the case of revised manuals on farming and housewifery, but both lay and clerical literature sometimes held some positions so adamantly that it simply vilified those people who disagreed.

The third category of literature used here, the letters,

diaries, and memoirs of contemporaries, helps to illustrate the dynamic relationship between the normative ideals of the professional writers and clergy and the practices of real families. These sources show the reactions to prescriptive literature among exactly those upper social strata most able to fulfill them. They testify that the laity believed that their ministers were, indeed, trying to give them rules for living which would enable them to understand and succeed in this world, without losing salvation in the world to come. Readers purchased and studied and discussed the sermons, catechisms, and prayer collections. They read and annotated the lay political and technical works. The memoirs reveal that families gave obeisance to the ideas embodied in these works, even if they carried them out at lagging speeds and only when material circumstances permitted. It was only as material conditions made it possible and necessary for more and more families to rely on the money income of the husband for subsistence that families could afford to live out the restrictive visions of the ideologues and actually limit the activities of their women.

The premature espousal of these ideals by families in the middle strata of society shown in these memoirs suggests the acceptance of the ideals by many lower strata families as well. It demonstrates, first, the varying speeds at which the ideals could be practiced: continuing economic dependence on wives could coexist with newly strict subordination of them. But, second, it shows that these ideals were reaching the lower strata—through sermons, household readings, catechisms— and suggests that they were not being opposed by an alternative vision. There is little evidence that any alternative theory justified a discrepancy between the kinds of lives their employers and ministers and teachers, in a word, their "superiors," told them to live and the kinds of lives they did live.

The suggestion that the lower orders accepted the ideology of their superiors is supported by the political works of members of those orders and of those who claimed to speak for them. By and large, radical sects in the civil war did not challenge the gender roles articulated by their political opponents.[12]

By the time massive testimony by the lower strata does become available, it is clear that they had, indeed, accepted the family structure laid out in these pages, although conclusive evidence for this acceptance in the seventeenth century is lacking.

The fourth and final category of literary source used in this study is drama. Drama plays a unique role in English culture, one at odds with the general trend of English literature to expand its relevance to mass audiences. In the late middle ages and early modern period, drama was a medium of truly popular culture. Villages, cities, and even individual guilds had commissioned dramatic works and performed them themselves, thus playing very active roles in the transmission of social attitudes through drama. The development of professional acting troupes and professional dramatists reduced the participation of community residents and guild members and increased the dependence of drama on aristocratic patronage.[13]

Two forms of drama are used herein. The first, the morality play, was a traditional form of entertainment and instruction. Often written and always adapted and performed by nonprofessionals, these plays were performed in yearly cycles, serving as year-round guides in "burgher morality." Commonly, various craft guilds of a town would take different biblical stories and present either the stories themselves or allegories based on them throughout the course of a year. The plays used here, *The Deluge, The Second Shepherd's Play*, and *Ralph Roister Doister*, reached their peak of popularity in the late fifteenth and early sixteenth centuries.

The second form of drama used in this study was written by professional actors and playwrights to be performed for a paying audience, rather than an entire town. These plays were written after 1600 and performed in London. The London audience was, by that time, composed of two disparate groups: the upper strata and the lower, the groundlings; the middle strata having largely replaced drama with sermons.[14] The plays are, therefore, representative of an aristocratic vision of society—as filtered, however, through the eyes and mouth of an aspirant to, rather than a member of, the aristocracy. The plays used were, again, all popular, as were their authors. Ben Jonson, for example, was recognized in his own time, as he is today, as a dramatic genius. The stepson of a bricklayer, Jonson attended the illustrious Westminster School and set up as a bricklayer before turning to the theater as an actor and dramatist. He became an early seventeenth-century court favorite for his spectacular masques while yet retaining the favor of groundlings for his sharply satirical comedies.[15] His play *Epicoene, or, the Silent Woman*, first performed in 1612, found favor with men of all strata although its topicality hindered its immediate commercial success. Thomas Middleton, in collaboration with Thomas Dekker, wrote *The Roaring Girl*, based on the story of a true-life Moll. Their play was one of the few seventeenth-century dramas portraying a strong and independent, albeit asexual, heroine. Middleton's popularity with London audiences led to his appointment in 1620 as City Chronologer.

The other dramatists used in this study wrote more narrowly for court and aristocratic circles. Francis Beaumont, whose collaboration with John Fletcher was regarded by contemporaries as "one of the marvels of the age,"[16] wrote mainly for private theaters and, on achieving marriage with a wealthy heiress in 1613, retired from playwriting. Fletcher continued without Beaumont, and himself achieved great commercial success as a playwright.[16] James Shirley's plays, which his biographer termed "fairly indicative of the fashionable drama of the time," also attained large commercial success and even greater success among court circles.[17] These latter playwrights attended either Cambridge or Oxford or both; some, including Shirley, taking orders and others going on to take legal educations. They were, and were educated as, gentlemen. Their plays depict women very differently from those of the morality plays, but very similarly to the ideal women of the clergy—with whom, after all, the playwrights shared an education and social background.

The social background of those whose diaries and letters are examined here is, in general, a step above that of the playwrights and many of the clerics. Most of the surviving records belong to members of the landed gentry, either by birth or by purchase. Moreover, the birth status of the women whose memoirs survive is almost uniformly high. It is unclear whether this reflects the unlikelihood of women of lower social strata compiling their thoughts in written form and recording their or their families' stories or the unlikelihood of such compilations surviving. As a rule, surviving memoirs are those of families who proposed—and remained in the same place long enough to accumulate records.

Almost all the women whose memoirs are used were of gentry status and entitled to be called ladies. Lady Margaret Cavendish, herself the daughter of upper gentry, married William Cavendish, the Duke of NewCastle, and used her high social position to escape some of the restrictions imposed on seventeenth-century women. Her publications during her lifetime scandalized many of her contemporaries who accepted works dealing with more typically "feminine" subjects by other female authors.[18] Lady Anne Halkett, a seventeenth-century woman of great vitality, intelligence, and wit, was the daughter of Thomas Murray, tutor and later secretary to Charles I. Orphaned by the time she reached her mid-twenties, she retained her place in court until her 1656 marriage to Sir James Halkett, a Scotsman who took her away from the political intrigue in which she had, apparently, shone.

Lady Anne Clifford (1590–1676) was the daughter of an earl and the wife of two earls. Her diary covers the year 1603 as reminiscence and 1616, 1617, and 1619 as daily journal. A prolific writer, she kept a daily journal until her death. Lady Anne Fanshawe (1625–1680), a close contemporary, was the daughter of a Customs officer—a devoted Royalist whose property was confiscated during the civil war. She married, early in the war, another devoted Royalist who seems to have ignored management of his property during his service to Charles. The mother of six sons and eight daughters, she outlived five of her sons and four daughters—her firstborn child dying in infancy amid the turmoil of war.

Lady Grace Mildmay, whose diary covers the third

quarter of the sixteenth century, was the daughter and heiress of a wealthy Wiltshire gentleman. In 1567 she married Anthony Mildmay, the son of a close adviser to Elizabeth. The son, although well connected in his own right and wealthy by his marriage, did not advance as far as his father in his political career. Lady Grace provided no notable aid. Lady Margaret Hoby, whose lifetime was contemporaneous with Lady Mildmay's— late sixteenth and early seventeenth centuries—received the militantly Protestant education fitting for her, the daughter of Anne Boleyn's nephew, but she received it in the homes of the aristocracy, as was fitting for the cousin of Elizabeth. Her first, early marriage ended with the death of her young husband, and William Cecil, Elizabeth's very close adviser, helped to persuade her to marry his nephew. They had no issue, although he had a bastard in 1602 whom he made his heir at Lady Hoby's death in 1605.

Lucy Hutchinson, whose autobiography details her own admittedly remarkable education, was the daughter of the keeper of the London Tower. Her mother took advantage of this high position to study with Sir Walter Raleigh and others of the famous men imprisoned there from time to time. She passed much of her knowledge thus garnered on to Lucy. Lucy and her husband were strong Parliamentarians during the war: in contrast to most of the other women discussed herein, Lucy's most severe financial problems came with the end of the war.

Dorothy Osborne, whose civil war correspondence to her suitor William Temple is examined, was another strong Royalist with many family ties to the aristocracy. Alice Thornton, her contemporary, shared with Dorothy the advantages of "good breeding" or gentle education in social graces but not the advantage of marrying well.[19] Alice Thornton's autobiography reveals the difficulties faced by women bred but not married well.

Finally, the civil war memoirs of the Verney family, compiled by a female descendant of the family, describe the efforts of what the compiler called "a remarkable household of capable women" to survive (and prosper) while their menfolk were absent at war or exile. During the war Lady Verney managed the family's great wealth in England while her husband Ralph was in exile on the continent. Miriam Slater has recently subjected these memoirs and their sources to a fruitful renewed analysis.

The male diarists, autobiographers, and letter writers studied were of similar high status. Sir Simonds D'Ewes and Sir Kenelm Digby were successful courtiers during the reigns of James and Charles. John Evelyn (1620–1706), heir to a gunpowder fortune, lived a quiet life of unostentatious wealth. His memoirs were dedicated to his grandson because all his sons predeceased him. Gervase Holles, who until the civil war lived a quiet life in Great Grimsby, exercising the "natural rule" of the gentry over their lesser countryfolk, was a strong Royalist who wrote his family history during his civil war exile. George Savile, the Marquess of Halifax, lived a life filled with considerable post-civil-war activity. His advice to his daughter distills the received wisdom about woman's role and social place in mid-seventeenth-century England.

Because these letters and diaries were private, sales figures offer no help in determining their relevance to the rest of English society. With the exceptions, however, of Bathsua Makin, who served as tutor to the children of Charles I despite her sex and who was frequently called the most learned woman of her day, the Duchess of NewCastle, and George Savile, the lives of these men and women appear to have conformed to social expectations. They thought of themselves as representative of, rather than standing out from, their peers. Their own assessments seem accurate: neither their lives nor their thoughts appear to have diverged remarkably from those of other upper-strata English in the sixteenth and seventeenth centuries.

In the case of professional writers, as already noted, there are clearer markers of the representativeness of a source. The works used here are those whose sales figures show them to have attracted large segments of their markets. It is worthwhile to recall, moreover, that the purchase of books in sixteenth- and seventeenth-century England was something of a novel phenomenon. There were no coffee-table editions or lending libraries or publishers willing to take prestigious losses. Bookselling was a growing business, and the sellers printed what they thought they could sell. Buyers purchased what they thought they could use.

The two husbandry books used here had both enormous popularity and longevity. Anthony FitzHerbert's *Book of Husbandry,* written by a gentleman farmer noted for his legal abilities more than his farming during his own lifetime, was first published in 1523. It went through more than twenty editions before the turn of the century. Thomas Tusser's *Points of Husbandry* was another huge seller, reprinted often during the sixteenth century and at intervals throughout the seventeenth century.

Cornelius Agrippa's *Treatise of the Nobilitie and Excellencie of Womankind* was first printed in England in 1542 and was reprinted in 1553. The version used here was from 1603. Thomas Eliot's *Defense of Good Women,* first printed in 1540 and reprinted by 1545, shared some of the popularity of the author's more famous *Book of the Governor.*

Thomas Smith's *De Republica Anglorum: A Discourse on the Commonwealth of England* was the result of much labor and research. Published in 1583, it sold well and was reprinted throughout the sixteenth, seventeenth, and eighteenth centuries. Its audience, however, was probably more interested in the political analysis of England than the discussion of household structure. The work is generally considered to be representative of "the ordinary attitude of thoughtful minds at that time."[20] John Stow's well-researched *Survay of London,* first published in 1598, reprinted in 1603, and afterward enlarged and reprinted in 1618 and 1633, also enjoyed respectable sales.

Other lay works on which this book relies include William Painter's *Palace of Pleasure,* a collection of dramatic tales surrounded by morals, and Phillip Stubbes's *Anatomy of Abuses* and his life of his wife. The *Anatomy of Abuses* was a smashing success, being first printed in May of 1583, reprinted in August of that year, and reaching a fifth edition by 1595. His biography of his wife rode the coattails of the success of *Anatomy of Abuses*, a work which sparked a rejoinder from one of sixteenth-century England's premier pamphleteers, Thomas Nashe, his own *Anatomy of Absurdity*. Works specifically addressed to women include Sir Hugh Plat's *Delights for Ladies* and *A Closet for Ladies*, frequently reprinted in the early seventeenth century, and Gervase Markham's very popular *The English Housewife* and *The Country Housewife's Garden*. Richard Braithwait's *The English Gentlewoman*, first printed in 1630 and already in its third edition by 1641, has also been used.

The clerical works discussed in this book, as noted above, were popular, prestigious, and powerful. As Louis B. Wright has pointed out, "Probably the political power of the clergy is less important than their subtle influence in the molding of social and cultural ideas,"[21] the subject of this study. The major sources used here for the early and mid-sixteenth century are the works of Thomas Becon, Hugh Latimer, and Miles Coverdale. Coverdale in 1541 translated *The Christian State of Matrimony*, a treatise by the famous continental reformer Henry Bullinger considered to be of marked influence in England. The work had seven reprints before 1575. Coverdale's influence was extended by his participation in the 1539 version of the English translation of the Bible. Latimer was one of the group of ministers known as the Commonwealthsmen for their sermons calling for social justice. He was martyred during the reign of Mary Tudor; his sermons were first printed in 1549 and were gathered together and reprinted throughout the late sixteenth century. Thomas Becon was another of the Commonwealthsmen but he survived through the early years of Elizabeth's reign. His *Goldē Boke of Christen Matrimonye* was first published in 1542, reprinted immediately in 1543, and published with other sermons in 1564.

Henry Smith, whose "Preparative to Marriage" is cited extensively, preached in the last quarter of the sixteenth century. Known as "Silver-Tongued Smith," he refused to take a parish in order to retain his freedom from the church hierarchy. Hired instead as a lecturer at St. Clement Dane, he drew admiring auditors from all social strata. Petitions supporting him were signed, according to Christopher Hill, by "ordinary tradesmen, as smiths, tailors, saddlers, hosiers, haberdashers, glaziers, cutlers and suchlike, most of whom could not write their names."[22] His collected sermons, first printed in the 1590s, went through numerous editions in the 1590s and early 1600s.

William Perkins, Smith's contemporary, rivaled his popularity among the masses and surpassed it among his fellow preachers. Called by Christopher Hill "the high priest of the Puritans," he exercised tremendous influence by means of his printed sermons.[23] Of him, William Haller has written, "No books, it is fair to say, were more often to be found upon the shelves of succeeding generations of preachers, and the name of no preacher recurs more often in later Puritan literature" than his.[24] Indeed, Matthew Griffith's 1633 *Bethel, or a Form of Families,* so popular that it was reprinted four times within the year, is, in many respects, but a summary of Perkins's "Christian Oeconomy." Perkins's sermons, of which "Christian Oeconomy" is one, were printed often and in various combinations in the seventeenth century.

Two other preachers from whose sermons this book draws extensively are William Gouge and Daniel Rogers. William Gouge preached at Blackfriars in London from 1608 to 1653. He was a very popular minister—people thronged in the aisles to hear him—and he participated actively in Puritan efforts to reach ever larger numbers of people through lectureships and publications. Termed "a Levite of Levites" by William Haller,[25] Gouge used the occasion of the publication of his sermons to answer any questions or criticisms raised in their oral delivery. In this way, he both exposed and stilled controversy. His *Of Domesticall Duties,* first published in 1622 and reprinted in 1623 and 1634, in content is very similar to the previously published *Bride-Bush* of William Whately, printed in 1616, 1619, and 1624. Louis Wright has commented that the concurrence of the well-known London minister added weight to the doctrines enunciated by Whately, a prosperous but lesser-known minister from Banbury.[26]

Daniel Rogers's *Matrimonial Honour*, first printed in 1642 and reprinted in 1650, despite Rogers's Royalist leanings, is the latest-written clerical work cited. Rogers, a contemporary of Gouge, appears to have taken some of Gouge's points to conclusions farther than those with which Gouge was comfortable.

The other clerical works used were also extremely well-selling, some going into many editions. Although their writers may have been less famous than the men just discussed, the ideas in the works are of a piece. Famous London preacher and obscure Yorkshire pastor were proselytizing to the same end. The measure of their success is the continued idealization of the strongly patriarchal household: employed father, housebound mother-wife, obedient child—"father knows best."

NOTES

Introduction: Pieces of a Puzzle

1. Historians generally agree with this statement, but there is widespread debate over the significance of particular events, over the rates at which change occurred, and even, in some senses, over who were the "bearers" of historical change. Although the debates are important, they do not bear on the work at hand.

2. 1688 was the year of the "Glorious Revolution." James II, brother of Charles II, was the next in line for the crown after Charles's death without legitimate issue. Although James was declared king, he was exiled shortly thereafter. Parliament invited his Protestant daughter and her Protestant husband to come to England and receive the crown. They peacefully and successfully did so. It should be noted here that the "demobbing" as it were, of the feudal aristocracy released thousands of former retainers, servants, and soldiers for other kinds of work. For a discussion of the Tudor state machinery, one would do well to begin with the works of G. R. Elton, such as *England Under the Tudors*.

3. K. Wrightson and David Levine, *Poverty and Piety in an English Village*, ch. 1; J. Thirk, ed., *The Agrarian History of England and Wales*, vol. 4 (1500–1640), esp. Alan Everitt, "The Marketing of Agricultural Produce," pp. 466–592, and Peter Bowden, "Agricultural Prices, Farm Profits, and Rents," pp. 593–695; Christopher Middleton, "The Sexual Division of Labour."

4. This enabled the crown to defend more securely the institutional and hierarchical aspects of the established church attacked by those who desired to reform the church "root and branch." Because the crown retained control of church institutions, it could block these radical reformers, forcing them to focus on institutions outside the church to spread their values. One of these institutions was the family, and the close attention paid by the reformers to the family served to alter its shape and its functions. See Michael Walzer, *The Revolution of the Saints*, pp. 188 ff. and William Hunt, *The Puritan Moment*, preface and pp. 130, 161. See also chapter 5.

5. Among the works which have considered women are the following: Walzer, *The Revolution of the Saints*, esp. pp. 188 ff.; Lawrence Stone, *The Family, Sex, and Marriage in England, 1500–1800*; William Haller, "Hail, Wedded Love"; Richard L. Greaves, *Society and Religion in Elizabethan England*, esp. pp. 142–45; Roberta Hamilton, *The Liberation of Women*; Ralph A. Houlbrooke, *The English Family, 1450–1750*; Mary Prior, ed., *Women in English Society*. Some of these works tend to view women and the effects of change on women through an unquestioning masculinist framework. This is much less of a problem with the recent works, some of which conclude that

women did not benefit as much as men from the new economic structures. For example, Miriam Slater's *Family Life in the Seventeenth Century* shows that upper-class Englishwomen had but one option for advancement or, even, to prevent derogation: marriage. She does not, however, attempt to explore social or economic reasons for women's impotence. And, on the other hand, John R. Gillis's *For Better, For Worse* suggests that the middling sort were only in the seventeenth century beginning to appreciate the housewife's economic contribution. Gillis sees a redefining of what he calls conjugal relations, but he suggests that the redefinition was an undermining of patriarchy. As will be seen in chapter 3, I agree with Gillis's assertion (p. 83) that the middling sorts did not mount an assault on patriarchy, but I contend that the Puritan redefinition was quite successful in reinforcing and strengthening patriarchy.

6. Elizabeth and her counselors feared rebellion by these feudal remnants for much of her reign—not without cause, as the pseudo-rebellion of Thomas, Duke of Norfolk in the late 1560s indicates. If a moment had existed, it would have been the peaceful accession of James I, but the royal counselors were very nervous about this, and James himself exhibited initial signs of insecurity and uneasiness. Yet, the seventeenth-century crown had nothing to fear from its old nemesis, the aristocracy, and much to fear from the strata it had raised to counterbalance the aristocracy.

7. John Donne, *Poetry and Prose*, p. 207.

8. And the greatest likelihood of their view surviving, physically as well as socially. See Sara Heller Mendelson, "Stuart Women's Diaries and Occasional Memoirs."

9. Wage workers, of course, did not gain political rights, but the discussion over extension of the franchise centered on the potential voter's freedom of thought and action—guaranteed, claimed radical Leveller and conservative property owner alike, by freedom from economic dependence on any one person. See C. B. MacPherson, *The Political Theory of Possessive Individualism*, especially his discussion on the Levellers, pp. 107–42; and A. MacFarlane's version, *The Origins of English Individualism*.

10. Keith Wrightson and David Levine, *Poverty and Piety in an English Village*, p. 172; David Levine, "Production, Reproduction, and the Proletarian Family in England, 1500–1850," pp. 3–8; F.L.M. Thompson, "Social Control in Victorian Britain," pp. 189–207; K. Wrightson, *English Society*.

11. See chapters 4–6; specifically, the cases of Lucy Hutchinson, the Verneys, and Kenelm Digby's mother.

12. This book uses an effective cutoff date of 1660, because in this year Charles II was "restored" to his crown and the tumults of the past 150 years were considered to be at end—order was "restored" with Charles. The essential elements of the new ideology of women and families were in place by 1660. What remained was the working out of these elements in the lives of men and women of succeeding centuries.

1. The Beginning of a New Age

1. William Harrison, *Elizabethan England*. But also see Christopher Hill, *Society and Puritanism in Pre-Revolutionary England*, p. 139, for discussion of different meanings of labor.

2. Keith Wrightson, *English Society*, p. 24; Ralph Houlbrooke, *The English Family*, pp. 23–24. In the description which follows, "gentry" is used as the English used

it, to include both genders. But, the English mainly meant by the term gentle*men* and ascribed to women born into the gentry different characteristics and different destinies.

3. Wrightson, *English Society*, p. 23.

4. The following discussion is based on Harrison's *Elizabethan England*, written in the mid-sixteenth century, and Sir Thomas Smith's *De Republica Anglorum*, pp. 42–45.

5. Wrightson, *English Society*, pp. 24–26.

6. See, for example, Michael Walzer, *The Revolution of the Saints*, pp. 247ff; and Louis B. Wright, *Middle-Class Culture in Elizabethan England*.

7. William Whately, *A Bride-Bush*, pp. 180–81.

8. Smith, *De Republica Anglorum*, pp. 42–43.

9. Harrison, *Elizabethan England*, pp. 7 and 8; see also Wrightson, *English Society*, p. 28; Lawrence Stone, *Crisis of the Aristocracy*; pp. 355–81; George Clarke, *A History of the Royal College of Physicians of London*; Houlbrooke, *The English Family*, p. 24; William J. Birken, "The Royal College of Physicians of London"; Brian P. Levack, *The Civil Lawyers in England*, pp. 9–16; Rosemary O'Day, *The English Clergy*; Lawrence Stone, "Social Mobility in England," pp. 25–70; M. Spufford, *Contrasting Communities*, pp. 49–90.

10. See David Levine, "Production, Reproduction"; Walzer, *Revolution of Saints*, pp. 248–49; and Gervase Holles, *Memorials of the Holles Family, 1493–1656*, pp. 18–19.

11. Smith, *De Republica Anglorum*, pp. 38–40.

12. For more detailed discussions, see Stone, *Crisis of the Aristocracy*, esp. introduction and conclusion; J. Thirsk, ed., *Agrarian History*, esp. pp. 161–255, 276–305.

13. Wrightson, *English Society*, pp. 130–35; Stone, *Crisis of the Aristocracy*, conclusion; Thirsk, ed., *Agrarian History*, pp. 276–305.

14. David Levine, *Family Formation in an Age of Nascent Capitalism*, p. 2; Tawney, *The Agrarian Problem in the Sixteenth Century*, p. 58.

15. Wrightson, *English Society*, pp. 33–35, 134–35; W. Hunt, *The Puritan Moment*, pp. 33–35; Levine, *Family Formation*, p. 12; see also Spufford, *Contrasting Communities*, pp. 49–95; Thirsk, ed., *Agrarian History*, pp. 1–112, 200–55.

16. Paul Seaver, "Introduction," pp. 7–10; D. C. Coleman, "Labour in the English Economy," and *The Economy of England*.

17. Thirsk, *Agrarian History*, pp. 200–55; Wrightson, *English Society*, pp. 222–27; Hunt, *The Puritan Moment*, pp. 79–83; Spufford, *Contrasting Communities*, pp. 90–104; P. Williams, *Tudor Regime*, pp. 241–42; 428–30; K. Wrightson, "Alehouses, Order, and the Reformation in Rural England," pp. 1–27.

18. The following monographs offer a full discussion of these points: Tawney, *The Agrarian Problem* and *Religion and the Rise of Capitalism*; Thirsk, ed., *Agrarian History*; Eric Kerridge, *The Agricultural Revolution*; and Levine, *Family Formation*.

19. Stone, "Social Mobility," pp. 25–70; R. S. Schofield and E. A. Wrigley, *The Population History of England, 1541–1871*; Spufford, *Contrasting Communities*, pp. 36–72; Thirsk, ed., *Agrarian History*, esp. pp. 396–465.

20. See, for discussion which holds up remarkably well, Mildred Campbell, *The English Yeoman under Elizabeth and the Early Stuarts*; see also, for discussion of early competitive capitalism, Robert Brenner, "The Origins of Capitalist Development"; David Levine, "Production, Reproduction," pp. 3–10.

21. For general discussion, see H. Lis and C. Soly, *Poverty and Capitalism in Pre-Industrial Europe*, pp. 30–60; also G. Unwin, *Industrial Organisation in the Sixteenth and Seventeenth Centuries* and *The Gilds and Companies of London;* W. Herbert, *The History of the Twelve Great Livery Companies of London.*

22. Everywhere there were local variations. Proximity to urban markets; what kind of land, arable or pasture; prevailing land tenure—and one's own tenure. I am making very broad generalizations, and they are, of course, subject to local caveats. Joan Thirsk in *English Peasant Farming* does an excellent job of making sense of the local variations. See also Thirsk, ed., *Agrarian History*, pp. 1–112 and Spufford, *Contrasting Communities*, pp. 50–150.

23. Cited in Wrightson, *English Society*, p. 150.

24. Cited in C. Hill, *Change and Continuity in Seventeenth-Century England*, p. 186. Morison assumes that the poor could get hold of weapons. However, by law only the gentry were entitled to possess weapons. See P. Williams, *The Tudor Regime*, pp. 17, 141, and Joel Samaha, *Law and Order in Historical Perspective;* J. A. Sharpe, *Crime in Seventeenth Century England.*

25. Cited in Hunt, *The Puritan Moment*, pp. 58–61.

26. Ibid., p. 51; Tawney, *Religion and the Rise of Capitalism*, pp. 149, 218; G. M. Trevelyan, *History of England*, 2:71–72; Christopher Hill, *The World Turned Upside Down*, pp. 16, 26, 33–35—Hill is particularly good on showing the ideas which so terrified the masters.

27. Cited in Hunt, *The Puritan Moment*, p. 61; see also A. Fletcher, *Tudor Rebellions;* Wrightson, *English Society*, pp. 173–79; Samaha, *Law and Order*, chs. 1 and 2.

28. Wrightson, *English Society*, p. 163; see also Samaha, *Law and Order*, ch. 1, and Sharpe, *Crime.*

29. J. E. Thorold Rogers, *Six Centuries of Work and Wages*, pp. 389–94; F. W. Tickner, *Women in English Economic History*, p. 412; also, of course, Alice Clark, *The Working Life of Women in Seventeenth Century England*, pp. 62–66, 72; Bertha Putnam, "Northhampton Wage Assessments."

30. Hunt, *The Puritan Moment*, pp. 70ff.

31. See Lis and Soly, *Poverty and Capitalism*, pp. 88–90; P. Williams, *The Tudor Regime*, pp. 198–202; D. Woodward, "The Background to the Statute of Artificers," pp. 32–34; E. M. Leonard, *The Early History of English Poor Relief*, pp. 22–40, 294–301; Joan Thirsk, *Economic Policy and Projects*, introduction.

32. Hunt, *The Puritan Moment*, p. 66; see also Lis and Soly, *Poverty and Capitalism*, pp. 30–60; and P. Williams, *The Tudor Regime*, pp. 17, 141; Samaha, *Law and Order*, pp. 11, 45; Wrightson, "Alehouses, Order, and Reformation," pp. 20–24.

33. Hunt, *The Puritan Moment*, pp. 75–76; K. Wrightson and D. Levine, *Poverty and Piety in an English Village*, pp. 128–31; for discussion, see Peter Laslett, *Family Life and Illicit Love in Earlier Generations.*

34. See E. M. Leonard, *The Early History of Poor Relief;* Wrightson, *English Society*, p. 158; Thirsk, *Economic Policy and Projects*, esp. ch. 1 and conclusion.

35. Cited in Hunt, *The Puritan Moment*, p. 81.

36. As noted, wages fell by half in real terms. Christopher Hill in *Society and Puritanism* pointed out that women's wages rose more slowly than men's, and all the secondary sources which actually cite the rates bear this out—without, however, ever call-

ing attention to it, as Hill did. See, for example, Rogers, *Six Centuries*, and Wrightson and Levine, *Poverty and Piety*, pp. 3–9.

37. Rogers in his *Six Centuries*, pp. 349–53, provides eloquent statements describing the effects of these policies on the men and women who could not survive without relief. See also Hunt, *The Puritan Moment*, p. 69 and Wrightson, *English Society*, pp. 142–48.

38. Again, see Rogers, *Six Centuries*, pp. 349–53, 389, 394.

39. Cited in Hill, *The World Turned Upside Down*, p. 17. The statement was made in 1633.

40. See, for example, Hunt, *The Puritan Moment*, p. 65; also Clark, *Working Life*, conclusion.

41. See Wrightson, *English Society*, pp. 109, 112 and Mary Prior, "Women and the Urban Economy." This is discussed in chapters 2 and 4.

42. Clark, *Working Life*, pp. 102–4; in the fifteenth and early sixteenth century, it was the *parents'* obligation to support the family, not the father's.

43. Cited in Hill, *Society and Puritanism*, p. 275.

2. Women and the New Economic Order

1. Alice Clark in her *Working Life of Women in Seventeenth Century England* did, of course, document the impact of some of these changes on the lives of women as workers, and I rely heavily on the statistics she amassed about women's participation in the market economy. No one has really taken up where Clark left off, following up or examining her arguments in greater depth or with more sophistication, although many historians have indicated the need to do so and several recent works address parts of Clark's arguments. Ms. Clark's book was reprinted in 1982, with an introduction by M. Chaytor and J. Lewis.

As will be evident, I am particularly concerned with the ideological aspects of new economic roles for women. This aspect of the sexual redivision of labor has been neglected in most accounts of women's place in economic orders. It is now particularly pertinent, in view of recent debates over the comparable worth of male and female labor, since it is through control over the evaluation of women's labor as well as control over the labor itself that women's labor has been constituted as a secondary and inferior segment of the labor market. The argument here is that women's labor is not necessarily less skilled or valuable than men's but has been, historically, differently skilled and less valued.

Heidi Hartman's "Capitalism, Patriarchy, and Job Segregation by Sex" in Zillah Eisenstein, ed., *Capitalist Patriarchy and the Case for Socialist Feminism* (New York: Monthly Review Press, 1979), pp. 206–47, provides the best introduction to theories of segmentation of the labor market by gender, but Hartman does not consider the significance of social evaluation of labor. Gayle Rubin's "The Traffic in Women" in R. Reiter, ed., *Towards an Anthropology of Women* (New York: Monthly Review Press, 1975) likewise provides a sharp, insightful, and provocative analysis of the value of women in the economic order without considering this aspect. I believe the failure of these authors to consider *attitudes* toward women's work and its comparability to men's renders their explanations of women's secondary place in economic orders only partially successful. As Michele Barrett has argued in *Women's Oppression Today: Problems in Marxist Feminist Analysis*, esp. pp. 99, 165–69, the division of labor is not without ideological dimensions. And, as will be seen in chapters 3–5, ideological dimensions have helped to shape the division of labor.

2. On the differences between the aristocrat and, even, the court lady and the gentlewoman of less social importance, see the different approaches to housewifery of Elizabeth, Countess of Shrewsbury and Lady Margaret Hoby: Louisa Stuart Costello, *Memoirs of Eminent Englishwomen*, 1:15, 16, 65–68; Lady Margaret Hoby, *Diary*. For more general information on the housewives of many strata, see Barbara Winchester, *Tudor Family Portrait* and Christina Hole, *The English Housewife in the Seventeenth Century;* see also Renata Bridenthal and Claudia Koonz, eds., *Becoming Visible: Women in European History*, especially Richard Vann, "Toward a New Lifestyle: Women in Preindustrial Capitalism"; Carole Shammas, "The Domestic Environment in Early Modern England and America"; Miranda Chaytor, "Household and Kinship: Ryton in the Late Sixteenth and Early Seventeenth Centuries"; Judith Bennett, "Spouses, Siblings, and Surnames: Reconstructing Families from Medieval Court Rolls." Suzanne Hull in *Chaste, Silent, and Obedient: English Books for Women, 1475–1640* discusses what literature wives read to help them carry out their tasks. Antonia Fraser, in *The Weaker Vessel*, examines women's roles inside and outside their homes. It should be noted, however, that the English vision of all women as housewives excluded the 10 percent of the population that never married at all. See L. Stone, *The Family, Sex, and Marriage in England*, pp. 43–46. These unmarried women were largely invisible to their contemporaries, and to many historians, existing mainly as paid or unpaid domestic servants. Their contemporaries did begin to notice them if they became pregnant. On the social derogation involved in spinsterhood and on women's efforts to avoid it, see M. Slater, *Family Life in the Seventeenth Century*, pp. 79–81, 106, 141. The fact remains that some women did not marry and, with the closing of the convents, these women remained in the world, often performing service or housewifely functions in the household of another.

3. W. B. Rye, ed., *England as seen by Foreigners in the day of Elizabeth and James the First*, p. 72.

4. Sir Thomas Smith, *De Republica Anglorum*, pp. 123–25.

5. *Ibid.*, pp. 123–25.

6. See Clark, *Working Life*, p. 153, and see William Herbert, *History of the Twelve Great Livery Companies*, e.g., pp. 84, 103–4, 117, 193, 419–23, 466–67; George Unwin, *Gilds and Companies*, p. 254.

7. See, for example, Lady Anne Clifford's *Diary;* Lady Anne's husband was so intent on selling her property that he enlisted the king's aid in persuading Lady Anne to give her permission. James I beseeched; he did not order. It took some time and continued abusive treatment of her and their children before Anne consented. When she finally did, a judge intervened in order to ascertain that her consent was "freely" given. Coercion was clearly involved, but there was an attempt made to prevent successful coercion. The expression "under couverture" meant that the wife's legal identity was subsumed in her husband's.

8. See Clark, *Working Life*, p. 54.

9. Household self-sufficiency obviously depended on individual and regional conditions and on local social and productive relations. For example, could the

poor cottager-housewife glean wool from grazing areas so that, despite her own lack of sheep, she was free from having to buy yarn for her own household and possibly could spin yarn for a cash income? Could families without ovens depend on an oven being made available for their use, at either a baker's or a local manor, so that it made sense for them to provide their own grain and bread, or should they purchase ready-made loaves? What were the minimal requirements in equipment to produce ale, and were there other ways of easily obtaining beverages—possibly better beverages? The answers to these questions varied considerably by region because soil conditions and social customs affected particular household responses. Thirsk, for example, in *English Peasant Farming,* noted that in the fenlands in the sixteenth century, many farmers had no arable land at all and purchased all their foodstuffs. However, they frequently purchased raw materials which they worked into food products rather than the products themselves, buying, for instance, barley and malt rather than ale or beer.

It is difficult to know who and how many maintained genuine self-sufficiency, and whether, among those who lost it, the loss was theft or resignation. The husbandman household was, by definition, self-sufficient. William Harrison in *Elizabethan England* observed that the husbandman ate "sows, brawn, bacon, fruitpies . . . fowl of sundry sorts, cheese, butter, eggs, etc. . . . by his own provision, which is the best hand and commonly the least charge" (p. 94). However, the Statute of Cottagers acknowledged that families would not survive with less than four acres unless they had wage income, and the category husbandmen clearly included many families with less than four acres. Husbandmen were self-sufficient, therefore, except when they were not.

Proximity to markets could determine and, Thirsk asserts in *English Peasant Farming,* did determine what crops the family would raise and therefore their self-sufficiency; i.e., did they sell food for money when, in fact, the food could have been eaten by the family? Where what Mildred Campbell in *The English Yeoman* calls "merchantable" and G. E. Fussell in the *English Rural Labourer* calls "industrial" crops replaced subsistence farming even among husbandmen, there remained the possibility that the wife could retain control of enough "garden land" to grow the barley, flax, wheat, or fruit necessary to feed her family, but the likelihood of her doing so decreased. The ideal of self-sufficiency remained normative but was less and less normal. D. C. Coleman has estimated that "In Stuart England, between a quarter and a half of the entire population were chronically below what contemporaries regarded as the official poverty line" (*The Economy of England,* p. 284). This statement shows the difficulty of analyzing the English situation in the seventeenth century "scientifically." The English during the Stuart period were very little concerned with official poverty line: the attempt to make do with very little was on the minds of most people, but we have little insight into exactly how they achieved this aim.

10. Hugh Latimer, *Fruitful Sermons,* p. 32; preached in 1552.

11. Rye, *England as seen by Foreigners,* p. xliv. Harrison, *Elizabethan England,* pp. 15–16. This contradicts the position of Peter Laslett, in *The World We Have Lost,* that English women went nowhere, except possibly church. The novels of William Painter repeatedly express—with great pride—that Englishwomen have the liberty to go anywhere. See, for example, Painter's comment that Milan women had "almost" the liberties that "ours" have; *Palace of Pleasure,* 3:46. Most markets were admittedly small during this time period, but they were not in the backyard and women did go to them.

12. For discussion of women's roles as consumers in markets, see the following: Dorothy Davis, *A History of Shopping;* E. P. Thompson, "The Moral Economy of the English Crowd in the Eighteenth Century," pp. 115–36.

13. Harrison, *Elizabethan England,* pp. 87–89. Harrison wrote, "prices were never so dear as in my time." See also David Levine, "Production, Reproduction," pp. 3–15; and Wrightson, *English Society,* pp. 134–37.

14. Harrison, *Elizabethan England,* pp. 93–94.

15. It is also the case that wheat bread was more suitable for urban dwellers, who tended to be more sedentary and to dwell in closer proximity to neighbors and co-workers than rural residents, because wheat bread is so much easier on the digestive tract. For an interesting discussion—and recipes—of English bread-eating habits see Elizabeth David, *English Bread and Yeast Cookery.* For a more scholarly look at English eating habits and who was able to provide for them, see J. C. Drummond and Anne Wilbraham, *The Englishman's Food,* and C. A. Wilson, *Food and Drink in Britain from the Stone Age to Recent Times.* See also Thompson, "The Moral Economy of the English Crowd," pp. 80–81.

16. See, for one example, Phillip Massinger, *The City Madam,* II, i; but this was a conventional subject, often addressed.

17. See, for example, Francis Bacon's words on wealth; "Riches are for spending, and spending for honour and good actions [and spending must be] order[ed] to the best show, that the bills might be less than the estimation abroad" ("Of Expense," *Essays*). See also G. P. V. Akrigg, *Jacobean Pageant,* pp. 166–70.

18. Harrison, *Elizabethan England,* pp. 87–88.

19. Gervase Markham, *The English Housewife,* p. 154.

20. See Mildred Campbell, *The English Yeoman,* p. 255.

21. See Margaret Hoby's *Diary,* for example; see also Davis, *A History of Shopping,* p. 121; Hole, *The English Housewife,* p. 58; Harrison, *Elizabethan England,* pp. 98–102.

22. See Levine, "Production, Reproduction," pp. 5–12; Hunt, *The Puritan Moment,* pp. 80–81, 129, 141–43; K. Wrightson, "Alehouses, Order, and the Reformation"; E. A. Wrigley, "Urban Growth and Agricultural Change."

23. See chapters 3 and 4 for discussion.

24. Mothers were not co-guardians of their children. The children of a marriage belonged to the father, and in his will he provided for guardianship of the children. Among the aristocracy, those who held their lands directly of the king were forced to attend the king's pleasure. In the sixteenth century, mothers frequently were appointed by their husbands to retain custody and control of the children, although this was less likely among the upper gentry than among the lower gentry and the nongentry where it was more likely that husband and wife had cooperated in productive activity during the marriage. For discussion of executorships and guardianships, see Pearl Hogrefe, *Tudor Women,* pp. 10–27 and Smith, *De Republica Anglorum,* pp. 126–28; Spufford, *Contrasting Communities,* pp. 88–90, 117. On guilds, see H. Lis and C. Soly, *Poverty and Capitalism,* pp. 30–60; and Mary Prior, "Women and the Urban Economy."

25. See T. Tusser, *Points of Husbandry,* pp. 40–41.

26. It did work both ways at times. As is the case today, heavy participation by women in a particular job itself serves to debase the job. If the job required skill,

would women do it? Then, as now, clearly not. The best documentations of women's exclusion from the trades remain Clark's *Working Life* and George Unwin's study of the organization and changing form and purposes of guilds in early modern England. Unwin does not single out women as a subject of investigation, but his analysis of how entry into trades was restricted may be interpolated with what else we know of women's circumstances to show the likely effects of the restrictions—and compared with statistics available on women to show that the likely effects did occur. See Unwin, *Industrial Organisation in the Sixteenth and Seventeenth Centuries;* also, his *The Gilds and Companies of London,* esp. pp. 254–63; F. S. Siebert, *Freedom of the Press in England, 1476–1776,* pp. 132–35.

27. Of the division of labor and the cheapness of goods, Adam Smith's classic *The Wealth of Nations* remains standard. See also Christopher Hill, *From Reformation to Industrial Revolution.* Margaret Cavendish, Duchess of NewCastle, recounted in the late seventeenth century that her friends had mocked her efforts at making paper flowers, telling her the people who made paper flowers for a living did so more cheaply than she—more speedily and with less waste (Cavendish, *Life*).

28. William Gouge, *Of Domesticall Duties,* pp. 442–45.

29. Unwin, *Industrial Organisation,* p. 128; Unwin, *Gilds and Companies,* pp. 254–56; Lis and Soly, *Poverty and Capitalism,* pp. 39–60.

30. Clark, *Working Life,* pp. 138–42.

31. Sir John Clapham, *A Concise Economic History of Britain from the Earliest Times to 1750,* esp. pp. 185–95. After agriculture, textiles were England's largest industry.

32. Clark, *Working Life,* pp. 102–4.

33. Anthony FitzHerbert, *Book of Husbandry,* p. 96.

34. E. Lipson, *The Economic History of England,* 2:50; R. Houlbrooke, *The English Family,* p. 108.

35. Joan Thirsk, "The Fantastical Folly of Fashion," pp. 50–74.

36. See, for a detailed discussion, Herbert A. Monckton, *A History of the English Public House;* see also Herbert, *Twelve Great Livery Companies,* 1:62. Thirsk, *Economic Policy and Projects,* p. 91; and Judith M. Bennett, "The Village Alewife: Women and Brewing in Fourteenth Century England"; John J. Butt, "The Transition of Privilege in Medieval Society."

37. Markham, *The English Housewife,* pp. 3–5.

38. For example, Lucy Hutchinson's mother learned through instruction by Walter Raleigh, presumably no mean instructor.

39. See, for detailed discussion, Thomas Rogers Forbes, *The Midwife and the Witch,* pp. 139–52; Clark, *Working Life,* pp. 242ff., 265–85; R. K. Merton, *Science, Technology, and Society in Seventeenth Century England,* pp. 124–28; George Clarke, *A History of the Royal College of Physicians,* pp. 180, 236–38, 253–54; Audrey Eccles, *Obstetrics and Gynecology in Tudor and Stuart England,* pp. 116–24.

40. A recent work by Martha Howell, *Women, Production, and Patriarchy in Late Medieval Cities* (Chicago: University of Chicago Press, 1986) examines the similar phenomenon, spread across much of northern Europe, of women being relegated to low-paying and low-status work. Howell argues that the women she studies had performed high-status work and that a significant element in ousting them from it was the establishment of work rules incompatible with women's other gender roles. The re-

moval of production from the household, she claims, was not a significant factor. It is the contention of this book, however, that although the establishment of new work rules may have helped to force women down in the labor hierarchy and market, these rules could have had this effect only because the flexibility of gender roles was being lost. It was not the new rigidity of work rules, in other words, that prevented women from participating in the high-status labor market, but the new rigidity of gender roles. In some specific cases women lost work because it left the home, in other specific cases they lost work because the new rules excluded them, and in still other specific cases the work left the home because of the new rules; but in all cases it was women's failure to adapt—to the move or the rules or both—which underlay and caused the loss. And this failure was the result of a new constriction of women's roles.

41. Davis, *A History of Shopping*, pp. 109–13; Prior, "Women and the Urban Economy."

42. See Clark, *Working Life*.

43. David Levine, *Family Formation in an Age of Nascent Capitalism*, pp. 12–15; see also discussion of various options for women in F. W. Tickner, *Women in English Economic History*, pp. 88–89, and R. Schofield, "English Marriage Patterns Revisited" for a discussion of population control through celibacy.

44. Dorothy Gardiner, *English Girlhood at School*, pp. 295–98.

45. See Levine, *Family Formation*, pp. 12–15; Thirsk, *English Peasant Farming*, pp. 23–40.

3. Women and Place

1. Even Gerrald Winstanley, notorious Digger—radical—allowed hierarchy; just a different hierarchy from that under which he lived. More's *Utopia* probably came closest to egalitarianism, but both More and Winstanley saw hierarchy as natural. Given equal opportunity, they thought, some men would rise to power and/or wealth because of their greater talents. Neither saw women capable of rising to power, albeit More espoused greater equality of education for women and provided excellent educations for his own daughters. See E.M.W. Tillyard, *The Elizabethan World Picture* for a fuller exposition of the Elizabethan concept of order and the great chain of being.

2. Henry Smith, "A Preparative to Marriage," *Sermons*, p. 29; see also Phillip Stubbes, *Anatomy of Abuses*, p. 75.

3. John Aylmer, *An Harborowe for Faithful and True Subjects*, p. 41.

4. Thomas Gataker, *Marriage Duties Briefly Couched Together*, p. 8.

5. Stubbes, *Anatomy of Abuses*, p. xii.

6. Thomas Becon, "The Goldē Boke of Christen Matrimonye," *Works*, p. 640.

7. Hannibal Gamon, *The Praise of a Godly Woman*, p. 26.

8. Richard Hooker, "Ecclesiastical Polity," p. 427.

9. See, for example, Christopher Hill, *Society and Puritanism*, pp. 125–44. See also Lis and Soly, *Poverty and Capitalism*, pp. 86, 116–17; the essays in Jean-Louis Flandrin, ed., *Families in Former Times*, demonstrate that the exaltation of labor was a European phenomenon, not only English or Protestant.

10. Stubbes, *Anatomy of Abuses*, p. xii; William Whately, *A Bride-Bush*, pp. 180–81.

11. C. Hill, *Society and Puritanism*, pp. 125–44; William Gouge, *Of Domesticall Duties*, pp. 560, 530. There were not, of course, massive opportunities for social mobility, but as shown in chapter 2, there were more opportunities, more openings, more movement than in traditional society. See also William Haller, *The Rise of Puritanism*, pp. 124 ff., and R. L. Greaves, *Society and Religion*, for discussions of the Puritan conception of calling.

12. See, for discussion, Hill, *Society and Puritanism*, pp. 124–44; Gervase Holles, *Memorials of the Holles Family*, pp. 18–19; J. Thirsk, *Economic Policy and Projects*, ch. 1 and pp. 34, 174; G.P.V. Akrigg, *Jacobean Pageant*, p. 168; P. Williams, *The Tudor Regime*, pp. 425ff. See also Rosemary O'Day, *The English Clergy*; Brian Levack, *The Civil Lawyers in England*; and George Clarke, *A History of the Royal College of Physicians* for examples of professionalization.

13. Matthew Griffith, *Bethel*, pp. 20–21.

14. Griffith, *Bethel*, pp. 118–19; Daniel Rogers, *Matrimonial Honour*, pp. 294–95; see also Thomas Gataker, *Paul's Desire*, pp. B1–B2. This also means that failure as a housewife is not a reflection of God's favor or lack thereof.

15. Gouge, *Of Domesticall Duties*, p. 18.

16. *Ibid.*, p. 280.

17. John Dod and William Hind, *Bathesheba's Instructions*, p. 57.

18. Stubbes, *Anatomy of Abuses*, p. 29, 50–61; quotation is from Gervase Babington, *A Very Fruitfull Exposition of the Commandements*, p. 272.

19. Margaret Cavendish, Countess of NewCastle, her autobiography attached to *The Life of William Cavendish*, p. 175.

20. See chapter 2 for discussion of need to regulate and "master" men. Men harmed property; women harmed men's souls. The work of poor men was obviously not highly valued. For both poor men and all women, labor was necessary discipline. But the new conception of women's labor ranked it even below that of the poor and unskilled men at the bottom of the male hierarchy. The social benefits of women's labor were indirect and negative: the restraint of evil. The labor of unskilled men was recognized as potentially an element in producing goods for public benefit and consumption, but the labor of women, *by definition*, if not in reality, produced goods for private consumption alone. Women's labor neither brought them closer to God nor contributed to the commonwealth. Some divines, as will be seen, denied even that the labor of women contributed to the weal of the family, attributing all family economic contributions to the labor of men, however poorly skilled or badly paid that labor.

21. Dod and Hind, *Bathesheba's Instructions*, p. 60.

22. William Whately, *A Bride-Bush*, p. 151; T. Becon, "New Catechism," *Works*, p. 530.

23. Dod and Hind, *Bathesheba's Instructions*, p. 44.

24. Gataker, *Marriage Duties*, pp. 20–21.

25. Becon, "New Catechism," *Works*, p. 530.

26. Edward Dering, "Catechism," no pagination available.

27. Thomas Gataker, *Marriage Duties*, pp. 20–21; see also Matthew Griffith, *Bethel*, pp. 118–19.

28. See Ian Maclean, *The Renaissance Notion of Woman*, for full, scholarly discussion of traditional notions of women. See also Ruth Kelso's standard, *Doctrine for a Lady of the Renaissance*. By patriarchal social structure, I mean a social-economic-political system in which men have a disproportionate access to social and material resources by virtue of their gender. "Sexist" is a more appropriate term in many contexts, but in sixteenth- and seventeenth-century England, there was an effort to justify men's advantages by virtue of the father's role.

29. See Aylmer, *An Harborowe*, pp. 6–8.

30. Gervase Markham, *The English Housewife*, p. 4.

31. Sir Kenelm Digby, *Private Memoirs*, pp. 6–8, 275–76.

32. Anon., *The Deluge*, ll. 203–8. Mrs. Noah's loyalty, one must note, does not save her friends. Noah beats her unconscious and drags her aboard. That Noah's action is represented to be in accord with God's will does suggest that women's loyalty to friends is taking on questionable overtones of virtue, pointing the way, perhaps, to Digby's assertion that women are incapable of true friendship.

33. Baldesar Castiglione, *The Courtier*, p. 215; Sir Thomas Smith, *De Republica Anglorum*, pp. 22–23.

34. Francis Beaumont and John Fletcher, *Knight of Malta*, II, v. Says the female protagonist about her fears: "Behold me in my sex." Also Beaumont in his *Knight of the Burning Pestle*, III, i, had these words coming out of a woman's mouth: "I am a woman, made of fear and love, a weak, weak woman" (p. 533).

35. G. C. Moore-Smith, ed., *Osborne Letters*, p. 176.

36. Edmund Spenser, *The Faerie Queene*, book VI, vi, 41–43; III, iii, 17; III, x, 11.

37. William Perkins, "A Discourse of the Damned Art of Witchcraft," *Collected Work* (1603), pp. 637–38.

38. John Fletcher, *Wild-Goose Chase*, III, i, 300 (p. 604).

39. As an example, see Francis Beaumont and John Fletcher, *The Maid in the Mill*, III, ii: A gentleman advises a nobleman to rape the low-born object of his desire who was resisting his advance: "Oh, force her, force her, sir, she longs to be ravished, / this before and after some have no pleasure but in violence" (p. 42). Cyril Tourneur's rapist in *The Revenger's Tragedy* III, iv, claims, "My fault was sweet sport which the world approves; / I die for that which every woman loves" (p. 39). The changing attitude embodied in drama is the subject of Suzanne Gossett's "Best Men are Molded Out of Faults: Marrying the Rapist in Jacobean Drama."

40. Thomas Heywood, *The General History of Women*, p. 226.

41. William Harrison, *Elizabethan England*, p. 79.

42. Rogers, *Matrimonial Honour*, p. 281.

43. For example, T. Smith, *De Republica Anglorum*, pp. 123–25.

44. Gervase Babington, *Notes upon Genesis*, p. 25.

45. H. Smith, "A Preparative to Marriage," *Sermons*, pp. 139, 35–39.

46. T. Smith, *De Republica Anglorum*, pp. 126–28.

47. See above, chapters 1 and 2.

48. Even if men were more productive, this advantage would be nullified, since guilds put limits on productivity—their object being to restrain and manage competition.

49. St. Augustine's *City of God* is a standard exposition of this view. Thomas

Starkey's *Dialogue Between Pole and Lupset*, by a minor official (with major hopes) of Henry VIII's court, is a sixteenth-century restatement.

50. Gouge, *Of Domesticall Duties*, p. 287; see also Gataker, *Marriage Duties*, p. 10.

51. Miles Coverdale, trans., *The Christian State of Matrimony*, p. 41; see also pp. 26–27.

52. Griffith, *Bethel*, pp. 114–15; Hannibal Gamon, *The Praise of a Godly Woman*, p. 11.

53. Rogers, *Matrimonial Honour*, pp. 253–54.

54. H. Smith, "A Preparative to Marriage," *Sermons*, p. 37.

55. See John Seldon, *Table Talk*, p. 126; Rogers, *Matrimonial Honour*, p. 303; John Brinsley, *A Looking Glass for Good Women*, p. 37.

56. See Maclean, *Renaissance Notion of Woman* and John Knox, *A Blast against the Monstrous Regiment of Women*.

57. Of course, Mary and Elizabeth were exceptions to women's more general exclusion from politics. But their reigns lasted more than fifty years, and despite Elizabeth's claims of a masculine and princely stomach, she did make use of her gender to organize and structure her court. See John E. Neale, *Elizabeth I*; Alison Heisch, "Queen Elizabeth I"; Larissa Taylor-Smither, "Elizabeth I: A Psychological Profile." On women as active participants in the public world as buyers and sellers, see, of course, Alice Clark, *Working Life*; Pearl Hogrefe, *Tudor Women* and *Women of Action in Tudor England*; Richard Vann, "Toward a New Lifestyle"; Antonia Fraser, *The Weaker Vessel*.

58. Lucy Hutchinson, *Memoirs*, p. 48.

4. The Woman Had the Keys

1. Doris Stenton, *The English Woman in History*, p. 74. But see also Barbara Winchester, *Tudor Family Portrait*; Christina Hole, *The English Housewife in the Seventeenth Century*; and Eileen Power, *Medieval Women*, and "The Position of Women."

2. The following works discuss Protestant family doctrine: Lawrence Stone, *The Family, Sex, and Marriage in England*; William Haller, "Hail, Wedded Love"; Mervyn James, *Family, Lineage, and Civil Society*; James Turner Johnson, *A Society Ordained by God*; Roberta Hamilton, *The Liberation of Women*; Michael Anderson, *Approaches to the History of the Western Family*. While these works offer clear presentations of many aspects of this doctrine and some, most notably Lawrence Stone (pp. 195–200), highlight its strongly patriarchal nature, none of these works has as a primary focus the effect of this doctrine on women's place in the family or social economy. For valuable comments on Stone, see Lois G. Schwoerer, "Seventeenth Century English Women," and Stephen Wilson, "The Myth of Motherhood a Myth." Steven Ozment's *When Fathers Ruled* does devote considerable attention to the effects of Protestant doctrine and practices on women. As is apparent, I strongly disagree with Ozment. See also Ralph Houlbrooke, *The English Family* and Antonia Fraser, *The Weaker Vessel*. Houlbrooke's book again seems to characterize the effects of Protestantism and capitalism on women as positive. Houlbrooke does lay out in informative and clear terms many of the social and economic changes described herein. Yet he interprets the ideological changes rather narrowly and, in some cases, strictly literally, when it is often the context which

is changing and which changes the implications of ideological expressions. The discussion below contrasting Thomas Gataker's prescriptions with those of Sir Thomas Smith illustrates how ideological change might be examined by Houlbrooke. See also Mark Poster, *Critical Theory of the Family;* C. L. Powell, *English Domestic Relations;* John Gillis, *For Better, For Worse.*

3. Anthony FitzHerbert, *Book of Husbandry,* pp. 95–98.

4. Sir Thomas Eliot, *The Defense of Good Women,* pp. 38–40.

5. Thomas Tusser, *Husbandry,* pp. 40–41.

6. *Ibid.,* p. 41.

7. Miles Coverdale, trans., *The Christian State of Matrimony,* p. 72.

8. Thomas Becon, "Goldē Boke of Christen Matrimonye," *Works,* p. 675. In many respects, Becon's work is but a reprise of Bullinger with, however, some revisions attempting to make the text more applicable to the English way of life.

9. See Clark, *Working Life;* FitzHerbert, *Book of Husbandry;* most texts on housewifery mention this.

10. Becon, "Goldē Boke of Matrimonye," *Works,* p. 676.

11. Thomas Becon, "New Catechism," *Works,* p. 530.

12. Sir Thomas Smith, *De Republica Anglorum,* p. 22; William Harrison, *Elizabethan England,* p. 78.

13. Becon, "New Catechism," *Works,* p. 530.

14. *Ibid.,* p. 515.

15. *Ibid.,* p. 514.

16. See Thomas More, "Letter to his wife," pp. 11–12. See also Sir Thomas Eliot, *Defense of Good Women,* p. 38; Smith, *De Republica Anglorum,* p. 22; Baldesar Castiglione, *The Courtier,* p. 215.

17. FitzHerbert, *Book of Husbandry,* pp. 96–97.

18. Tusser, *Husbandry,* pp. 40–41.

19. FitzHerbert, *Book of Husbandry,* p. 96.

20. See, for example, Frances Parthenope Verney, ed., *Memoirs of the Verney Family During the Civil War,* and Miriam Slater's work on the same family, *Family Life in the Seventeenth Century;* see also Alison Plowden, *Tudor Women,* p. 38 and Margaret Hoby's *Diary.*

21. Nicholas Breton, "The Good and the Bad," p. 29.

22. Margaret Hoby, *Diary.* The diary is filled with lists noting the completion of these chores.

23. John Evelyn, *Memoires for my Grandson,* p. 70. Evelyn is but a drop in a storm of criticism. See below.

24. Castiglione, *The Courtier,* p. 241.

25. Sir Phillip Sidney, *Countess of Pembroke's Arcadia,* p. 242.

26. Cornelius Agrippa, *A Treatise of the Nobilitie and Excellencie of Womankind.* No pagination available.

27. John Stow, *Survay of London,* pp. 481, 496–97, 871, 874–75.

28. Henry Smith, "Banquet of Job's Children," *Sermons,* p. 471.

29. Coverdale, trans., *Christian State of Matrimony,* p. 69.

30. Henry Medwall, *Fulgens and Lucrece,* I, 280–82; see also Phillip Sidney, "The Lady of May," *Miscellaneous Prose.* It should be noted that Dorothy MacLaren in "Marital Fertility and Lactation" argues that wealthy families viewed the reproduction

of children differently from poorer families—wealthy folk hoping for large numbers—partially because the wealthy had less success in raising their children to adulthood. Because women from poor families—and she implies, all but wealthy families—breastfed their own children, and breastfeeding served more effectively as birth control in the sixteenth than the twentieth century, nonwealthy families had longer birth intervals and thus lower infant mortality. The argument is not entirely successful. Even MacLaren acknowledges that large numbers of "middling status" women sent their babies out to nurse in London—so widespread a phenomenon was wet-nursing in sixteenth- and seventeenth-century London that it started almost an industry in the suburbs (pp. 28–29). The truth is, as she notes (p. 28), our knowledge of maternal breastfeeding in preindustrial England is extremely limited. We know that divines urged mothers to breastfeed. We know that some physicians and women believed breastfeeding to be effective birth control. We know that infant mortality statistics were very high, and we know that rich and poor alike strove to have enough grown children that the children could provide for the parents in their old age. (On mortality statistics, see Stone, *Family, Sex, and Marriage*, p. 58 and Schofield, "English Marriage Patterns Revisited.") We do not know that sixteenth-century families in the strata below the aristocracy saw breastfeeding as an important means of achieving this, and there are suggestions that these families found the mother's economic contribution too valuable immediately to forego for the sake of the next generation.

31. Tusser, *Husbandry*, p. 162.

32. Becon, "New Catechism," *Works*, p. 516.

33. Tusser, *Husbandry*, p. 162.

34. See below on motherhood, but, as was noted above, our knowledge of this subject is limited.

35. Tusser, *Husbandry*, p. 162.

36. Thomas Bentley, *Monument of Matrones*, 3:33–35.

37. Gervase Markham, *The English Housewife*, pp. 2–3.

38. Dorothy Leigh, *The Mother's Blessing*, pp. 58–59.

39. *Ibid.*, pp. 24, 46.

40. Phillip Stubbes, *Anatomy of Abuses*, pp. 170ff.; Arthur Dent, *The Plain Man's Pathway to Heaven*, p. 315; see also Roger Ascham, *The Scholemaster*, and Richard Mulcaster, *Positions*, p. 18.

41. Smith, *De Republica Anglorum*, pp. 22–23.

42. Becon, "New Catechism," *Works*, p. 516.

43. Bentley, *Monument of Matrones*, 3:67, 85.

44. *Ibid.*, p. 67.

45. Gervase Babington, *Notes upon Genesis*, p. 66.

46. Evelyn, *Memoires for my Grandson*, p. 70.

47. See, for example, Phillip Massinger's *The City Madam*, II, ii, James Shirley's *The Lady of Pleasure*, II, i, or Thomas Dekker's *The Shoemaker's Holiday*, III, ii.

48. Babington, *Notes upon Genesis*, p. 66.

49. See G.P.V. Akrigg, *Jacobean Pageant*, pp. 166–70; as Francis Bacon wrote: "Riches are for spending, and spending for honour and good actions" ("Of Expense," *Essays*).

50. Rachel Weigall, "An Elizabethan Gentlewoman: The Journal of Lady Mildmay," pp. 120–21.

51. Richard Braithwait, *The English Gentlewoman*, p. 297.

52. Sir Hugh Plat, *Delights for Ladies*, p. 1) 2. See also, Elizabeth David, *English Bread and Yeast Cookery*, p. 145, and Plat, *A Closet*.

53. George Savile, Marquis of Halifax, "Advise to a Daughter," *Works*, pp. 24–25.

54. *Ibid.* pp. 20, 24–25.

55. Henry Smith, "A Preparative to Marriage," *Sermons*, p. 31.

56. Savile, "Advise to a Daughter," *Works*, pp. 24–25.

57. *Ibid.*

58. William Perkins, "Christian Oeconomy," *Works*, p. 700.

59. *Ibid.*, p. 698.

60. William Gouge, *Of Domesticall Duties*, p. 259.

61. Thomas Gataker, *Marriage Duties*, pp. 20–21.

62. J. Dod and W. Hind, *Bathesheba's Instructions*, p. 34.

63. Daniel Rogers, *Matrimonial Honour*, p. 292.

64. Markham's works were addressed both to women who had idle time on their hands and to those raised as if they would. Some of these latter women did not marry well; they may indeed have needed his very basic instructions in order to perform essential housewifely tasks and, as in *Cheap and good Husbandry*, to do so with real economy.

65. Perkins, "Christian Oeconomy," *Works*, p. 693; also, Coverdale, trans., *Christian State of Matrimony*, p. 76, and see Lawrence Stone, *The Family, Sex, and Marriage in England*, p. 159.

66. Gervase Babington, *Notes upon Genesis*, p. 85.

67. Stone, *The Family, Sex, and Marriage in England*, pp. 114, 427–28. However, Stone points out that among the aristocracy, the shift was slow. Maternal breastfeeding, he says, did not come "into fashion" until the eighteenth century. For a viewpoint emphasizing the slowness of the spread, see Audrey Eccles, *Obstetrics and Gynecology*, pp. 97–99. MacLaren in "Marital Fertility" points out that wet-nursing was becoming more costly in the seventeenth century; the calculations that the housewife would make might thus tilt in favor of maternal nursing simply because wet-nurses were relatively more expensive and the housewife's role relatively less valued.

68. Gouge, *Of Domesticall Duties*, p. 515.

69. *Ibid.*, p. 515; see also for very similar statements, Rogers, *Matrimonial Honour*, p. 291. For other observations on the novelty of the mother's role, see Barbara Harris, "Marriage Sixteenth-Century Style," p. 371, and Shulamith Shahar, *The Fourth Estate*, pp. 98–103.

70. Thomas Dekker and John Webster, *Westward Ho!*, I, ii. (p. 22).

71. Alice Thornton, *Autobiography*, p. 3.

72. Anne, Lady Fanshawe, *Memoirs*, pp. 18, 43–45.

73. F. P. Verney, ed., *Memoirs*, 1:103–4, 2:294. See also Gouge, *Of Domesticall Duties*, p. 515 and Clark, *Working Life*, p. 58. See also Miriam Slater, "The Weightiest Business" and "Debate: The Weightiest Business," plus Sara H. Mendelson, "Debate: The Weightiest Business."

74. Mulcaster, *Positions*, pp. 172, 174, 176–77, 281.

75. *Ibid.*, p. 174.

76. *Ibid.*, pp. 177–81. But Markham and Plat, et al., moved in to fill this void. See also Suzanne Hull, *Chaste, Silent, and Obedient.*

77. Smith, "A Preparative to Marriage," *Sermons*, p. 20.

78. See Mulcaster, *Positions*, "To the Reader"; Alison Heisch, "Queen Elizabeth I," pp. 31–56 and R. Greaves, *Society and Religion*, pp. 310–11; Fraser, *The Weaker Vessel*, and Elizabeth H. Hageman, "Recent Studies in Women Writers."

79. Nicholas Breton, "An Old Man's Lesson," pp. 14–15. See also Juan Luis Vives, *The Instruction of a Christen Woman.*

80. Pearl Hogrefe, *Tudor Women*, pp. 95–99; C. S. Lewis, "English Literature in the Sixteenth Century," p. 307; Bentley, *Monument of Matrones*, p. 230; Hageman, "Recent Studies"; Hull, *Chaste, Silent, and Obedient.*

81. Lawrence Stone, "The Educational Revolution"; D. Cressy, *Literacy and the Social Order*, chs. 1 and 2.

82. Mulcaster, *Positions*, pp. 176–79.

83. Ben Jonson's *Epicoene* is, in no small part, an attack on "learned ladies."

84. John Marston, *The Dutch Courtesan*, IV, i, 49–53 (p. 259).

85. See Gervase Markham, *The English Housewife* and *The Country Housewife's Garden.*

86. Thornton, *Memoirs*, p. 8; and see Cressy, *Literacy and the Social Order*, pp. 30–35.

87. Rogers, *Matrimonial Honour*, p. 305.

88. Braithwait, *The English Gentlewoman*, p. 398.

89. Gervase Babington, *The Commandements*, pp. 185–86; Smith, "A Preparative to Marriage," *Sermons*, p. 43; Braithwait, *The English Gentlewoman*, p. 398.

90. See William Haller, *The Rise of Puritanism*; P. Williams, *The Tudor Regime.* Henry VIII legislated limitations on reading; the limitations were by status and gender.

91. D. Gardiner, *English Girlhood at School*, pp. 195–96 and Clark, *Working Life.*

92. Thornton, *Autobiography*, pp. 100–1; Fanshawe, *Memoirs*, pp. 22–23.

93. Gervase Holles, *Memorials of the Holles Family*, p. 219.

94. Hutchinson, *Memoirs*, pp. 18–19.

95. Fanshawe, *Memoirs*, p. 12.

96. Gouge, *Of Domesticall Duties*, p. 431.

97. Tusser, *Husbandry*, p. 41.

98. Becon, "New Catechism," *Works*, p. 530.

99. Smith, *De Republica Anglorum*, pp. 22–23.

100. Tusser, *Husbandry*, pp. 26–45; Thomas Becon, "Goldē Boke of Matrimonye," *Works*, p. 649.

101. Richard Braithwait, "as every man's house is his castle, so is his family a private commonwealth" (*The English Gentleman*, p. 87).

102. Griffith, *Bethel*, p. 223.

103. Perkins, "Christian Oeconomy," *Works*, pp. 670–71.

104. *Ibid.*, p. 700.

105. Rogers, *Matrimonial Honour*, p. 187.

106. Whately, *A Bride-Bush*, pp. 174–75.

107. Rogers, *Matrimonial Honour*, p. 289.

108. Gouge, *Of Domesticall Duties*, p. 303.

109. Smith, "A Preparative to Marriage," *Sermons*, p. 35.

110. Whately, *A Bride-Bush*, pp. 81–83.

111. Rogers, *Matrimonial Honour*, p. 303.

112. Gouge, *Of Domesticall Duties*, p. 303.

113. Gataker, *A Wife Indeed*, p. 18. See for other examples, Smith, "A Preparative to Marriage," *Sermons*, pp. 9–13; Whately, *A Bride-Bush*, p. 60.

114. Becon, "New Catechism," *Works*, p. 545, "Goldē Boke of Matrimonye," *Works*, pp. 667–68.

115. Rogers, *Matrimonial Honour*, pp. 160–61.

116. Whately, *A Bride-Bush*, p. 180.

117. Rogers, *Matrimonial Honour*, p. 292; Gouge, *Of Domesticall Duties*, p. 259.

118. Whately, *A Bride-Bush*, p. 151.

119. Rogers, *Matrimonial Honour*, pp. 294–95.

120. Gouge, *Of Domesticall Duties*, p. 259.

121. Gataker, *Marriage Duties*, pp. 20–21.

122. Perkins, "Christian Oeconomy," *Works*, p. 700.

123. Whately, *A Bride-Bush*, pp. 150–51.

124. Rogers, *Matrimonial Honour*, p. 250.

125. Gouge, *Of Domesticall Duties*, p. 309.

126. Gerrard Winstanley, *The Law of Freedom in a Platform*, pp. 146–47.

127. Gouge, *Of Domesticall Duties*, p. 259; see also Whately, *A Bride-Bush*, p. 89.

128. Jonson, *Epicoene*, IV, i, 212–15 (p. 124); see also Rogers, *Matrimonial Honour*, p. 304; Gataker, *A Wife Indeed*, p. 16.

129. Rogers, *Matrimonial Honour*, p. 289.

130. See Gouge, *Of Domesticall Duties*, pp. 505–10.

131. Rogers, *Matrimonial Honour*, p. 198.

132. G. Savile, "Advise to a Daughter," *Works*, pp. 24–25.

133. Rogers, *Matrimonial Honour*, p. 161.

134. G. Moore-Smith, ed., *Osborne Letters*, p. 155.

135. Whately, *A Bride-Bush*, p. 60.

5. Legendary Hearts

1. See, for example, Steven Ozment, *When Fathers Ruled*. Others who espouse less extreme versions of this theory than Ozment include Lawrence Stone, *Family, Sex, and Marriage*, where, on pp. 195–203, Stone presents the "other side," despite his conclusion that, on the whole, the Protestant elevation of marriage was a boon to women. Thomas Max Safley's *Let No Man Put Asunder: The Control of Marriage in the German Southwest: A Comparative Study 1550–1600* (Kirksville, Mo.: Sixteenth Century Journal, 1984) suggests that Protestantism per se changed little in women's family status and that the significant difference was that it opened the possibilities for true divorce. Should this be shown to be true, the question remains, could women afford to explore those possibilities? See also Roberta Hamilton, *The Liberation of Women*; James Turner Johnson, *A Society Ordained by God*; R. L. Greaves, *Society and Religion*; Edmund

Leites, "The Duty to Desire"; William and Mandeville Haller, "The Puritan Art of Love"; A. MacFarlane, *The Family of Ralph Josselin*.

2. Daniel Rogers, *Matrimonial Honour*, p. 325; William Perkins, "Christian Oeconomy," *Works*, pp. 689–90.

3. See Christopher Hill, *Society and Puritanism*; William Haller, *The Rise of Puritanism*; Gordon Schochet, *Patriarchalism in Political Thought*, for discussion of the family as the model of civil society. Thomas Hobbes demonstrates the pervasiveness of this dogma. See his *Man and Citizen*, B. Gert, ed. (New York: Anchor Books, 1972), pp. 212–19; *Leviathan*, C. B. MacPherson, ed. (New York: Pelican, 1971), pp. 253, 383, 224.

4. Thomas Becon, "Goldē Boke of Matrimonye" *Works*, p. 649; see also Henry Smith, "A Preparative to Marriage," *Sermons*, p. 13.

5. William Perkins, "Christian Oeconomy," *Works*, pp. 670–71.

6. William Gouge, *Of Domesticall Duties*, p. 494.

7. *Ibid.*, p. 560.

8. Matthew Griffith, *Bethel*, pp. 3–8, 223–24.

9. Rogers, *A Practical Catechisme*, pp. 66–67; see also, Gouge, *Of Domesticall Duties*, p. 287.

10. Griffith, *Bethel*, p. 223; Perkins, "Christian Oeconomy," *Works*, pp. 670–71; Thomas Gataker, *Marriage Duties*, pp. 10–13; John Aylmer, *An Harborowe*, p. 41; Richard Hooker, "Ecclesiastical Polity," *Work*, p. 427.

11. Richard Hooker, "Ecclesiastical Polity," *Work*, p. 427; Nicholas Byfield, *A Commentary upon Peter*, p. 73; Hugh Latimer, *Fruitfull Sermons*, p. 106; Perkins, "Christian Oeconomy," *Works*, p. 698, William Whately, *A Bride-Bush*, pp. 188–89.

12. On the "excellency of marriage," see the following: Miles Coverdale, trans., *Christian State of Matrimony*, pp. 2–6; Becon, "Goldē Boke of Matrimonye," *Works*, pp. 564–68; Smith, "A Preparative to Marriage," *Sermons*, p. 9; Griffith, *Bethel*, pp. 20–21, 28.

13. Griffith, *Bethel*, pp. 20–21. His implication, moreover, rested on ever stronger material supports.

14. Gouge, *Of Domesticall Duties*, p. 331; Whately, *A Bride-Bush*, p. 60.

15. Alexander Nowell, *Catechisme*, p. 12; Gervase Babington, *The Commandements*, pp. 185–86.

16. Thomas Middleton, *Women Beware Women*, II, i.

17. Phillip Massinger, *The Virgin Martyr*, I, i; Gouge, *Of Domesticall Duties*, p. 3.

18. Gouge, *Of Domesticall Duties*, p. 3.

19. *Ibid.*, p. 396; Thomas Gataker, *A Good Wife God's Gift*, pp. 22–23; Perkins, "Christian Oeconomy," *Works*, p. 692.

20. Lady Anne Clifford, *Diary*, pp. 62–69.

21. E. M. Thompson, ed., *Hatton Correspondence*, 1:50; see also Barbara Harris, "Marriage Sixteenth-Century Style" and Alice T. Friedman, "Portrait of a Marriage" for similar descriptions of the dependence of fatherless wives on their husbands early in this time.

22. Phillip Massinger, *City Madam*, III, ii. Other examples may be found in Thomas Bentley, *Monument of Matrones*, who says marriages between nonequals are "irksome to men, burdensome to earth and intolerable in a commonwealth," 3:55; and Robert Greene, *Arcadia*, and Edmund Tilney, *The Flower of Friendship*.

23. See previous chapter for discussion of husbands owning all, including the fruits of the women's labor.

24. See, for example, Shakespeare's *Taming of the Shrew;* Phillip Massinger, *The City Madam* and James Shirley, *The Lady of Pleasure;* John Dod and William Hind, *Bathsheba's Instructions,* p. 28; Rogers, *Matrimonial Honour,* p. 255; and Gataker, *A Good Wife God's Gift,* p. 20.

25. Whately, *A Bride-Bush,* pp. 188–91.

26. Griffith, *Bethel,* p. 8.

27. George Savile, "Advise to a Daughter," *Works,* pp. 18–19.

28. Alice Thornton, *Autobiography,* pp. 213–14.

29. Smith, "A Preparative to Marriage," *Sermons,* p. 31.

30. R. W. Blencowe, ed., *Sydney Papers,* p. 138; G. Holles, *Memorials,* p. 109; J. P. Cooper, ed., *Wentworth Papers,* pp. 304–5. Also see Harris, "Marriage Sixteenth-Century Style"; Friedman, "Portrait of a Marriage"; and Miriam Slater, *Family Life in the Seventeenth Century.*

31. Lady Anne Halkett, *Autobiography,* pp. 6, 72–73, 100–1.

32. Thornton, *Autobiography,* pp. 62, 78–79.

33. See, for example, G. Moore-Smith, ed. *Osborne Letters,* p. 155; see also Slater, *Family Life in the Seventeenth Century.*

34. Verney, ed., *Verney Memoirs,* 2:143, 365; see also Slater, *Family Life in the Seventeenth Century,* pp. 78–91.

35. John Evelyn, *Memoires for my Grandson,* p. 13–14; also Slater, *Family Life in the Seventeenth Century,* pp. 106, 144.

36. Smith, "A Preparative to Marriage," *Sermons,* p. 13; Gervase Babington, *Notes upon Genesis,* p. 12.

37. Gataker, *A Wife Indeed,* pp. 18–19.

38. Whately, *A Bride-Bush,* p. 61.

39. John Seldon, *Table Talk,* p. 126; John Brinsley, *A Looking Glass for Good Women,* p. 37.

40. Babington, *Notes upon Genesis,* p. 64.

41. Whately, *A Bride-Bush,* pp. 188–90; Aylmer, *An Harborowe,* pp. 6–8.

42. Richard Hooker, "Ecclesiastical Polity," *Work,* pp. 150–53, 427–29.

43. Gouge, *Of Domesticall Duties,* p. 423.

44. See Whately, *A Bride-Bush,* pp. 188–89; see also Gouge, *Of Domesticall Duties,* p. 273; Babington, *Notes upon Genesis,* p. 20.

45. Rogers, *Matrimonial Honour,* p. 305.

46. *Ibid.*

47. Gouge, *Of Domesticall Duties,* p. 236.

48. Rogers, *Matrimonial Honour,* p. 266.

49. Smith, "A Preparative to Marriage," *Sermons,* p. 38.

50. Thomas Gataker, *Marriage Duties,* p. 13; see also Gouge, *Of Domesticall Duties,* p. 337.

51. Griffith, *Bethel,* p. 318.

52. See, for example, N. Udall's *Ralph Roister Doister;* Thomas Tusser, *Husbandry,* p. 25; Smith, "A Preparative to Marriage," *Sermons,* p. 18; Lawrence Stone, *Crisis of the Aristocracy,* pp. 594 ff.

53. See, for example, Tusser, *Husbandry*, pp. 175, 177; A. FitzHerbert, *Book of Husbandry*, p. 95; Harris, "Marriage Sixteenth-Century Style," pp. 371–82.

54. Tusser, *Husbandry*, p. 177.

55. Sir Walter Raleigh, "Instructions to his Son," pp. 7–9.

56. Tusser, *Husbandry*, p. 177; FitzHerbert, *Book of Husbandry*, p. 95.

57. Edmund Tilney, *The Flower of Friendship*, p. Diiij.

58. George Savile, "Advise to a Daughter," *Works*, pp. 7–8.

59. Gouge, *Of Domesticall Duties*, p. 234; see also K. Wrightson and D. Levine, *Poverty and Piety*, pp. 135–41; D. Levine, "Production, Reproduction," pp. 3–15; Harris, "Marriage Sixteenth-Century Style," pp. 375–77; and Friedman, "Portrait of a Marriage," p. 546.

60. Dod and Hind, *Bathesheba's Instructions*, p. 28; E. Leites, "The Duty to Desire," p. 388.

61. Whately, *A Bride-Bush*, p. 31.

62. Baldesar Castiglione, *The Courtier*, p. 189.

63. George Gascoigne, "Tale of Mrs. Frances." Ralph Houlbrooke, *The English Family*, cites on p. 116 Robert Greene's 1592 "Conversion of an English Courtesan."

64. R. Braithwait, *English Gentlewoman*, p. 293; G. Moore-Smith, ed., *Osborne Letters*, p. 125.

65. Thomas Dekker and Thomas Middleton, *The Roaring Girl*, III, i, 100–4.

66. Savile, "Advise to a Daughter," *Works*, pp. 10–11.

67. Gouge, *Of Domesticall Duties*, pp. 219–21; see also Miles Coverdale, trans., *The Christian State of Matrimony*, pp. 26–27, 41.

68. Gouge, *Of Domesticall Duties*, pp. 223–24; Griffith, *Bethel*, p. 239–40; Smith, "A Preparative to Marriage," *Sermons*, p. 13.

69. As contrasted, that is, with the housewife who managed the family economy.

70. Rogers, *Matrimonial Honour*, pp. 253–55.

71. Gataker, *A Mariage Praier*, p. 20.

72. Gouge, *Of Domesticall Duties*, p. 270.

73. Whately, *A Bride-Bush*, p. 192.

74. Sir Kenelm Digby, *Private Memoirs*, pp. 270–72; Sir Walter Raleigh, "Instructions to his Son," p. 7; James Shirley, *The Lady of Pleasure*, II, ii.

75. Becon, "Goldē Boke of Matrimonye," *Works*, pp. 647, 665; Whately, *A Bride-Bush*, p. 31; Coverdale, trans., *The Christian State of Matrimony*, pp. 45–54.

76. J. P. Cooper, ed., *Wentworth Papers*, p. 20.

77. Digby, *Private Memoirs*, pp. 270–72.

78. Robert Greene, *Arcadia*, p. 20j; Francis Beaumont and John Fletcher, *The Maid in the Mill*, III, i (p. 39); Braithwait, *English Gentlewoman*, p. 345; *English Gentleman*, p. 145.

79. Francis Bacon, "Of Marriage and Single Life," *Essays*, p. 23.

80. Gataker, *A Mariage Praier*, pp. 18–19.

81. Gataker, *A Wife Indeed*, p. 53.

82. Rogers, *Matrimonial Honour*, p. 295; see also Thomas Gataker, *Paul's Desire*, pp. B1–B2.

83. Verney, ed., *Verney Memoirs*, 2:370; Raleigh, "Instructions to his Son," p. 7.

84. Richard Braithwait, *A Ladies Love Lecture*, p. 425.

85. Margaret Cavendish, *Life*, pp. 156–58.

86. Bathsua Makin in M. R. Mahl and H. Koon, eds., *The Female Spectator: English Women Writers Before 1800*, p. 135.

87. *Ibid.*

88. *Ibid.*, pp. 127–31, 134.

89. *Ibid.*, p. 137; Braithwait, *English Gentlewoman*, p. 319; Cooper, ed., *Wentworth Papers*, p. 21.

90. Braithwait, *English Gentlewoman*, p. 312; Evelyn, *Memoires for my Grandson*, pp. 13–14; Cooper, ed., *Wentworth Papers*, p. 21.

91. From a letter to Anne Oxinden, of gentry status, from her mother on the occasion of Anne's marriage, 1632. The mother added that she could not fill a request of her daughter, for although her "husband seems to give me power . . . I have no power." D. Gardiner, ed., *The Oxinden Letters*, p. 87. See also Slater, *Family Life in the Seventeenth Century*, pp. 80–81, 106, 144 on women unable to provide for themselves.

92. It was Daniel Rogers who called attention to the lack of intellectual stimulation in the nursery, *Matrimonial Honour*, p. 161; but see also Gouge, *Domesticall Duties*, p. 546.

93. J. Dod and W. Hind, *Bathsheba's Instructions*, p. 3.

94. Rogers, *Matrimonial Honour*, p. 161.

95. Sir Simonds D'Ewes, *Autobiography*, pp. 24–40.

96. Savile, "Advise to a Daughter," *Works*, p. 56.

97. See Gordon Schochet, *Patriarchalism*, ch. 4, and John Bramhall, *Castigations of Mr. Hobbes*.

98. Gouge, *Of Domesticall Duties*, p. 486.

99. *Ibid.*, p. 431.

100. *Ibid.*, p. 484–85.

101. G. Moore-Smith, ed., *Osborne Letters*, p. 34.

102. Savile, "Advise to a Daughter," *Works*, p. 2.

103. Thomas Tusser on "cockering," *Husbandry*, p. 163; Thomas Becon, "New Catechism," *Works*, pp 518–22; Dorothy Leigh, *The Mother's Blessing*, pp. 11–12.

104. Matthew Griffith, *Bethel*, pp. 319, 335–38; see also John Foxe, *Book of Martyrs*, p. 1110 on parents preferring their children alive in sin to dead in perfect martyrdom.

105. Leigh, *The Mother's Blessing*, pp. 11–12; see also E. M. Thompson, ed., *Hatton Correspondence*. The clergy suspected—and some modern historians agree—that those women who were, as per ministerial instruction, lavishing love and care on their infants were also practicing birth control in order to limit the number of infants who required this care and children who would require, again as per ministerial instruction, some stock or capital to set them up in life. Samuel Hieron in the early seventeenth century complained that some of his congregants "would prescribe the Lord how many [children] he should give them and set him down a stint which he must not exceed." Hieron called this "a notable evidence of a miserable and faithless mind" (*Sermons*, p. 408). On the contrary, it may easily be seen as evidence of maternal effort to perform the new tasks of childrearing faithfully and competently. The clergy's call for maternal

breastfeeding, coupled with their anger at attempts at birth control, suggests that the amenorrheal effects of lactation were not quite so well known as D. MacLaren alleges in "Marital Fertility."

106. Gouge, *Of Domesticall Duties*, pp. 428–29.

107. Lucy Hutchinson, *Memoirs*, p. 287; William Painter, *Palace of Pleasure*, vol. 1, novel 23.

108. See, for example, anon., *The Sacrifice of Isaac;* also John Foxe, *Book of Martyrs*, p. 1110. There is a general discussion of this in E. Badinter's *Mother Love* and a particular discussion in Joseph Illick's "Childrearing in Seventeenth Century England." The ministers and Foxe attest to parental affection *contra* Badinter and Illick.

109. William Harrison, *Elizabethan England*, pp. 87–88; Gouge, *Of Domesticall Duties*, p. 486.

6. Putting the Pieces Together

1. For example, Matthew Griffith, *Bethel*, p. 414; see also Miles Coverdale, trans., *Christian State of Matrimony*, pp. 73–74.

2. Phillip Stubbes, "Life of His Wife" in *Anatomy of Abuses*, pp. 198–99.

3. Quotation is from Gervase Babington, *Notes upon Genesis*, p. 134; but see also the works of Thomas Nashe, especially "Anatomy of Absurdity," and Nicholas Breton. Both were popular pamphleteers of late sixteenth-century England.

4. Babington, *Notes upon Genesis*, p. 134.

5. Richard Baxter, *A Breviate of the Life of Margaret, Wife of Richard Baxter*, pp. 64–65; William Harrison in the mid-sixteenth century had praised clerical marriage exactly because ministers' wives made so notable a contribution to poor relief; *Elizabethan England*, pp. 78–79.

6. R. Greene, *Arcadia* (1580s); Edmund Tilney, *Flower of Friendship*, and, of course, Phillip Stubbes in *Anatomy of Abuses* in the sixteenth century. Baxter in the seventeenth century (*Breviate*) was willing for his talented wife to go where she would.

7. This is the process expounded in chapters 4 and 5.

8. Alice Thornton, *Autobiography*, pp. 54, 239–48.

9. William Gouge, *Of Domesticall Duties*, pp. 406, 97.

10. See Louis B. Wright, ed., *Advice to a Son*. Burghley, Raleigh, and Wentworth stood together on this issue.

11. J. P. Cooper, ed. *Wentworth Papers*, p. 20.

12. Michael Walzer, *The Revolution of the Saints*, pp. 217–18. See also E. M. Leonard, *The Early History of English Poor Relief*.

13. Anne, Lady Fanshawe, *Memoirs*, p. 20; Gervase Holles, *Memorials*, pp. 25–26.

14. Gouge, *Of Domesticall Duties*, p. 265.

15. See John Stow's *Survey of London;* William Herbert, *The Twelve Great Livery Companies*.

16. Gouge, *Of Domesticall Duties*, p. 404.

17. See, for example, William Perkins, "Christian Oeconomy," *Works*, pp. 689–90; William Whately, *A Bride-Bush*, pp. 9–14.

18. See, for example, Griffith, *Bethel*, pp. 228–30.

19. Daniel Rogers, *Matrimonial Honour,* p. 163.

20. Perkins, "Christian Oeconomy," *Works,* p. 690. Again, see E. Leites, "The Duty to Desire."

21. Perkins, "Christian Oeconomy," *Works,* pp. 689–90.

22. Griffith, *Bethel,* pp. 239–40; Henry Smith, "A Preparative to Marriage," *Sermons,* p. 13; Gouge, *Of Domesticall Duties,* pp. 223–24.

23. Perkins, "Christian Oeconomy," *Works,* pp. 689–90; see also Gouge, *Of Domesticall Duties,* pp. 218–23.

24. See discussions of adultery in chapter 5.

25. J. Dod and W. Hind, *Bathesheba's Instructions,* p. 26.

26. Francis Beaumont and John Fletcher, *The Maid in the Mill,* III, ii (p.44).

27. Margaret Cavendish, *Life,* p. 161.

28. As was seen in chapter 5, neither the clergy nor important agents of political power approved of mewing up wives to control them. The clergy insisted upon cohabitation that the woman might demonstrate her humble subjection, the husband might receive it, and the whole family be instructed on life as it should be. James's counselors feared "mewing up" would leave country areas without their natural male leaders and thus fail to promote the natural and stable order of society as desired by cleric and counselor alike. See also G.P.V. Akrigg, *Jacobean Pageant;* Braithwait, *English Gentlewoman,* p. 293; K. Digby, *Private Memoirs,* pp. 98–102; George Savile, "Advise to a Daughter," *Works,* pp. 1, 27.

29. William Cecil (Lord Burghley), "Certain Precepts," p.10.

30. *Ibid.*

31. "Advice to My Son" in J. P. Cooper, ed., *Wentworth Papers,* p. 20.

32. *Ibid.,* p. 21. See also Sir Walter Raleigh, "Instructions to his Son," p. 22.

33. See chapter 5 for more detail on Lady Hoby.

34. Gervase Markham, *The English Housewife,* p. 4.

35. Braithwait, *English Gentlewoman,* p. 397.

36. Again, religious ministers and council ministers criticized husbands who allowed—or forced—their wives to such freedom. See Akrigg, *Jacobean Pageant* and A. T. Friedman, "Portrait of a Marriage."

37. Daniel Rogers, *Matrimonial Honour,* pp. 160–61.

38. Cooper, ed., *Wentworth Papers,* p. 21, J. Evelyn, *Memoires for my Grandson,* pp. 13–14; see also R. S. Schofield, "The Measurement of Literacy in Pre-Industrial England," pp. 311–25; D. Cressy, *Literacy and the Social Order,* pp. 38–70.

39. Babington, *Notes upon Genesis,* p. 66.

40. For a fuller discussion, see Patricia Higgins, "The Reactions of Women," pp. 180–225 and Ellen A. McArthur, "Women Petitioners," pp. 698–709; F. S. Siebert, *Freedom of the Press* on the subject of mercury women, pp. 208–24; F. P. Verney, ed., *Verney Memoirs,* 2:86; and Keith Thomas, "Women and the Civil War Sects," pp. 42–62.

41. Siebert, *Freedom of the Press,* pp. 208–24.

42. See, for example, the Verney women, Anne Fanshawe, and Anne Halkett, mentioned earlier.

43. J. Goodwin, "Anti-Cavalierism," p. 222.

44. Lucy Hutchinson, *Memoirs,* p. 236; Verney ed., *Verney Memoirs,* 2:283–87, 307.

45. Verney, ed., *Verney Memoirs*, 2:283–87; Slater, *Family Life in the Seventeenth Century*.

46. Rogers, *A Practical Catechisme*, pp. 66–67.

47. Gouge, *Of Domesticall Duties*, p. 287.

48. Hutchinson, *Memoirs*, p. 49; *Macbeth* also provides insight into general "public opinion" on women participating in political events.

49. Verney, ed., *Verney Memoirs*, 2:86.

50. R. Braithwait, *The English Gentleman*, p. 87.

51. Rogers, *Matrimonial Honour*, pp. 160–61.

7. Much Remains to Be Done

1. See the autobiographies of Alice Thornton, Lady Anne Fanshawe, Lucy Hutchinson—and chapter 4 of this work.

2. See Michael Walzer, *The Revolution of the Saints*, pp. 247–52 and William Hunt, *The Puritan Moment*, pp. 112–40.

3. See chapters 3 and 4.

4. This is a dominant view in many feminist histories and is also widespread in other branches of the social sciences. See, for example, Marianne A. Ferber, "Women and Work: Issues of the 1980s," *Signs* (Winter 1982) 8(2):273–95; Carl Degler, *At Odds: Women and the Family in America from the Revolution to the Present* (New York and Oxford: Oxford University Press, 1980).

5. The husband may have needed to challenge the existing distribution of social resources more than ever since he alone was responsible for providing his family with their share. But he was in less of a position to take any risky actions challenging that distribution, since if anything happened to him or if he ceased to bring in wages, the family could starve.

Appendix: Literary Sources

1. Recent research suggests that the widespread increase in literacy was mediated through the changes in social stratification discussed in chapter 2, and that it intensified a growing polarization between the rich and poor. By 1700, it is broadly true that most of the rich (men) could read while most of the poor could not. However, this broad generalization disguises some significant variations.

The first is the great upsurge of literacy in the early years of the English reformation. The initial impulse of English reformers was to foster literacy among rich and poor, men and women alike. The English shared the desire voiced by the noted continental humanist Erasmus to spread the gospel (suitably purged of Roman abuses) by offering the Bible to the plowman at his plow and the housewife at her spinning wheel. The reformers seem to have enjoyed great success in offering the Bible to the masses—they sponsored several widely purchased translations of the Bible into English, and they provided instruction even in many "dark corners" of England. They were not so successful in spreading the gospel, finding, to their dismay, that it was not only through the papists that the devil quoted scripture. Women and the poor, too, offered the devil an open forum.

Henry VIII was ready in the early 1540s to deny women unmediated access to the Bible, forbidding them to read it themselves. Most reformers, however, were daunted but not defeated: throughout the sixteenth century, they continued to encourage Bible reading by all Christians—but they encouraged Christians to read the newly translated and annotated Bibles they themselves provided, Bibles designed to render clear and unprovoking the "unclear" passages which might have engendered questioning of the social order. The annotations provided Christians with explicit statements of the gospel they aimed to share with all the English through sermons, oral and printed. Their early efforts to spread literacy among the poor masses do appear to have flagged by the turn of the century, especially relative to their efforts to spread their gospel among their social peers, the "better inhabitants" of the parishes and the nation.

But—and this phenomenon somewhat negates the polarizing effects of the class-specificity of literacy—the reformers expected their peers to impose their gospel on everyone else. The clergy made very clear that it was the religious duty of employers, parents, and indeed, all "superiors" to instruct and train inferiors in religious and biblical precepts and to use all possible means to enforce the behavior prescribed by the clergy in their biblical exegeses and their more wide-ranging sermons. Thus, they called upon the literate to provide daily readings for the illiterate under their governance. They required heads of households to conduct daily prayer sessions and to question children and servants on the catechism. They mounted vigorous campaigns to ensure that every Englishperson attended Sunday church services, where the illiterate could hear the minister deliver the same sermon that the literate could later read for themselves. Hence the illiterate were exposed to the same religious culture developing among the literate, and they were exposed in such a way as to deprive them of opportunities to subject the doctrines expounded to critical analysis.

The second significant variation hidden by the generalization that the rich could read and the poor could not is that urban residents were far more literate than their rural counterparts. Large and growing percentages of apprentices, artisans, and craftspeople in seventeenth-century English cities could read, while in rural areas, even some very prosperous yeomen were still illiterate. This phenomenon suggests both that literacy was more necessary for social advancement and, possibly, survival in the cities than in the slower-paced rural areas and that urban dwellers were more likely than rural residents to be directly addressed by authors. I readily acknowledge that many of the attitudes discussed in this book were initially applicable mainly to the city dwellers but argue that the attitudes, like literacy itself, filtered back and were adopted in the countryside.

See, for extensive discussion, Lawrence Stone, "The Educational Revolution in England," pp. 41–80; see also Kenneth Charlton, *Education in Renaissance England;* D. Cressy, *Literacy and the Social Order,* esp. pp. 13–59; Margaret Spufford, *Small Books and Pleasant Histories,* pp. 22–40, and ch. 3; Suzanne Hull, *Chaste, Silent, and Obedient;* H. S. Bennett, *English Books.* See, for an example of the needs generated by a new literacy, R. Cawdrey, *Dictionary.*

2. Joan Simon, *Education and Society in Tudor England,* p. 15; Alison Plowden, *Tudor Women,* p. 38; Louis B. Wright, *Middle-Class Culture in Elizabethan En-*

gland, pp. 44–48; Lawrence Stone, *The Family, Sex, and Marriage*, pp. 202–4; Stone, "Educational Revolution," p. 64; Pearl Hogrefe, *Women of Action in Tudor England*, pp. x–xi; Sir Simonds D'Ewes, *Autobiography*, pp. 63–64; Lucy Hutchinson, *Memoirs*, pp. 21–22; Richard Mulcaster, *Positions*, pp. 138–39.

3. R. S. Schofield, "The Measurement of Literacy in Pre-Industrial England," p. 311; the diaries of Lady Anne Clifford and Lady Margaret Hoby both demonstrate the role that mistresses of households played in providing for "readings" to be given for female servants. The functionally illiterate received oral expositions of the values mistresses wanted shared. See Cressy, *Literacy and the Social Order*, pp. 13–14; K. Wrightson, *English Society*, pp. 188–98; Margaret Spufford, *Contrasting Communities*, pp. 171–200; J. Goody and I. Watt, "The Consequences of Literacy."

4. C. S. Lewis, "English Literature in the Sixteenth Century," p. 62.

5. For a discussion of the reading tastes of the middle strata of Tudor society, Louis B. Wright's *Middle-Class Culture in Elizabethan England* remains unsurpassed. But see also Margaret Spufford, *Small Books and Pleasant Histories*; Suzanne Hull, *Chaste, Silent, and Obedient*; J. J. Jusserand, *The English Novel in the Time of Shakespeare*.

6. William Painter, *The Palace of Pleasure*, "To the reader," 1:12–13.

7. Sir Phillip Sidney, "Defense of Poesie," *Miscellaneous Prose*, pp. 87, 81–82. That form of lay literature directed at a general audience which took this formula most seriously was the treatise on morality and society. A very popular form of prose in the late sixteenth and seventeenth centuries in England, these treatises were generally very harsh and condemnatory of both men and women. Frequently humorous, the treatises excoriated current corruption and set forth ideal behavior patterns (Oh! the days when wives were Penelopes!). Those cited herein by Nicholas Breton, Thomas Nashe, and Phillip Stubbes were among the best-selling during the period 1550–1650. Some of these works were so popular that they were translated into French. Again, it is unlikely that readers actually lived according to the prescriptions of these works, but it is likely that purchasers took some of these prescriptions fully to heart. For a fuller exposition of this point, see Lewis, *English Literature in the Sixteenth Century*, pp. 394–429.

8. Daniel Rogers, *Matrimonial Honour*, p. 325.

9. Christopher Hill, *Society and Puritanism in Pre-Revolutionary England*, pp. 32–33. See also R. Greaves, *Society and Religion*, pp. 329–33; P. Williams, *The Tudor Regime*, p. 6; K. Wrightson and D. Levine, *Poverty and Piety*, pp. 12–14; P. Zagorin, *The Court and the Country*, pp. 182–84; Gordon Schochet, *Patriarchalism in Political Thought*, p. 74.

10. Hill, *Society and Puritanism*, pp. 32–60.

11. See Greaves, *Society and Religion*; Ralph Houlbrooke, *The English Family*, p. 6, and Thomas Safley, *Let No Man Put Asunder: The Control of Marriage in the German Southwest: A Comparative Study 1550–1600* (Kirksville, MO: Sixteenth Century Journal, 1984).

12. See, for example, Gerrard Winstanley's *The Law of Freedom in a Platform* and William Haller, ed., *Tracts on Liberty in the Puritan Revolution, 1638–1647*. The Quakers were somewhat of an exception to this, in that, to a limited degree, they allowed women an independent religious voice. The Leveller Wildman, some of whose writings are available in Haller's collection, may also have been less wedded to the traditional patriarchal notions of women's place.

13. See the following for a fuller discussion of this: Brian Gibbons, *Jacobean City Comedy;* David Bevington, *Tudor Drama and Politics;* Henry H. Adams, *English Domestic or Homiletic Tragedy;* M. C. Bradbrook, *Themes and Conventions of Elizabethan Tragedy.*

14. Gibbons, *Jacobean City Comedy* and Bevington, *Tudor Drama and Politics* address this issue; see also A. L. Rowse, *Tudor Cornwall,* p. 437.

15. S. Barnet, M. Berman, W. Burto, eds., *The Genius of the Early English Theater,* p. 238.

16. R. Fraser and N. Rabkin, eds., *Drama of the English Renaissance,* 2:549.

17. R. S. Forsythe, *Shirley's Plays,* p. 13.

18. See, for example, Dorothy Osborne's comments on the Duchess of New-Castle: Dorothy believed the Duchess's assertive writings showed her to be "a little distracted" and wondered that her friends let so aggressive a woman "go abroad." G. C. Moore-Smith, ed., *Osborne Letters,* pp. 37, 41. See also Sara H. Mendelson, "Stuart Women's Diaries." The biographies of most of the men and women whose journals are used herein may be perused in the *Dictionary of National Biography.*

19. G. C. Moore-Smith, ed., *Osborne Letters,* p. xxi; Alice Thornton, *Autobiography,* introduction.

20. G. P. Gooch, *English Democratic Ideas in the Seventeenth Century,* 2d ed., with notes by H. J. Laski (New York: Harper and Row, 1927; Harper Torchbook reprint, 1959), p. 32; see also G.J.R. Parry, "William Harrison and Holinshed's Chronicles."

21. Wright, *Middle-Class Culture,* p. 276.

22. Cited in Hill, *Society and Puritanism,* p. 83; see also William Haller, *The Rise of Puritanism.*

23. Hill, *Society and Puritanism,* p. 140.

24. Haller, *The Rise of Puritanism,* p. 65.

25. *Ibid.,* p. 67.

26. Wright, *Middle-Class Culture,* p. 222.

SELECTED
BIBLIOGRAPHY

Plays Cited

Anonymous. *The Deluge.* In J. Q. Adams, ed., *Chief Pre-Shakespearean Dramas: A Selection of Plays Illustrating the History of English Drama from Its Origins down to Shakespeare.* Cambridge, Mass.: Houghton Mifflin, 1924; reprint ed., 1952.

——*The Sacrifice of Isaac.* In J. Q. Adams, ed., *Chief Pre-Shakespearean Dramas: A Selection of Plays Illustrating the History of English Drama from Its Origins down to Shakespeare.* Cambridge, Mass.: Houghton Mifflin, 1924; reprint ed., 1952.

——*The Second Shepherd's Play.* In S. Barnet, M. Berman, and W. Burto, eds., *The Genius of the Early English Theater.* New York: New American Library, 1962.

Beaumont, Francis. *The Knight of the Burning Pestle.* In Russell A. Fraser and Norman Rabkin, eds., *Drama of the English Renaissance,* vol. 2. New York: Macmillan, 1976.

Beaumont, Francis, and John Fletcher. *The Knight of Malta.* In A. R. Waller, eds., *The Work of Francis Beaumont and John Fletcher,* vol. 5. Cambridge: Cambridge University Press, 1907.

——*The Maid in the Mill.* In A. R. Waller, ed., *The Work of Francis Beaumont and John Fletcher,* vol. 5. Cambridge: Cambridge University Press, 1907.

Dekker, Thomas. *The Shoemaker's Holiday.* In Robert G. Lawrence, ed., *Early Seventeenth Century Drama.* London: J. G. Dent, Everyman's Library, 1963.

Dekker, Thomas, and Thomas Middleton. *The Roaring Girl.* In Russell A. Fraser and Norman Rabkin, eds., *Drama of the English Renaissance,* vol. 2. New York: Macmillan, 1976.

Dekker, Thomas, and John Webster. *Westward Ho.* In *The Works of John Webster,* vol. 3. Annotated by the Rev. Alexander Dyce. London: William Pickering, 1830.

Fletcher, John. *The Wild-Goose Chase*. In Russell A. Fraser and Norman Rabkin, eds., *Drama of the English Renaissance*, vol. 2. New York: Macmillan, 1976.

Jonson, Ben. *Epicoene, or, the Silent Woman*. In Russell A. Fraser and Norman Rabkin, eds., *Drama of the English Renaissance*, vol. 2. New York: Macmillan, 1976.

Marston, John. *The Dutch Courtesan*. In Russell A. Fraser and Norman Rabkin, eds., *Drama of the English Renaissance*, vol. 2. New York: Macmillan, 1976.

Massinger, Philip. *The City Madam*. In Robin Chapman and Allan Grant, eds., *The City and the Court: Five Seventeenth-Century Comedies of London Life*. San Francisco: Chandler, 1968.

——*The Virgin Martyr*. In Arthur Symons, ed., *Philip Massinger*, vol. 2. The Mermaid Series: The Best Plays of the Old Dramatists, Havelock Ellis, ed. London, 1889.

Medwall, Henry. *Fulgens and Lucrece*. In Frederick S. Boas, ed., *Five Pre-Shakespearean Comedies*. Reprint ed., Oxford: Oxford University Press, 1970. Originally in the World's Classics Series, 1934.

Middleton, Thomas. *Women Beware Women*. Edited by Roma Gill. A Mermaid Dramabook. New York: Hill and Wang, 1968.

Shirley, James. *The Lady of Pleasure*. In Robin Chapman and Allan Grant, eds., *The City and the Court: Five Seventeenth-Century Comedies of London Life*. San Francisco: Chandler, 1968.

Tourneur, Cyril. *The Revenger's Tragedy*. In Russell A. Fraser and Norman Rabkin, eds., *Drama of the English Renaissance*, vol. 2. New York: Macmillan, 1976.

Udall, Nicholas. *Ralph Roister Doister*. In Frederick S. Boas, ed., *Five Pre-Shakespearean Comedies*. Reprint ed., Oxford: Oxford University Press, 1970. Originally in the World's Classics Series, 1934.

Other Works

Adams, Henry Hitch. *English Domestic or Homiletic Tragedy, 1575–1642*. New York: Columbia University Press, 1943.

Adams, Joseph Quincy, ed. *Chief Pre-Shakespearean Dramas: A Selection of Plays Illustrating the History of English Drama from Its Origins down to Shakespeare*. Cambridge, Mass.: Houghton Mifflin, 1924; reprint ed., 1952.

Agrippa, H. Cornelius. *A Treatise of the Nobilitie and Excellencie of Womankind*. Translated by David Clapham. London: 1st printed, 1542; this ed., 1603.

Akrigg, G.P.V. *Jacobean Pageant or The Court of King James I.* Cambridge, Mass.: Harvard University Press, 1962.

Anderson, Michael. *Approaches to the History of the Western Family, 1500–1914.* London: Macmillan, 1980.

Ascham, Roger. *The Scholemaster, or plain and perfect way of teaching children.* London, 1571.

Aylmer, John. *An Harborowe for Faithful and True Subjects, against the Late blowne Blast, concerning the Government of Wemen.* London, 1559.

Babington, Gervase. *Certain Plaine, briefe, and Comfortable Notes upon every Chapter of Genesis.* London, 1592.

——*A Very Fruitfull Exposition of the Commandements.* London: 1st ed., 1583; this (3d) ed., 1590.

Bacon, Francis. *Essays.* Introduction by Oliphant Smeaton. London: J. M. Dent, 1906; reprint ed., 1939.

Badinter, Elisabeth. *Mother Love: Myth and Reality—Motherhood in Modern History.* New York: Macmillan, 1981.

Barnet, Sylvan, Morton Berman, and William Burto, eds. *The Genuis of the Early English Theater.* New York: New American Library, 1962.

Barrett, Michelle. *Women's Oppression Today: Problems in Marxist Feminist Analysis.* London: Verso and New Left Books, 1980.

Baxter, Richard. *A Breviate of the Life of Margaret, the daughter of Francis Charlton of Apply in Shropshire, Esq. And Wife of Richard Baxter. With the character of her mother, truly described in her published funeral sermon, reprinted at her daughter's request.* London, 1681.

Becon, Thomas. *The Works of Thomas Becon.* Vol. 1, including "A New Catechism" and "The Goldē Boke of Christen Matrimonye." London, 1564.

Bennett, H. S. *English Books and Readers, 1603–1640, Being a Study in the History of the Book Trade in the Reigns of James I and Charles I.* Cambridge: Cambridge University Press, 1970.

Bennett, Judith. "Spouses, Siblings, and Surnames: Reconstructing Families from Medieval Village Court Rolls." *Journal of British Studies* (Fall 1983), 23(1):24–46.

——"The Village Alewife: Women and Brewing in Fourteenth Century England." Paper delivered at the American Historical Association Convention, December 1982.

Bentley, Thomas. *The Monument of Matrones: Containing Seven Several Lamps of Virgnity, or distinct treatises; whereof the first five concern prayer and meditation: the other last two, precepts and examples as the worthy works partly of men, partly of women.* London, 1582.

Bevington, David. *Tudor Drama and Politics: A Critical Approach to Topical Meaning.* Cambridge, Mass.: Harvard University Press, 1968.

Birken, William Joseph. "The Royal College of Physicians of London and Its Support of the Parliamentary Cause in the Civil War." *Journal of British Studies* (Fall 1983), 23(1):47–62.

Blencowe, R. W., ed. *Sydney Papers, consisting of a Journal of the Earl of Leicester, and Original Letters of Algernon Sydney.* London, 1825.

Boas, Frederick S. *An Introduction to Stuart Drama.* Oxford: Oxford University Press, 1946.

——, ed. *Five Pre-Shakespearean Comedies.* Reprint ed., Oxford: Oxford University Press, 1970. Originally published 1934.

Bradbrook, M. C. *Themes and Conventions of Elizabethan Tragedy.* Cambridge: Cambridge University Press, 1969.

Braithwait, Richard. *The English Gentleman and English Gentlewoman, both in one volume couched, the third edition, revised, corrected and enlarged; with a Ladies Love Lecture, and a Supplement Lately Annexed, and Entitled The Turtles Triumph.* London: 1st printed, 1630; this ed., 1641.

Bramhall, John. *Castigations of Mr. Hobbes 1658.* London and New York: Garland, Garland Reprints Series, 1977.

Brenner, Robert. "The Origins of Capitalist Development: A Critique of Neo-Smithian Marxism." *New Left Review* (July–August 1977), 104:25–93.

Breton, Nicholas. "The Good and the Bad"; "An Old Man's Lesson"; and "Of a Quiet Woman." In Alexander Grosart, ed., *The Works in Verse and Prose of Nicholas Breton,* vol. 2: *Prose.* Edinburgh: Anglistica and Americana Series of Reprints, 1879.

Bridenthal, Renata and Claudia Koontz, eds. *Becoming Visible: Women in European History.* Boston: Houghton Mifflin, 1977.

Brinsley, John. *A Looking Glass for Good Women.* London, 1645.

Butt, John J., Jr. "The Transition of Privilege in Medieval Society: A Study of the English Brewers." Ph.D dissertation, Rutgers University, 1982.

Byfield, Nicholas. *A Commentary or Sermons upon the Second Chapter of the First Epistle of St. Peter.* London, 1623.

Campbell, Mildred. *The English Yeoman Under Elizabeth and the Early Stuarts.* New Haven: Yale University Press, 1942.

Castiglione, Baldesar. *The Book of the Courtier.* Translated by Charles S. Singleton. New York: Doubleday, Anchor, 1959.

Cavendish, Lady Margaret. *The Life of William Cavendish, Duke of NewCastle, to which is added the true relation of my birth, breeding, and life, by the Duchess of NewCastle.* Annotated by C. H. Firth. London and New York: Routledge and E. P. Dutton, 1903.

Cawdrey, Robert. *A Table Alphabeticall of Hard Usual Words (1604): The First English Dictionary.* Edited by Robert A. Peters. Gainesville, Fla.: Scholars Facsimiles and Reprints, 1966.

Cecil, William (Lord Burghley). "Certain Precepts for the Well-Ordering of a

Man's Life." In Louis B. Wright, ed., *Advice to a Son*, pp. 7–14. Ithaca: Cornell University Press for the Folger Library, 1962.

Chapman, Robin and Allan Grant, eds. *The City and the Court: Five Seventeenth Century Comedies of London Life.* San Francisco: Chandler, 1968.

Charlton, Kenneth. *Education in Renaissance England.* London: Routledge and Kegan Paul, 1965.

Chaytor, Miranda. "Household and Kinship: Ryton in the Late Sixteenth and Early Seventeenth Centuries." *History Workshop Journal* (1980), 10:25–60.

Clapham, Sir John. *A Concise Economic History of Britain from the Earliest Times to 1750.* Cambridge: Cambridge University Press, 1949.

Clark, Alice. *The Working Life of Women in the Seventeenth Century.* London and New York: E. P. Dutton, 1919. Reissued with an Introduction by Miranda Chaytor and Jane Lewis. London: Routledge and Kegan Paul, 1982.

Clarke, George. *A History of the Royal College of Physicians of London.* Oxford: Clarendon Press, 1964.

Clarke, John. *Holy Incense for the Censers of the Saints.* London, 1634.

Clifford, Lady Anne. *The Diary of Lady Anne Clifford.* Edited and with an introduction by Vita Sackville West. London: William Heinemann, 1923.

Coleman, D. C. *The Economy of England, 1450–1750.* London: Oxford University Press, 1977.

——"Labour in the English Economy of the Seventeenth Century." In Paul S. Seaver, ed., *Society in an Age of Revolution*, pp. 111–38. New York: New Viewpoints, 1976.

Cooper, J. P., ed. *Wentworth Papers, 1597–1628.* London: Royal Historical Society, Camden Society 4th ser., vol. 12, 1973.

Costello, Louisa Stuart. *Memoirs of Eminent English Women*, vol. 1. London: Richard Bentley, 1844.

Coverdale, Miles, trans. *The Christian State of Matrimony wherein husbands and wives may learn to keep house together with love, by Henry Bullinger.* London, 1543.

Cressy, David. *Literacy and the Social Order: Reading and Writing in Tudor and Stuart England.* New York: Cambridge University Press, 1980.

David, Elizabeth. *English Bread and Yeast Cookery.* London: Allan Lane, Penguin Books, 1977.

Davis, Dorothy. *A History of Shopping.* London: Routledge and Kegan Paul, 1966.

Dent, Arthur. *The Plain Man's Pathway to Heaven.* London, 1603.

Dering, Edward. "A Brief and Necessary Catechism or Instruction, very needful to be known of all Householders." In *Mr. Dering's Works More at large than ever hath here-to-fore been Printed in any one Volume.* London, 1597.

D'Ewes, Sir Simonds, Bart. *The Autobiography of Sir Simonds D'Ewes, Bart., during the reigns of James I and Charles I.* Edited by J. O. Halliwell. London: Richard Bentley, 1845.

Digby, Sir Kenelm. *Private Memoirs of Sir Kenelm Digby, Gentleman of the Bedchamber to King Charles the First, written by Himself.* Edited by Nicholas H. Nicholas. London: Saunders and Otley, 1927.

Dod, John and William Hind. *Bathesheba's Instructions to her Son Lemuel Containing a fruitful and plain Exposition of the last chapter of the Proverbs. Describing the duties of a Great-man and the Virtues of a Gracious Woman.* London, 1614.

Donne, John. *John Donne: Poetry and Prose.* Edited by Frank J. Warnke. New York: Random House, Modern Library Paperback, 1967.

Drummond, J. C. and Anne Wilbraham. *The Englishman's Food: A History of Five Centuries of English Diet.* London: Jonathan Cape, 1939.

Eccles, Audrey. *Obstetrics and Gynecology in Tudor and Stuart England.* Kent, Ohio: Kent State University Press, 1982.

Eliot, Sir Thomas. *The Defense of Good Women.* Edited by Edwin Johnston Howard. Oxford, Ohio: Anchor Press, 1940.

Elton, G. R., ed. *England Under the Tudors.* London: Methuen, 1960.

Evelyn, John. *Memoires for my Grandson.* Edited and with a preface and notes by Geoffrey Keynes. Oxford: Nonesuch Press, 1926.

Fanshawe, Anne Lady. *The Memoirs of Anne Lady Fanshawe, 1600–1672.* Edited by M. H. Nicholas. London: John Lane, 1907.

FitzHerbert, Sir Anthony. *The Book of Husbandry by Sir Anthony FitzHerbert.* Edited by Walter Skeat. London: English Dialect Society, 1882.

Flandrin, J. L. *Families in Former Times: Kinship, Household, and Sexuality.* Translated by Richard Southern. Cambridge: Cambridge University Press, 1979.

Fletcher, Anthony. *Tudor Rebellions.* London: Longman's, Green, 1973.

Forbes, Thomas Rogers. *The Midwife and the Witch.* New Haven: Yale University Press, 1966.

Forsythe, Robert Stanley. *The Relations of Shirley's Plays to the Elizabethan Drama.* New York: B. Blum, 1965.

Foxe, John. *Acts and Monuments of these latter and perilous days (The Book of Martyrs).* London, 1563.

Fraser, Antonia. *The Weaker Vessel.* New York: Alfred A. Knopf, 1984.

Fraser, Russell A. and Norman Rabkin, eds. *Drama of the English Renaissance,* vol. 2. New York: Macmillan, 1976.

Friedman, Alice T. "Portrait of a Marriage: The Willoughby Letters, 1585–1586." *SIGNS: Journal of Women in Culture and Society* (Spring 1986), 11(3):542–56.

Fussell, G. E. *The English Rural Laborer: His Home, Furniture, Clothing, and Food from Tudor to Victorian Times.* London: Batchworth Press, 1949.

Gamon, Hannibal. *The Praise of a Godly Woman. A Sermon Preached at the Solemn Funeral of the Right Honourable Ladie, The Ladie Frances Roberts, at Lanhide Rock Church in Cornwall, the tenth of August, 1626.* London, 1626.

Gardiner, Dorothy. *English Girlhood at School: A Study of Women's Education Through Twelve Centuries.* London: Oxford University Press, 1929.

——, ed. *The Oxinden Letters, 1607–1642: Being the Correspondence of Henry Oxinden of Barham and his Circle.* London: Constable, 1933.

Gascoigne, George. "The Tale of Mrs. Frances." In Edward J. O'Brien, ed., *Elizabethan Tales.* Boston and New York: Houghton Mifflin, 1938.

Gataker, Thomas. *A Good Wife God's Gift and A Wife Indeed: Two Marriage Sermons.* London: 1st printed, 1620; this (3d) ed., 1624.

——*Marriage Duties Briefly Couched Together.* London, 1620.

——*A Mariage Praier.* London, 1624.

——*Paul's Desire of Dissolution and Death's Advantage. A Sermon Preached at the Funeral of that right virtuous and religious Gentlewoman Mrs. Rebecca Crisp, together with the Testimonie then given unto her.* London, 1620.

Gibbons, Brian. *Jacobean City Comedy: A Study of Satiric Plays by Jonson, Marston, and Middleton.* Cambridge, Mass.: Harvard University Press, 1968.

Gillis, John R. *For Better, for Worse: British Marriages 1600 to the Present.* New York: Oxford University Press, 1985.

Goodwin, John. "Anti-Cavalierism." In William Haller, ed., *Tracts on Liberty in the Puritan Revolution,* 2:218–71. New York: Octagon, 1965.

Goody, Jack and Ian Watt. "The Consequences of Literacy." In Jack R. Goody, ed., *Literacy in Traditional Societies,* pp. 27–68. Cambridge: Cambridge University Press, 1968.

Gossett, Suzanne. "Best Men Are Molded Out of Faults: Marrying the Rapist in Jacobean Drama." *English Literary Renaissance* (Fall 1985), 14(3):305–27.

Gouge, William. *Of Domesticall Duties, Eight Treatises.* London, 1623.

Greaves, Richard L. *Society and Religion in Elizabethan England.* Minneapolis: University of Minnesota Press, 1981.

Greene, Robert. *Greene's Arcadia; or Menaphon.* London, 1616.

Griffith, Matthew. *Bethel, or a Form for Families: In which all sorts, of both sexes, are so squared and framed by the word of God, as they may best serve in their several places, for useful pieces in God's building.* London, 1633. Printed by Richard Badger for Henry Tanton.

Hageman, Elizabeth H. "Recent Studies in Women Writers of Tudor England." *English Literary Renaissance* (Fall 1985), 14(3):409–25.

Halkett, Lady Anne. *The Autobiography of Lady Anne Halkett.* Edited by John Gough Nichols. London: Camden Society, n.s. 13, 1875.

Haller, William. "Hail, Wedded Love." *ELH: A Journal of English Literary History* (June 1946), 13:79–97.

——*The Rise of Puritanism, or, The Way to the New Jerusalem as set forth in Pulpit and Press from Thomas Cartwright to John Lilburne and John Milton.* New York, 1938; reprint ed., Philadelphia: University of Pennsylvania Paperback, 1972.

——*Tracts on Liberty in the Puritan Revolution.* Vol. 2. New York: Octagon, 1965.

Haller, William and Mandeville Haller. "The Puritan Art of Love." *Huntingdon Library Quarterly* (January 1942), 5(2):235–72.

Hamilton, Roberta. *The Liberation of Women: A Study of Patriarchy and Capitalism.* London: Allen and Unwin, 1978.

Harris, Barbara. "Marriage Sixteenth-Century Style: Elizabeth Stafford and the Third Duke of Norfolk." *Journal of Social History* (Spring 1982), 15(3):371–82.

Harrison, William. *Elizabethan England.* Edited by Lothrop Withington, with an introduction by F. J. Furnivall. London: Walter Scott, 1889.

Heisch, Alison. "Queen Elizabeth I: Parliamentary Rhetoric and the Exercise of Power." *SIGNS: Journal of Women in Culture and Society* (Autumn 1975), 1(1):31–56.

Herbert, William. *The History of the Twelve Great Livery Companies of London.* 2 vols. Privately printed, 1837; reprint ed., New York: August M. Kelley, 1968.

Heywood, Thomas. *The General History of Women, containing the lives of the Most Holy and Prophane, the most famous and infamous, in all ages, exactly described not only from poeticall fictions but from the most Ancient, Modern, and Admired Historians to our Times.* London, 1657.

Hieron, Samuel. *All the Sermons of Samuel Hieron, Minister of God's word.* Including "The Marriage Blessing" and "The Bridegroom." London, 1614.

Higgins, Patricia. "The Reactions of Women, with Special Reference to Women Petitioners." In Brian Manning, ed., *Politics, Religion, and the English Civil War,* pp. 179–225. London: Edward Arnold, 1973.

Hill, Christopher. *Change and Continuity in Seventeenth Century England.* Cambridge, Mass.: Harvard University Press, 1975.

——*From Reformation to Industrial Revolution: A Social and Economic History of Britain, 1530–1780.* London: Weidenfeld and Nicolson, 1967.

——*Society and Puritanism in Pre-Revolutionary England.* 2d ed. New York: Schocken, 1972.

——*The World Turned Upside Down: Radical Ideas During the English Revolution.* New York: Viking Press, 1972.

Hobbes, Thomas. *Leviathan.* Edited by C. B. MacPherson. New York: Pelican, 1971.

——*Man and Citizen.* Edited by Bernard Gert. New York: Anchor Books, 1972.

Hoby, Lady Margaret. *The Diary of Lady Margaret Hoby, 1599–1605.* Edited by Dorothy M. Meads. London: Routledge, 1930.

Hogrefe, Pearl. *Tudor Women: Commoners and Queens.* Ames: Iowa State University Press, 1975.

——*Women of Action in Tudor England: Nine Biographical Sketches.* Ames: Iowa State University Press, 1977.

Hole, Christina. *The English Housewife in the Seventeenth Century.* London: Chatto and Windus, 1953.

Holles, Gervase. *Memorials of the Holles Family, 1493–1656.* Edited by A. C. Wood. London: Camden Society, 3d ser., vol. 55, 1937.

Hooker, Richard. "Ecclesiastical Polity." In *The Work of That Learned and Judicious Divine Mr. Richard Hooker.* With an account of his life and death by Isaac Walton; arranged by John Keble; revised by R. W. Church and F. Paget. London, 1841; reprint ed., New York: Burt Franklin, 1970.

Houlbrooke, Ralph A. *The English Family, 1450–1750.* Edited by J. Stevenson. Themes in British Social History series. New York and London: Longman, 1984.

Hull, Suzanne W. *Chaste, Silent, and Obedient: English Books for Women, 1475–1640.* San Marino, Calif.: Huntingdon Library, 1982.

Hunt, William. *The Puritan Moment: The Coming of Revolution in an English County.* Cambridge, Mass.: Harvard University Press, 1983.

Hutchinson, Lucy. *Memoirs of the Life of Colonel Hutchinson with the fragment of an autobiography of Mrs. Hutchinson.* Edited by James Sutherland. London: Oxford University Press, 1973.

Illick, Joseph E. "Childrearing in Seventeenth Century England and America." In Lloyd deMause, ed., *The History of Childhood,* pp. 303–50. Reprint ed., New York: Harper and Row, 1975.

James, Mervyn. *Family, Lineage, and Civil Society: A Study of Society, Politics, and Mentality in the Durham Region, 1500–1640.* Oxford: Clarendon Press, 1974.

Johnson, James Turner. *A Society Ordained by God: English Puritan Marriage Doctrine in the First Half of the Seventeenth Century.* Nashville, Tenn.: Abingdon Press, 1970.

Jusserand, J. J. *The English Novel in the Time of Shakespeare.* Translated by Elizabeth Lee. Rev. ed. New York: AMS Press, 1965.

Kelso, Ruth. *Doctrine for a Lady of the Renaissance.* Urbana: University of Illinois Press, 1956.

Kerridge, Eric. *The Agricultural Revolution.* London: Allen and Unwin, 1967.

Knox, John. *A Blast against the Monstrous Regiment of Women.* Strasbourg, 1558.

Laslett, Peter. *Family Life and Illicit Love in Earlier Generations: Essay in Historical Sociology.* Cambridge: Cambridge University Press, 1977.

——*The World We Have Lost.* London: Methuen, 1965.

Latimer, Hugh. *Fruitfull Sermons Preached by the right Reverend Father, and constant Martyr of Jesus Christ, Master Hugh Latimer.* London, 1635.

Leigh, Dorothy. *The Mother's Blessing: or, The Godly Counsaile of a Gentlewoman, not long since deceased, left behind for her children.* London: 7th printing, 1621.

Leites, Edmund. "The Duty to Desire: Love, Friendship, and Sexuality in Some Puritan Theories of Marriage." *Journal of Social History* (Spring 1982), 15(3):383–408.

Leonard, E. M. *The Early History of English Poor Relief.* Cambridge: Cambridge University Press, 1900; reprint ed., London: Cass, 1965.

Levack, Brian P. *The Civil Lawyers in England, 1603–1641: A Political Study.* Oxford: Clarendon Press, 1973.

Levine, David. *Family Formation in an Age of Nascent Capitalism.* San Francisco: Academic Press, 1977.

——"Production, Reproduction, and the Proletarian Family in England, 1500–1850." Paper presented at Rutgers University, New Jersey, May 1983.

Lewis, C. S. "English Literature in the Sixteenth Century, Excluding Drama." In *The Oxford History of English Literature,* vol. 3. General editors Bonamy Dobree and Norman Davis. Oxford: Oxford University Press, 1944.

Lipson, E. *The Economic History of England,* vol. 2: *The Age of Mercantilism.* London: A. and C. Black, 1931.

Lis, Hugo and Catharina Soly. *Poverty and Capitalism in Pre-Industrial Europe.* London: Harvester Press, 1979.

McArthur, Ellen A. "Women Petitioners and the Long Parliament." *English Historical Review* (October 1909), 24:698–709.

McCance, R. A. and E. M. Widdowson. *Breads White and Brown: Their Place in Thought and Social History.* London: Sir Isaac Pitman, 1959.

MacFarlane, Alan. *The Family of Ralph Josselin, a Seventeenth-Century Clergyman: An Essay in Historical Anthropology.* Cambridge: Cambridge University Press, 1970.

——*The Origins of English Individualism: The Family, Property, and Social Transition.* London: Basil Blackwell, 1978.

MacLaren, Dorothy. "Marital Fertility and Lactation, 1520–1720." In Mary Prior, ed., *Women in English Society,* pp. 22–54. London and New York: Methuen, 1985.

MacLean, Ian. *The Renaissance Notion of Woman: A Study in the Fortunes of Scholasticism and Medical Science in European Intellectual Life.* Cambridge: Cambridge University Press, 1980.

MacPherson, C. B. *The Political Theory of Possessive Individualism: Hobbes to*

Locke. London: Clarendon Press, 1962; Oxford University Paper ed., 1964.

Mahl, M. R. and H. Koon, eds. *The Female Spectator: English Women Writers Before 1800.* Bloomington: Indiana University Press, 1977.

Markham, Gervase. *Cheap and good Husbandry for the Well-Ordering of all Beasts and Fowls, and for the general cure of their diseases.* London: 6th ed., 1631.

——*The Country Housewife's Garden, Containing Rules for Herbs and Seeds of Common Use, with their times and seasons when to set and sow them. Together with the Husbandry of Bees, published with secrets necessary for every housewife.* London, 1637.

——*The English Housewife, Containing the inward and outward virtues which ought to be in a complete woman.* London: 1st printing, 1615; this ed., 1637.

Mendelson, Sara Heller. "Debate: The Weightiest Business: Marriage in an Upper-Gentry Family in Seventeenth Century England." *Past and Present* (November 1979), 85:126–35.

——"Stuart Women's Diaries and Occasional Memoirs." In Mary Prior, ed., *Women in English Society,* pp. 181–210. London and New York: Methuen, 1985.

Merton, Robert K. *Science, Technology, and Society in Seventeenth Century England.* With a new introduction by the author. New York: Harper Torchbooks, 1970.

Middleton, Christopher. "The Sexual Divison of Labour in Feudal England." *New Left Review* (January–April 1979), pp. 113–14, 147–68.

Monckton, Herbert Anthony. *A History of the English Public House.* London: Bodley Head, 1969.

Moore-Smith, G. C., ed. *The Letters of Dorothy Osborne to William Temple.* Oxford: Clarendon Press, 1928.

More, Thomas. "Letter to his wife." In W. Baptiste Scoones, ed., *Four Centuries of English Letters: Selections from the Correspondence of 150 Writers from the Period of the Paston Letters to the Present Day.* New York, 1880.

Mulcaster, Richard. *Positions wherein those Primitive Circumstances be Examined which are necessary for the Training Up of Children either for skill in their books, or health in their body.* With an appendix by Robert Herbert Quick. London: Longman's, Green, 1888.

Nashe, Thomas. "The Anatomy of Absurdity." In Ronald W. McKerrow, ed., *The Works of Thomas Nashe,* vol. 1. London: A. H. Bullen, 1904.

Neale, John E. *Queen Elizabeth I: A Biography.* New York: Doubleday, Anchor, 1957.

Nowell, Alexander. *A Catechisme, or First Instruction and Learning of Christian Religion.* Translated from the Latin by T. Norton. London, 1570.

O'Brien, Edward J., ed. *Elizabethan Tales*. Boston and New York: Houghton Mifflin, 1938.

O'Day, Rosemary. *The English Clergy: The Emergence and Consolidation of a Profession, 1558–1642*. Leicester: Leicester University Press, 1979.

Ozment, Steven. *When Fathers Ruled: Family Life in Reformation Europe*. Cambridge, Mass.: Harvard University Press, 1983.

Painter, William. *The Palace of Pleasure*. 3 vols. New York: Dover, 1966.

Parry, G.J.R. "William Harrison and Holinshed's Chronicles," *Historical Journal* (December 1984), 27(4):789–810.

Perkins, William. *The Collected Works of William Perkins*. Vol. 3. Including "Christian Oeconomy, or A Short Survey of the Right Manner of Erecting and Ordering a Family," "A Discourse of the Damned Art of Witchcraft," "An Exposition on Jude." Translated by Thomas Pickering. London, 1635.

Plat, Sir Hugh. *A Closet for Ladies and Gentlewomen. Or the Art of Preserving, conserving, and candying, with the manner how to make diverse kinds of syrups, and all kind of banquetting stuffs. Also divers sovereign Medicines and salves for sundry diseases*. London, 1632.

——*Delights for Ladies, to Adorn their Persons, Tables, Closets, and Distillators, with Beauties, Banquets, Perfumes, and Waters. Reade, practice, and censure*. London, 1632.

Plowden, Alison. *Tudor Women: Queens and Commoners*. New York: Atheneum, 1979.

Poster, Mark. *Critical Theory of the Family*. New York: Seabury Press, 1978.

Powell, Chilton Latham. *English Domestic Relations, 1487–1653*. New York: Columbia University Press, 1917.

Power, Eileen. *Medieval Women*. Cambridge: Cambridge University Press, 1975.

——"The Position of Women." In C. G. Crump and E. F. Jacob, eds., *The Legacy of the Middle Ages*, pp. 400–30. Oxford: Clarendon Press, 1926.

Prior, Mary. "Women and the Urban Economy, 1500–1800." In Mary Prior, ed., *Women in English Society*, pp. 93–117. London and New York: Methuen, 1985.

——, ed. *Women in English Society*. London and New York: Methuen, 1985.

Putnam, Bertha M. "Northhampton Wage Assessments of 1560 and 1667." *Economic History Review* (January 1927), 1:124–34.

Raleigh, Sir Walter. "Sir Walter Raleigh's Instructions to his son and to Posterity." In Louis B. Wright, ed., *Advice to a Son*, pp. 15–32. Ithaca: Cornell University Press for the Folger Library, 1962.

Rogers, Daniel. *Matrimonial Honour: or, The Mutual Crown and Comfort of godly, loyal, and chaste Marriage*. London, 1642.

——*A Practicall Catechisme*. London, 1633.

Rogers, James E. Thorold. *Six Centuries of Work and Wages: The History of English Labour*. With a new preface by G.D.H. Cole. London: George Allen and Unwin, 1949.

Rowse, A. L. *Tudor Cornwall: Portrait of a Society*. London: Jonathan Cape, 1941.

Rye, William Benchley. *England as seen by Foreigners in the day of Elizabeth and James the First*. London: John Russell Smith, 1865.

Samaha, Joel. *Law and Order in Historical Perspective*. New York and London: Academic Press, 1974.

Savile, George, Duke of Savile. *The Complete Works of George Savile, First Marquess of Halifax*. Edited by Walter Raleigh. Including "Advise to a Daughter." Oxford: Clarendon Press, 1912.

Schochet, Gordon J. *Patriarchalism in Political Thought: The Authoritarian Family and Political Speculations and Attitudes, Especially in Seventeenth-Century England*. New York: Basic Books, 1975.

Schofield, Roger. "English Marriage Patterns Revisited." *Journal of Family History* (Spring 1985), 10(1):2–20.

——"The Measurement of Literacy in Pre-Industrial England." In Jack R. Goody, ed., *Literacy in Traditional Societies*, pp. 311–25. Cambridge: Cambridge University Press, 1968.

Schofield, Roger and E. A. Wrigley. *The Population History of England, 1541–1871*. Cambridge: Cambridge University Press, 1981.

Schwoerer, Lois G. "Seventeenth Century English Women: Engraven in Stone." *Albion* (Winter 1984), 16(4):389–403.

Seaver, Paul. "Introduction." In Paul Seaver, ed., *Society in an Age of Revolution*, pp. 1–25. New York: New Viewpoints, 1976.

Seldon, John. *The Table Talk of John Seldon*. Edited by Samuel Harvey Reynolds. Oxford: Clarendon Press, 1892.

Shahar, Shulamith. *The Fourth Estate: A History of Women in the Middle Ages*. London and New York: Methuen, 1983.

Shammas, Carole. "The Domestic Environment in Early Modern England and America." *Journal of Social History* (Fall 1980), 14:3–24.

Sharpe, J. A. *Crime in Seventeenth Century England: A County Study*. London: Cambridge University Press, 1983.

Sidney, Sir Philip. *The Countess of Pembroke's Arcadia written by Sir Philip Sidney*. Edited by Albert Feuillerat. 4th ed. Cambridge: Cambridge University Press, 1965.

——*Miscellaneous Prose of Sir Phillip Sydney*. Edited by Katherine Duncan-Jones and Jan van Iorsten. Oxford: Clarendon Press, 1973.

Siebert, Frederick Seaton. *Freedom of the Press in England, 1476–1776*. Urbana: University of Illinois Press, 1952; reprint ed., 1965.

Simon, Joan. *Education and Society in Tudor England*. Cambridge: Cambridge University Press, 1966.

Slater, Miriam. "Debate: The Weightiest Business: Marriage in an Upper-Gentry Family in Seventeenth Century England." *Past and Present* (November 1979), 85:136–41.

——*Family Life in the Seventeenth Century: The Verneys of Claydon House*. London and Boston: Routledge and Kegan Paul, 1984.

——"The Weightiest Business: Marriage in an Upper-Gentry Family in Seventeenth Century England." *Past and Present* (August 1976), 72:25–54.

Smith, Henry. *The Sermons of Master Henry Smith, gathered together in one volume*. Including "A Preparative to Marriage," "The True Trial of the Spirits," "The Wedding Garment," "The Bridegroom," "The Way to Walk In," and "The Banquet of Job's Children." London, 1600.

Smith, Sir Thomas. *De Republica Anglorum: A Discourse on the Commonwealth of England by Sir Thomas Smith*. Edited by L. Alston and with a preface by F. W. Maitland. Cambridge: Cambridge University Press, 1906.

Spenser, Edmund. *The Faerie Queene*. Edited by Thomas P. Roche, Jr. and C. Patrick O'Donne. London: Penguin English Library, 1978.

Spufford, Margaret. *Contrasting Communities: English Villagers in the Sixteenth and Seventeenth Centuries*. Cambridge: Cambridge University Press, 1974.

——*Small Books and Pleasant Histories: Popular Fiction and Its Readership in Seventeenth Century England*. London: Methuen, 1981.

Starkey, Thomas. *A Dialogue Between Reginald Pole and Thomas Lupset by Thomas Starkey*. Edited by Kathleen Burton. London: Chatto and Windus, 1948.

Stenton, Doris Mary. *The English Woman in History*. New York: Macmillan, 1957.

Stone, Lawrence. *The Crisis of the Aristocracy, 1558–1641*. Oxford: Clarendon Press, 1965.

——"The Educational Revolution in England, 1560–1640." *Past and Present* (July 1964), 28:41–80.

——*The Family, Sex, and Marriage in England, 1500–1800*. New York: Harper and Row, 1977.

——"Social Mobility in England, 1500–1700." In Paul Seaver, ed., *Society in an Age of Revolution*, pp. 25–70. New York: New Viewpoints, 1976.

Stow, John. *The Survay of London: containing the Original, Antiquity, Encrease and more Modern Estate of the said famous Citie. As also, the Rule and Government thereof (both Ecclesiasticall and Temporall) from time to time, revised and enlarged by A. M. Leonard*. London, 1618.

Stubbes, Phillip. *Phillip Stubbes's Anatomy of the Abuses in England in Shakspere's Youth A.D. 1583 (Collated with other editions in 1583, 1585, and*

1595). With estracts from Stubbes's Life of his Wife, 1591. Edited by Frederick J. Furnivall. London: New Shakspere Society, 1879.

Tawney, R. H. *The Agrarian Problem in the Sixteenth Century.* London: Longmans, Green, 1912.

——*Religion and the Rise of Capitalism.* New York: Harcourt Brace, 1926; Mentor paperback, 1954.

Taylor-Smither, Larissa J. "Elizabeth I: A Psychological Profile." *Sixteenth Century Journal* (Spring 1984), 15(1):47–73.

Thirsk, Joan. *Economic Policy and Projects: The Development of a Consumer Society in Early Modern England.* Oxford: Clarendon Press, 1978.

——*English Peasant Farming: The Agrarian History of Lincolnshire from Tudor to Recent Times.* London: Routledge and Kegan Paul, 1957.

——"The Fantastical Folly of Fashion: The English Stocking Knitting Industry, 1500–1700." In N. B. Harte and K. G. Ponting, eds., *Textile History and Economic History: Essays in Honour of Miss Julia de Lacy Mann,* pp. 50–74. Manchester: Manchester University Press, 1973.

——"Seventeenth Century Agriculture and Social Change." In Paul S. Seaver, ed., *Society in an Age of Revolution,* pp. 71–110. New York: New Viewpoints, 1976.

——, ed. *The Agrarian History of England and Wales,* vol. 4: *1500–1640.* Cambridge: Cambridge University Press, 1967.

Thomas, Keith. "Women and the Civil War Sects." *Past and Present* (April 1958), 13:42–62.

Thompson, Edward Maunde, ed. *Correspondence of the Family of Hatton being chiefly letters addressed to Christopher, 1st Viscount Hatton, A.D. 1601–1704.* 2 vols. London: Camden Society, n.s., 1878.

Thompson, E. P. "The Moral Economy of the English Crowd in the Eighteenth Century." *Past and Present* (February 1971), 50:76–136.

Thomson, F.L.M. "Social Control in Victorian Britain." *English Historical Review,* 2d ser. (1981), 34:189–207.

Thornton, Alice. *The Autobiography of Mrs. Alice Thornton of East Newton, Co. York.* Edited by Charles Jackson. London: Andrews for the Surtees Society, 1873.

Tickner, F. W. *Women in English Economic History.* London: J. M. Dent, 1923.

Tillyard, E.M.W. *The Elizabethan World Picture.* New York: Macmillan, 1944.

Tilney, Edmund. *A Briefe and Pleasant Discourse of Duties in Marriage, called the Flower of Friendship.* London: 1st printed, 1568; this ed., 1577.

Trevelyan, G. M. *History of England,* vol. 2: *The Tudors and the Stuart Era.* Rev. ed. New York: Doubleday, Anchor, 1953.

Tusser, Thomas. *Thomas Tusser 1557 Floruit His Good Points of Husbandry.* Edited by Dorothy Hartley. London: Country Life, 1931.

Unwin, George. *The Gilds and Companies of London.* London: Methuen, 1909.

———*Industrial Organisation in the Sixteenth and Seventeenth Centuries.* With an introduction by T. S. Ashton. London: Cass, 1957.

Vann, Richard T. "Toward a New Lifestyle: Women in Preindustrial Capitalism." In Renate Bridenthal and Claudia Koonz, eds. *Becoming Visible: Women in European History,* pp. 192–215. Boston: Houghton Mifflin, 1977.

Verney, Frances Parthenope, ed. *Memoirs of the Verney Family during the Civil War.* 2 vols. London: Longman's, Green, 1892.

Vives, Juan Luis. *A Very Frutefull and Pleasant Boke Called the Instruction of a Christen Woman.* London, 1529.

Walzer, Michael. *The Revolution of the Saints: A Study in the Origins of Radical Politics.* 3d ed. New York: Atheneum, 1970.

Weigall, Rachel. "An Elizabethan Gentlewoman: The Journal of Lady Mildmay, circa 1570–1617." *Quarterly Review* (July 1911), 428:119–39.

Whately, William. *A Bride-Bush, or, A Direction for Married Persons.* London: 1st printed, 1616; this (3d) ed. 1623.

Williams, Penry. *The Tudor Regime.* Oxford: Clarendon Press, 1979.

Wilson, C. Anne. *Food and Drink in Britain from the Stone Age to Recent Times.* London: Constable, 1973.

Wilson, Steven. "The Myth of Motherhood a Myth: The Historical View of European Childrearing." *Social History* (May 1984), 9(2):181–98.

Winchester, Barbara. *Tudor Family Portrait.* London: Jonathan Cape, 1955.

Winstanley, Gerrard. *The Law of Freedom in a Platform, or, True Magistracy Restored.* Edited by Robert W. Kenny. New York: Shocken Books, 1973.

Woodward, D. "The Background to the Statute of Artificers: The Genesis of Labour Policy, 1558–1563." *English Historical Review,* 2d ser. (1980), 33:32–34.

Wright, Louis B. *Middle-Class Culture in Elizabethan England.* Chapel Hill: University of North Carolina Press, 1935; reprint ed., Ithaca: Cornell University, 1965.

———, ed. *Advice to a Son.* Ithaca: Cornell University Press for the Folger Library, 1962.

Wrightson, Keith. "Alehouses, Order, and Reformation in Rural England, 1590–1660." In Eileen Yeo and Steven Yeo, eds., *Popular Culture and Class Conflict: Explorations in the History of Labour and Leisure,* pp. 1–27. Brighton, Sussex: Harvester Press, 1981.

———*English Society, 1580–1680.* New Brunswick, N.J.: Rutgers University Press, 1982.

Wrightson, Keith and David Levine. *Poverty and Piety in an English Village: Terling, 1525–1700.* San Francisco: Academic Press, 1979.

Wrigley, E. Anthony. "Urban Growth and Agricultural Change: England and the Continent in the Early Modern Period." *Journal of Interdisciplinary History* (Spring 1985), 15(4):683–728.

——, ed. *An Introduction to English Historical Demography from the Sixteenth to the Nineteenth Century*. New York: Basic Books, 1966.

Zagorin, Perez. *The Court and the Country: The Beginning of the English Revolution*. New York: Atheneum, 1969.

Index